Muhammad's Heirs

Muslim scholars are a vital part of Islam and are sometimes considered "heirs to the prophets," continuing Muhammad's work of establishing Islam in the centuries after his death. But this was not always the case: indeed, Muslims survived the turmoil of their first century largely without the help of scholars. In this book, Jonathan Brockopp seeks to determine the nature of Muslim scholarly communities and to account for their emergence from the very beginning of the Muslim story until the mid-tenth century. By analyzing coins, papyri, and Arabic literary manuscripts from the ancient mosque-library of Kairouan, Tunisia, Brockopp offers a new interpretation of Muslim scholars' rise to positions of power and influence, serving as moral guides and the chief arbiters of Muslim tradition. This book will be of great benefit to scholars of comparative religion and advanced students in Middle Eastern history, Islamic Studies, Islamic Law, and early Islamic literature.

Jonathan E. Brockopp is an associate professor of History and Religious Studies at Pennsylvania State University. He is the editor of and contributor to *The Cambridge Companion to Muḥammad* (Cambridge University Press, 2010).

Cambridge Studies in Islamic Civilization

Editorial Board

Chase F. Robinson, *The Graduate Center, The City University of New York (general editor)*

Michael Cook, *Princeton University*
Maribel Fierro, *Spanish National Research Council*
Alan Mikhail, *Yale University*
David O. Morgan, *Professor Emeritus, University of Wisconsin–Madison*
Intisar Rabb, *Harvard University*
Muhammad Qasim Zaman, *Princeton University*

Other titles in the series are listed at the back of the book.

Muhammad's Heirs

The Rise of Muslim Scholarly Communities, 622–950

JONATHAN E. BROCKOPP
Pennsylvania State University

CAMBRIDGE
UNIVERSITY PRESS

CAMBRIDGE
UNIVERSITY PRESS

University Printing House, Cambridge CB2 8BS, United Kingdom

One Liberty Plaza, 20th Floor, New York, NY 10006, USA

477 Williamstown Road, Port Melbourne, VIC 3207, Australia

314-321, 3rd Floor, Plot 3, Splendor Forum, Jasola District Centre, New Delhi - 110025, India

79 Anson Road, #06-04/06, Singapore 079906

Cambridge University Press is part of the University of Cambridge.

It furthers the University's mission by disseminating knowledge in the pursuit of education, learning and research at the highest international levels of excellence.

www.cambridge.org
Information on this title: www.cambridge.org/9781107106666
DOI: 10.1017/9781316227145

First published 2017

A catalogue record for this publication is available from the British Library

Library of Congress Cataloging in Publication data
Names: Brockopp, Jonathan E., 1962– author.
Title: Muhammad's heirs : the rise of Muslim scholarly communities, 622–950 / Jonathan E. Brockopp.
Description: New York, N.Y. : Cambridge University Press, 2017. | Series: Cambridge studies in Islamic civilization | Includes bibliographical references and index.
Identifiers: LCCN 2017007087 | ISBN 9781107106666 (Hardback)
Subjects: LCSH: Learning and scholarship–Islamic Empire–History. | Ulama–History. | Muslim scholars. | BISAC: HISTORY / Middle East / General.
Classification: LCC DS36.855 .B76 2017 | DDC 297.6/109021–dc23
LC record available at https://lccn.loc.gov/2017007087

ISBN 978-1-107-10666-6 Hardback
ISBN 978-1-107-51437-9 Paperback

Contents

Figures

Acknowledgments

A work such as this registers many debts, and it is my pleasure to thank the individuals and institutions that have made my efforts possible. Just as I insist here on the importance of the rise of scholarly *communities*, so also I am deeply aware just how much my work is dependent on the support of others. Pride of place goes to my philosopher-wife Paula Droege, whose sharp mind and commitment to cogency helps me strive for clarity in argument, and to Asma Afsaruddin, who generously read the entire final draft of this book, offering extremely useful comments, critiques, and encouragement.

I am privileged to hold a tenured position at the Pennsylvania State University, and I thank my department and colleagues for supporting my work with research leaves as well as stimulating conversations. A sabbatical leave in fall 2012 combined with a fellowship at Penn State's Institute for the Arts and Humanities in spring 2013 allowed for the completion of a first draft. The idea for this book, however, was formed earlier in 2012 during a month-long seminar on Mediterranean Studies sponsored by the National Endowment for the Humanities; I am grateful to leaders Brian Catlos and Sharon Kinoshita, as well as my colleagues at the seminar. I presented ideas from this project at the NEH seminar in Barcelona, as well as at national meetings of the Middle East Studies Association and at the American Academy of Religion, leading to separate, but related, articles on the origins of Islam that have now appeared in *History of Religions* and the *Journal of the American Academy of Religion.* The many generous comments and critiques from colleagues too numerous to name here helped shape and improve the final product. In particular, I would like to thank the anonymous reviewers for those journals and for Cambridge University Press, who went above and beyond the call to make copious notes on earlier versions of this book. In the increasingly competitive world of academia, where we are judged on the length of our CV, conscientious anonymous reviews are a thankless task. I trust the reviewers will read this note, however, and know just how much I appreciate their careful attention to argument and detail.

A special note of thanks is due to the editorial board of the Cambridge series on Islamic Civilization, especially Chase Robinson and the late Shahab Ahmad, both of whom offered encouragement and constructive criticism. The staff and editors at Cambridge have also been a delight to work with. Lauren Golder and Bill Cossen helped with compiling the bibliography and securing permissions for the many images in this book, and librarians and staff at libraries in Heidelberg, Paris, Dublin, and above all Raqqada have my thanks. But it is the Penn State librarians who helped keep the task of revisions on schedule; I kept giving them what I thought were impossible tasks, and they kept finding the books and articles I needed.

Finally, it is difficult to express in words my debt to Miklos Muranyi, who back in 1992 opened up his personal library to an American graduate student. His generosity and support, not to mention his unparalleled publications, have been the inspiration for my work ever since, and I dedicate this book to him.

Note on Transliteration and Dates

To simplify the text for nonspecialists, I reserve diacritics for Arabic technical terms, which are always italicized. Arabic names and terms that have become part of English are written without italics or diacritics, though I chose the slightly more correct Muhammad and Qur'an instead of Mohamed and Koran. Full diacritics are included in the footnotes and the bibliography.

As has become commonplace in our field, death dates of specific persons are identified first with the Muslim date (sometimes marked AH for *anno hegirae*), followed by the Common Era (CE) date, for example, Malik b. Anas (d. 179/795). Occasionally, I will also refer to a century in this way, such as the second/eighth century. When a century or date is not otherwise identified, it should be read as referring to the Common Era.

Unless otherwise noted, all translations are my own.

Introduction

Seventeen years ago, I was giving a lecture on the history of Islamic law at the University of Fez–Sais in Morocco. The students were bright, perceptive, and patient with my halting Arabic, but they objected to my main argument. My topic was a unique genre in the Arabic literary tradition, biographies of scholars, and my focus was on Qadi Iyad b. Musa (d. 544/1149), the great polymath from Ceuta, a figure well known to my Moroccan audience. What they could not accept was my suggestion that when writing biographies of the great figures from the early Islamic centuries, Iyad subtly manipulated their stories to fulfill his notion of what a great legal scholar should be.

The students pelted me with questions: Are you a Muslim? How long have you been studying Arabic? Why aren't you a Muslim? My host, Professor Hamid Lahmar, was embarrassed and told the students they should focus on the substance of my talk, not on my personal characteristics. But I welcomed these questions and answered them as honestly as I could. Then I asked the students why they felt such questions were important: could it be that the accidents of my personal history (American, Christian, trained in the United States, Germany, and Egypt) could affect my reading of history? If this is so for me, then why not for Iyad b. Musa? It was one of those moments every teacher lives for; suddenly they understood that all readers of history are biased.

No matter how much we may try, we cannot study history for purely antiquarian interests. Not only is our reading of the past shaped by what we think is important, it is also limited by our individual capacities to understand human societies and motivations. When Iyad wrote about Malik or Sahnun (two great scholars from the past), he lived in a world where dreams, prophecies, and miraculous events were as real as dates of death and places of residence, what we normally call "facts." Moreover, from Iyad's perspective, dreams and prophecies might well be more indicative of the truth of the matter: that Malik and Sahnun were exemplary scholars, worthy of emulation. As a scholar of religion, I am as interested in what Iyad makes of these exemplary scholars as I am in who "they actually were."[1] Yet in order to understand precisely what Iyad is doing with the historical material in front of him we must first, to the extent possible, reconstruct that history from materials not subject to his interpretations. Only then can we see the subtle manipulation of meaning by Iyad and other biographers. This book is therefore an attempt to reconstruct the history of Muslim scholars based primarily on documentary sources.

It is important to note, however, that the preponderance of early material sources derives from the Muslim west. The Umayyad caliphate had its seat in Damascus, but most of the administrative correspondence from that era has survived in Egypt. Likewise, we are told that Medina, Kufa, Baghdad, and other eastern cities were hotbeds of scholarly activity, yet the largest cache of early scholarly manuscripts comes from Kairouan in North Africa. Therefore, my methodological commitment to documentary evidence tilts this book west, and so it is western sources, such as Qadi Iyad's writings, that I call on most for their view of history. This book is not, however, merely a history of Muslim scholarship in North Africa; it rather attempts to define the very concept of a Muslim scholarly community and to account for the emergence of these communities from the very beginning of the Muslim story until the mid-tenth century.[2] Furthermore, as I demonstrate below, early Muslim scholarly communities were highly connected with one another. The very mercantilism that grew the wealth of Fustat and Baghdad also allowed for an active exchange of books, letters, and ideas as scholars traveled widely throughout the Islamic world. In this one North African library, we see clear evidence of these activities, and so this collection can be used as a foundation for a much broader history.

[1] Or, in the words of positivist Leopold von Ranke "*wie es eigentlich gewesen ist*" (as it actually was). See Fred Donner, *Narratives of Islamic Origins: The Beginnings of Islamic Historical Writing*, Studies in Late Antiquity and Early Islam, No. 14 (Princeton: Darwin Press, 1998), 26 n.

[2] This is why I have resisted the suggestions from two reviewers of earlier drafts that I use a narrower title for the book to underscore the large amount of North African material.

The Kairouan collection, however, only begins to take shape two hundred years after the death of the Prophet Muhammad. By that time, these scholars, known in Arabic as "people of knowledge" (*ahl al-ʿilm*) or simply "knowers" (*ʿulamāʾ*), were already well established. By the time that Iyad b. Musa is writing history in the twelfth century, these people, mostly but not all men, were marked off from other believers in several ways. Their schooling, their interaction with political authorities, their dress and public comportment – all were visible signs not only that they had mastered important facts about Islamic law, theology, and history, but also that they were keepers of a sacred trust. The knowledge they had was itself a gift from God, one of the ways that he guides his community along the straight path. Whether jurists, judges, theologians, or muftis, they continue to perform many functions in Muslim societies, and it is quite difficult to imagine Islam without them.

It is the very task of this book, however, to imagine Islam without the scholarly institutions that arose only centuries after Muhammad's death. Part of the confusion lies in our English translation of the Arabic *ʿulamāʾ*, because the word "scholars" seems to suggest "schools," that is, places of learning and a formal curriculum of study. But the Arabic word *ʿulamāʾ* is not so clear; it merely means "people who possess *ʿilm*." That last word also is hard to comprehend, because *ʿilm* can mean both knowledge that is acquired over years of study and also knowledge that is gained directly from God as a grace from him.[3] Further, these categories are generally thought to be related, such that great achievement in the mastery and interpretation of the sources is often taken to be a sign of God's grace; exceptional individuals were even identified as *mujaddidūn*, renewers of the age. To be an *ʿālim*, then, is to be recognized as having knowledge, and with this knowledge comes a kind of charisma. It is a divine gift, an intrinsic personal quality, and also a social phenomenon with tangible effects.

All three of these elements (divine, personal, and social) are important, and in stories about the Prophet's companions, scholars are portrayed as having had them all, in part. Later writers lionized this earliest generation, but they could not have functioned in Medinan society the way that scholars of the twelfth century (much less the twenty-first century) did; they may well have been people of knowledge, even with divine

[3] Franz Rosenthal, *Knowledge Triumphant: The Concept of Knowledge in Medieval Islam* (Leiden: E. J. Brill, 1970). Claude Gilliot, "ʿUlamāʾ," in *Encyclopaedia of Islam*, 2nd ed. (Leiden: E. J. Brill, 1962–2001).

dispensations, but they had no schools and no program of training. Therefore, I shall refer to these first generations as proto-scholars, individuals the memory of whom would be important for later generations, apart from what they actually may have accomplished. As I will discuss below, it is the process of memory by which writers such as Iyad b. Musa made these proto-scholars (Ali, Ibn Abbas, Abdullah b. Umar, and others) into exemplary individuals who, along with the "founders of legal schools," would carve out a clear path for future scholars, thereby helping to establish that third, social, element of their scholarly nature.

So while today the existence and importance of the *ʿulamāʾ* is well understood to be a central and vital part of this major world religious tradition, it was not always the case. Indeed, at various times and places it has not been scholars who led the community of Muslims but direct descendants of the Prophet, political leaders, Sufi mystics, and various other sorts of charismatic leaders, all of whom were held to be possessors of knowledge. This is certainly true in our own time, when many *madrasas* have become instruments of state control, and when politicians, physicians, journalists, and terrorists gladly speak in the name of Islam. Some observers, such as Khaled Abou El Fadl, have mourned this decline in the authority of the scholar as a particularly negative development of the modern age.[4] It seems to me, however, that scholarly authority has always been in conflict with other forms of Muslim religious authority. Especially in the first two centuries of Islam's history, when the role of scholars was vague and ill defined, there was little hint of the powerful institutions that would arise to guide Muslims when sultans and caliphs had seemingly abandoned religion.

Abou El Fadl's notion of scholarly interaction is less a historical description than an aspiration for the future. I am not saying that his depiction of a time when scholars freely debated with one another on the basis of reasoned analysis is inaccurate, only that it is incomplete. Further, his historical analysis is explicitly a call to Muslims to support this sort of scholarly authority today. This is a reasonable use of history, but it is not my purpose in this book. Far from seeing scholarly authority as a natural, inevitable development, deriving from the Prophet's own example, I see it as one of many competing visions of religious authority among early followers of Muhammad. Its development into a powerful and influential

[4] Khaled Abou El Fadl, *Conference of the Books: The Search for Beauty in Islam* (Lanham, MD: University Press of America, 2001). See also Shahab Ahmed, *What Is Islam? The Importance of Being Islamic* (Princeton: Princeton University Press, 2015).

institution strikes me as not at all inevitable, and yet the roots of this institution have never been fully examined in the light of documentary evidence.

APPROACHES TO EARLY MUSLIM HISTORY

Most books on the early history of Islam depend heavily on popular Muslim accounts that describe a satisfying story arc; it begins with Gabriel appearing to a humble prophet, moves to the establishment of an early Muslim state, and quickly jumps to Islam as a world religion with a splendid capital in Baghdad.[5] Fred Donner calls this the "descriptive approach" because it simply refashions the Muslim narrative sources without subjecting them to critical analysis.[6] Unfortunately, this approach runs the risk of glossing over some of the most interesting evidence. Over the past two hundred years, archeologists, papyrologists, numismatists, and other experts have patiently amassed an astounding trove of material from the early Islamic period. Much of this research has been published in obscure academic journals, and few have taken the time to survey the evidence in a systematic way.[7] But coins, glass weights, diplomatic correspondence, architecture, and other forms of material culture are a vital source for reconstructing early Islamic history. The stories told by these artifacts, however, do not neatly match the memory of early Muslim historians, writing centuries after the facts. These discrepancies have led to the rise of what Donner calls the "skeptical" view that casts doubt both on the dating of the Qurʾan and also (in its most radical

[5] The speed of such presentations elides decades of history, because as Steven Judd has pointed out "modern scholars have marginalized the Umayyad period" (*Religious Scholars and the Umayyads; Piety-Minded Supporters of the Marwānid Caliphate* [New York: Routledge, 2014], 12).

[6] Donner (*Narratives*, 16–26) distinguishes several different strands in recent historiography, ranging from this "descriptive approach" to "skeptics"; Herbert Berg, making a slightly different distinction, refers to "sceptical" and "sanguine" writers (*The Development of Exegesis in Early Islam: The Authenticity of Muslim Literature from the Formative Period,* Curzon Studies in the Qurʾān [Richmond, Surrey: Curzon, 2000], 111–113). Both Berg and Donner's typologies break down upon application to individuals (it is hard to know how Asma Afsaruddin, Matthew Gordon, or Miklos Muranyi would fit in). For a detailed analysis of these approaches, and an argument for a new common ground in the study of Islamic origins, see Jonathan Brockopp, "Islamic Origins and Incidental Normativity," *Journal of the American Academy of Religion* 84 (2016), 121–147.

[7] Notable exceptions include Andrew Rippin, *Muslims: Their Religious Beliefs and Practices*, 4th ed. (New York: Routledge, 2011), and Fred Donner, *Muhammad and the Believers: At the Origins of Islam* (Cambridge, MA: Harvard University Press, 2010).

form) on the historicity of Muhammad.[8] These scholars reject Muslims' accounts and attempt to describe the rise of Islam solely on the basis of these bits and pieces of evidence that serendipity has preserved for us.

Not surprisingly, the stories that these two groups try to tell diverge strongly one from another. On the one hand, we have the familiar description of Muhammad as a prophet, initially rejected by his people, but eventually founding a community of believers in Medina. The scriptures revealed to him inspired a new movement after his death, one that struggled initially to find its identity through a series of civil wars, but which eventually triumphed, establishing a world empire in a few short decades that stretched from the Atlantic to the borders of India and China. Islam, in this view, was complete just before the Prophet's death as the Qurʾan itself seems to state in one of the last verses said to have been revealed: "Today I have perfected for you your religion and completed my favor on you and chosen for you Islam as a religion" (Qurʾan 5:3). On the other hand, the most ardent skeptics spin a yarn that begins not with Muhammad's life, but with the establishment of empire by Arab leaders decades after Muhammad's supposed death. There are no Muslims in this depiction; rather, the Arabs are Christian, devoted to Jesus as a "praised messenger of God" (*muḥammad rasūl Allāh*).[9] Arising from the wars between the Byzantine and Persian empires, with their variant forms of Christianity, these "believers" cobble together recitations (*qurʾān*) from local churches and establish yet another form of Christian church. Eventually, an adjective initially referring to Jesus as one to be praised (*muḥammad*) is anthropomorphized into an Arabian prophet, and a back story of hardship, intrigue, and triumph is imagined for this character.

The first of these stories presents Islam as a triumph of God in history; the second presents Islam as a sham, built on borrowed foundations. As for which one is true, that depends on one's previous commitments. Since both accounts ignore evidence, they reveal more about those writing history rather than what actually happened. In my view, the mistake made by both these groups of scholars is the granting of an identity and

[8] Donner, *Narratives*, 26, calls this the "radically skeptical argument," a position that I believe is no longer tenable. For a fuller description and criticism of the skeptical position, see Jonathan Brockopp, "Interpreting Material Evidence: Religion at the 'Origins of Islam'," *History of Religions* 55 (2015), 121–147.

[9] Christoph Luxenberg, "A New Interpretation of the Arabic Inscription in Jerusalem's Dome of the Rock," in Karl-Heinz Ohlig and Gerd Puin (eds.), *The Hidden Origins of Islam* (Amherst, MA: Prometheus Books, 2010), 141.

a substance to the notion of seventh-century Islam far out of proportion to what either the evidence or sociological theory would support. Modern scholars who adopt a descriptive approach (and consider the Qurʾan and early literary sources trustworthy) must take seriously the fact that even these sources do not support any unified narrative of the rise of Islam. The Qurʾan's excoriating of the Bedouin for being merely *muslim* (obedient to Muhammad) and not *muʾmin* (true believers in the faith) in Sura 49:14 is precursor to divisive wars (of "apostasy" and *fiṭna*) that the Muslim historians record in great detail. It is instructive to note that later generations do not depict these various groups as being non-Muslims, but as unacceptable forms of Muslim: hypocrites, apostates, secessionists, or extremists. This is direct evidence that the legacy of Muhammad was contested, and that there were many different ideas on how best to be a "Muslim" during the seventh and eighth centuries. Further, such "Muslims" as may have existed after Muhammad's death must have been a small minority in a world that continued to be dominated by Christian, Jews, and Zoroastrians for centuries.

It is not really surprising that so many writers succumb to this descriptive approach; after all, the triumphal interpretations of Muslim historians make for a much better story. We should not expect "skeptical" scholars to make the same mistake, yet they do just that when they presume that the only possible form for Islam in the seventh century must have been the Islam of the ninth century, where Muhammad and the Qurʾan were recognized sources of knowledge and faith.[10] The truth, I suggest, is much more interesting. Based both on what we know of the history of other world religions and also on a sociological understanding of the emergence of new religious movements, we should expect that the utter lack of institutions to enforce any single notion of Muhammad, the Qurʾan, or Islam during this early period made for a very wide variety of views. Some individuals in the seventh century may well have been

[10] The late Patricia Crone, writing about putative seventh-century Muslims, found it hard to imagine that "they could have had a scripture containing legislation *without* regarding it as a source of law" ("Two Legal Problems Bearing on the Early History of the Qurʾān," *Jerusalem Studies in Arabic and Islam* 18 [1984], 1–37, at 14). She was right that they often did not regard it as a source of law, but wrong to imagine that this proves the nonexistence of the Qurʾan. As I will discuss below, physical evidence makes it clear that the Qurʾan existed in the seventh century. But the fact that early Muslims did not always pay close attention to Qurʾanic law also complicates comparative analysis, such as that done recently by Holger Michael Zellentin in *The Qurʾān's Legal Culture: The Didascalia Apostolorum as a Point of Departure* (Tübingen: Mohr Siebeck, 2013).

convinced of the reality of Muhammad and the truth of his message, but these individuals seem to have differed widely on the details. Also, individual groups of devotees must have been small, disconnected, and without any power to impose their views on others. Those of us committed to understanding this history need to develop methodologies for entertaining contradictory and even competing narratives,[11] including theories of how scholars came to be the arbiters of Islam and of Islamic history.

There is more: we should expect that individuals in the past were just as complex as people in the present. For example, we would certainly be mistaken if we thought that a powerful figure like the Umayyad Caliph Abd al-Malik b. Marwan held on to precisely the same set of motivations throughout his life. Similarly, we should not imagine that a magnificent and complex monument, such as the Dome of the Rock built by Abd al-Malik, should have been built with a single set of intentions.[12] Finally, we should expect that public engagement with such a structure would be even more variant, with each individual bringing his or her own set of presumptions to the experience. We may draw the same conclusions about other sources on which we build our history – a coin from Muʿawiya's reign, a historical account written two hundred years after the fact, even the Qurʾan itself – all must be subject to the same interpretive process. We cannot afford to ignore any of them, though we should not expect them to tell a single story. Rather, each piece of evidence is something like a broken fragment of a holograph. They all preserve information on the subject from a particular point of view; through careful analysis it is possible to use several fragments together to shed light on the whole. At the same time, that larger story should not detract from the integrity of the individual piece of evidence.

ORGANIZATION OF THIS BOOK

I opened this book with a story about Qadi Iyad's manipulation of stories, because I am concerned with both history and memory. By history, I mean the actual sociological circumstances that helped shape the

[11] As one example, François Déroche points out that scholars working on early Qurʾan manuscripts tend to try to organize them all into a single dating scheme, when it makes more sense that they were produced by different communities; see *Qurʾans of the Umayyads:* A First Overview (Leiden: E. J. Brill, 2014), 54.

[12] Chase Robinson does an admirable job of opening up possibilities in his *ʿAbd al-Malik* (Oxford: Oneworld, 2005), a book that provides more questions than answers. See his discussion of the Dome of the Rock on pages 3–9; cf. Rippin, *Muslims*, 63–67.

ʿ*ulamāʾ* into a community of authoritative individuals. That history is partially reflected in artifacts – coins, papyri, architecture – that happen to have been preserved. By memory, I mean the stories that people like Iyad tell about those artifacts and the people who produced them. The very coherence of these stories reveals them to be interpretive acts; they give meaning to those lives, weaving them into broader narratives of power and legitimation.[13] I want to be perfectly clear, however, that I consider both history and memory to be equally important, and I am well aware that in criticizing the interpretive acts of Qadi Iyad (along with those of Goldziher, Schacht, and others) I am also weaving a narrative out of scraps of evidence. I cannot claim my version is better, only that it is responding to a different set of interests.

After an overview of the sources here in this introduction, I begin in Chapter 1 by addressing the evidence about that first community, Muslims who are thought to have lived with the Prophet Muhammad in Medina, some of whom lived to see the establishment of the Umayyads in Damascus. Chapter 2 follows this chronological order, ending in 750 when I believe a true scholarly class begins to form. In a very real sense, however, the originating kernel of this book is found in Chapter 3, the early Abbasid period, when we finally have solid evidence that this scholarly community has emerged. In Chapters 4 and 5, I delve deeply into this documentary evidence to demonstrate how it can be used to undergird a history of early scholarly communities.[14] Much of this evidence derives from a single community in North Africa, allowing for an extraordinarily detailed account of scholarly activity during this period. Because that community was strongly connected with similar communities in Andalusia, Egypt, Arabia, and Iraq, however, the evidence also allows for some preliminary judgments about the rise of scholarly communities in the rest of the Muslim world.

This focus on North Africa is dictated by a unique set of ancient Arabic manuscripts more than one thousand years old. Not only are they among the earliest known examples of literary Arabic, they preserve texts from the late second and early third Islamic centuries (about 770–850 CE). In

[13] They are attempts at, in Shahab Ahmed's words, "hermeneutical engagement" (*What Is Islam*, 345). I do not go quite so far as Ahmed El Shamsy in ascribing a collective power to memory (*The Canonization of Islamic Law: A Social and Intellectual History* [Cambridge: Cambridge University Press, 2013], 9–10).

[14] I wish here to reiterate my gratitude to the anonymous reviewers of the first draft of this book for their many suggestions, comments, and criticisms, but primarily for suggesting the addition of a fifth chapter.

other words, these manuscripts are actual artifacts of a scholarly community that, beginning in the early ninth century, wrote copies of texts that were produced generations earlier. In doing so, they give us direct evidence of scholarly communities active by 780 at the latest. Chapters 1 and 2 are my attempt to push the boundary even earlier than 780, speculating on the rise of early scholarly communities even while maintaining my methodological commitments to depending primarily on material remains. The earlier we push this boundary, the thinner the evidence and so therefore the more speculative the arguments, but the result, I hope, is a consistent account of how the *ʿulamāʾ* may have arisen as a sociological force.

A REVIEW OF THE SOURCES

The primary sources for this study vary considerably from one period to the next. Documentary evidence for the seventh century is sparse – items of more durable material (coins, epigraphy) are represented out of proportion to other materials (such as papyri), and nearly all of these are from Egypt, which Muslim historical sources represent as either a province or a borderland (*thaghr*), not as a seat of either empire or scholarship. Our first dated witness to Arabic literary writing does not arise until 229/844, and it is a history of King David (attributed to Wahb b. Munabbih, d. 110/728 or 114/732) that has as much a Jewish character as an Islamic one.[15] At about the same time, Abd al-Malik b. Habib (d. 238/852) was said to have composed his "History," a copy of which has survived, although its authenticity has been questioned. The late date of manuscripts for this and other literary texts, along with the manipulation of memory by historians, has led some modern scholars to reject literary sources altogether. But I believe this is an error. As I discuss in Chapter 1, an analysis of Ibn Habib's account reveals some surprising insights into the individuals I term "proto-scholars." Further, we do not have to depend solely on Muslim historians to learn about the ancient Muslim past; three other categories of evidence can help us reconstruct this early period: (1) material remains, such as documents, coins, architecture, and epigraphy; (2) historical accounts from non-Muslims; and (3) the ancient manuscripts from Kairouan.

[15] See discussion in Chapter 2.

Material Evidence

Civilizations leave traces of their passing, and we have a surprising wealth of material sources for our study, even of the earliest period. From Arabic graffiti in caves to dated tax receipts on papyri, the rapid development of an Arabic (and perhaps Islamic) civilization in the seventh century is undeniable. Much of this material has been described by experts, but it is very hard to interpret; in fact, the same evidence can be drawn upon to support widely differing theories of the development of Islam. For our purposes, we must admit that coins, papyrus, and architecture give us almost no direct information about early Muslim scholars,[16] but they do establish an important framework of fundamental information.

In 622, Middle Persian and Greek were the main languages represented in the sources, with some Coptic documents as well. Arabic may have been widespread as a spoken language, but written Arabic had only lately been derived from the Nabatean script and was still in the process of development.[17] Already by 643, however, we have our first dated example of Arabic correspondence preserved on papyrus (Figure I.1).

Like many other early papyri, this one is composed in both Arabic and Greek, part of a group of twenty-two papyri from Egypt, dating from the period AH 22–57 (643–677 CE).[18] The Arabic here is formal and clear,

[16] For this reason, most historians of Islamic law simply ignore them. For example, neither Steven Judd (*Religious Scholars and the Umayyads*) nor Wael Hallaq (*The Origins and Evolution of Islamic Law* [Cambridge: Cambridge University Press, 2005]) address the important cache of papyri from the chancery of Qurra b. Sharik, and Judd claims that analysis of papyrus is "in its infancy" (p. 17). As I will try to demonstrate in this book, this over-dependence on Arabic literary sources has led legal historians to underestimate the importance of Jewish and Christian scholarly communities and misconstrue the role of writing among Muslim proto-scholars.

[17] Beatrice Gruendler, *The Development of the Arabic Scripts, from the Nabatean Era to the First Islamic Century According to Dated Texts*, Harvard Semitic Series, 43 (Atlanta: Scholars Press, 1993).

[18] Alan Jones, "The Dotting of a Script and the Dating of an Era: The Strange Neglect of PERF 558," *Islamic Culture* 72, no. 4 (1998), 95–103. See also Yūsuf Rāġib, "Les premiers documents arabes de l'ére musulmane," in Constantine Zuckerman (ed.), *Constructing the Seventh Century* (Paris: Assocation des Amis du Centre d'Histoire et Civilisation de Byzance, 2013), 679–726 at 702–703; idem, "Un papyrus arabe de l'an 22 de l'hégire," in Ghislaine Alleaume, Sylvie Denoix, and Michel Tuchscherer (eds.), *Histoire, archéologies et littératures du monde musulman: mélanges en l'honneur d'André Raymond* (Cairo: Institut Francais d'Archéologie Orientale, 2009), 363–372; Lejla Demiri and Cornelia Römer, *Texts from the Early Islamic Period of Egypt: Muslims and Christians at Their First Encounter; Arabic Papyri from the Erzherzog Rainer Collection, Austrian National Library, Vienna* (Vienna: Phoibos, 2009), 8–9; Gruendler, *Development*, 22.

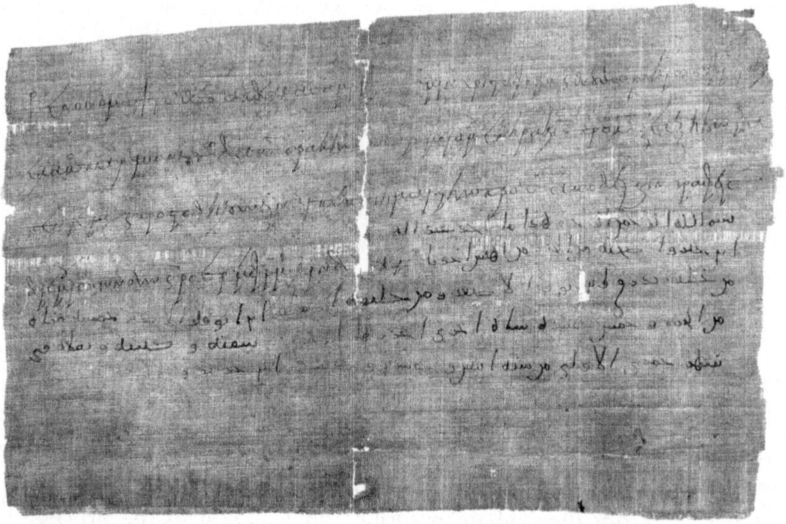

Figure I.1: Arabic correspondence dated to Jumada I, 22/April 643 (G 39726 Pap; PERF 558. 23 × 36 cm)

with a surprisingly early use of dots to differentiate consonants, but it is the continued appearance of Greek in these papyri over the next hundred years that is of greatest interest, since it demonstrates that the new Arab rulers continued to use Byzantine forms. Persian influence is also manifest. For example, the first datable use of the name Muhammad on an artifact is found not in the Arabic script, but in Pahlavi, inscribed on coins that continued to employ the iconography of the fallen Sasanid Empire: a Zoroastrian fire altar and the visage of the Emperor.[19] Coins minted by Arabs in former Byzantine territories likewise bore crosses and depictions of the Byzantine Emperor.

This continuity of usage is everywhere visible, from mundane tax receipts from Egypt[20] to the spectacular Dome of the Rock (completed 72/691), which combines Arabic inscriptions with Byzantine architectural

[19] Heinz Gaube, *Arabosasanidische Numismatik* (Braunschweig: Klinkhardt u. Biermann, 1973), 18–37.

[20] Kosei Morimoto, *The Fiscal Administration of Egypt in the Early Islamic Period* (Kyoto: Dohosha, 1981). Morimoto, p. 59, argues that a new Arabic ideal soon held sway.

style. Not for another century would Arabic completely displace these other languages,[21] and even then Persian (written in Arabic script) would see a revival. Cross-cultural influences in architecture would never fully disappear.

These cross-cultural influences are also apparent in the Qur'an, our sole literary text from the seventh century. I consider the Qur'an to be an early seventh-century document for several reasons. First, while our earliest dated Qur'ans are no earlier than other dated literary texts, we have far more ancient, dated manuscripts for the Qur'an than for any other text (fourteen fragments dated to the third Islamic century).[22] Second, some undated manuscripts of the Qur'an can be reasonably argued to have been written before 700;[23] no other literary text can make this claim. Third, the content of the Qur'an is quite dissonant, in both substance and style, from classical Arabic texts of the ninth century.[24] While Muslims may regard it as a record of revelation, given to the Prophet Muhammad piecemeal over the course of twenty-three years, I treat it as an archaic document that may well preserve material from the early seventh century and before.[25]

[21] Adolf Grohmann, "Aperçu de papyrologie arabe," *Études de papyrologie* 1 (1932) : 77–79.

[22] See François Déroche, "Les manuscrits arabes datés du IIIe/IXe siècle," *Revue des Études Islamiques* 55–57 (1987–1989), 343–379. Déroche finds no Qur'an fragments to be securely dated before 229; I was privileged to review several ancient fragments during a research trip in July 2015. I am grateful to Dr. Marie-Geneviève Guesdon at the Bibliothèque National de France and Dr. Elaine Wright at the Chester Beatty Library in Dublin for facilitating my research.

[23] An excellent summary of recent finds is found in Nicolai Sinai, "When Did the Consonantal Skeleton of the Quran Reach Closure?" *Bulletin of the School of Oriental and African Studies* 77, no. 2 (2014), 273–292 and 77, no. 3 (2014), 509–521, at 273–275 (my thanks to Chase Robinson for this reference). Detailed analysis is found in Déroche, *Qur'ans of the Umayyads*. As I discuss in Chapter 2, I agree with Déroche's reservations on the results of recent radiocarbon dating.

[24] For examples, see chapter 1 of Donner, *Narratives*, 35ff.

[25] By writing "seventh century and before" I am tacitly accepting the possibility proposed by Marco Schoeller ("Post-Enlightenment Academic Study of the Qur'ān," in Jane McAuliffe [ed.], *Encyclopaedia of the Qur'an* [Leiden: E. J. Brill, 2001–2006]) that the heart of Wansbrough's thesis of exegetical communities can be saved if the date for the compilation of the text is moved to the seventh century. In coming to this conclusion, I am reacting to both the internal nature of the Qur'an and also historical memory that places other "books of recitation" in the hands of Muhammad's rivals, including the anti-Prophet Musaylima.
For a fuller response to Wansbrough's original thesis, see Donner's extended argument in *Narratives*, 37–42.

To understand this document, however, several important caveats about its sociological function must be kept in mind. First, the written Qur'an was secondary to the memorization and oral performance of the text – the manuscripts we possess are, in part, mnemonic devices that aided in its teaching and memorization. Second, this ritual and performative nature of the text was its primary function in the early period, represented by the talismanic usage of quotations in the earliest coins, architecture, and some papyri.[26] Third, systematic attempts to connect specific verses to historical events, or to build legal or theological doctrines on specific verses, or to analyze grammatical usages – in short, systematic exegeses of any kind – date from the second/eighth century at the earliest.[27] In other words, I find that the evidence suggests that the compilation of the Qur'an occurred only a decade or two after the death of the Prophet; at the same time, I hold that the canonization of the Qur'an as the primary source of divine knowledge was a much longer process that took centuries.[28] In the present study, the Qur'an therefore has three distinct roles: (1) a record of Muhammad's views of scholars and scholarship in the early seventh century (or, more piously expressed, God's views as revealed through Muhammad); (2) a material witness to the activities of proto-scholars who wrote the earliest manuscript fragments we now possess; and (3) a religious authority invoked by and interpreted by later groups of scholars.

Non-Arabic Literary Sources

Given the sheer weight of Islamic history, it is hard to regard the Qur'an and other documentary evidence outside the powerful interpretive lens of Muslim memory. Contemporary accounts in Greek, Syriac, Coptic, and Persian are therefore particularly valuable, as they also bore witness to the rise of this new Arab polity. Numerous references to the conquering Arabs in non-Arabic sources give us a complex picture, though once again direct information on Islam or scholars is lacking. Sophronius, Patriarch of Jerusalem, offers us some of our first impressions of the Arab

[26] Sinai, "Consonantal Skeleton," 290–291.

[27] I discuss the problems of reconstructing early texts that claim to be systematic works from the first Islamic century in Chapter 2.

[28] I am in agreement with the overall argument in Sinai, "Consonantal Skeleton;" however, it is worth noting that even his "emergent canon" theory addresses only the question of when the *rasm* was fixed, not the process of the text becoming canon in Muslim law and theology.

conquests in his Christmas sermon from 634.[29] An account from one "Thomas the Presbyter" gives us our first datable mention of Muhammad in non-Muslim accounts, noting that "there was a battle between the Romans and the Arabs of Muḥammad (*ṭayyāyē d-Mḥmṭ*) in Palestine twelve miles east of Gaza."[30] As with accounts from Arab historians, these literary impressions were often collected and written down centuries after the events themselves, yet they offer us a valuable perspective on the period.[31] The names given to these conquerors were *ṭayyāyē* (meaning Arab), Saracen, and *mhaggrāyē*, a Syriac version of the Arabic *muhājir*.[32] The terms Muslim and Islam do not appear in the earliest of these sources, just as they are not found in coins or papyri from the earliest period.

This absence is a useful reminder that in the perspective of the broader world of the seventh century, Islam did not yet exist. Nonetheless, I do not agree with those skeptics who doubt the existence of Muhammad, nor even with Fred Donner, who suggests that we call these people the "believers' movement" and that "it would be historically inaccurate to call the early Believers' movement 'Islam'."[33] As I have argued elsewhere, such assertions conflate public expression of religion with the religion itself.[34] What we can say is that such Muslims as may have existed in the

[29] Sebastian Brock, "Syriac Views of Emergent Islam," in G. H. A. Juynboll (ed.), *Studies on the First Century of Islamic Society* (Carbondale: Southern Illinois University Press, 1982), 9–21, at 9; Robert Hoyland, *Seeing Islam as Others Saw It. A Survey and Analysis of the Christian, Jewish and Zoroastrian Writings on Islam* (Princeton: Darwin Press, 1997), 70–71; David Thomas and Barbara Roggema (eds.), *Christian Muslim Relations: A Bibliographical History*, Volume 1 (600–900) (Leiden: E. J. Brill, 2009), 124–125, with references.

[30] Hoyland, *Seeing Islam*, 120.

[31] Thomas and Roggema, *Christian Muslim Relations*, is particularly valuable in this regard as full bibliographic information is given, including information on the manuscripts that serve as witnesses to this material. See also Maged Mikhail, *From Byzantine to Islamic Egypt: Religion, Identity and Politics after the Arab Conquest* (London: I. B. Taurus, 2014). For an instructive analysis of non-Muslim sources for the history of the Muslim conquest, see Phil Booth, "The Muslim Conquest of Egypt Reconsidered," in Zuckerman (ed.), *Constructing the Seventh Century*, 639–679.

[32] Brock, "Syriac Views," 15; Hoyland, *Seeing Islam*, 180 (see his notes for discussion of alternative meanings). This term is the source of Patricia Crone's Hagarism to reflect these Christian impressions of the early Muslim movement (*Hagarism: The Making of the Islamic World* [Cambridge: Cambridge University Press, 1980]).

[33] Fred Donner, *Muhammad and the Believers*, 195. Also Donner, "From Believers to Muslims: Confessional Self-Identity in the Early Islamic Community," *Al-Abhath: Journal of the Faculty of Arts and Sciences of the American University of Beirut* 50–51 (2002–2003), 9–53.

[34] Brockopp, "Interpreting Material Evidence." I do not go quite so far as Gregor Schoeler (*The Genesis of Literature in Islam: From the Aural to the Read*, Shawkat Toorawa

seventh century were part of a small, private, minority movement within already established Christian, Zoroastrian, and Jewish religious worlds. And many of the early Muslims may not have strongly distinguished themselves from their Christian (or Jewish or Zoroastrian) neighbors. That a new religion emerged intact from this sectarian environment at all is remarkable, and that, I will argue, is the chief legacy of the emerging scholarly community.

The Manuscripts of Kairouan, Tunisia

As I suggested above, the treasures of the mosque-library of Kairouan have dramatically changed our knowledge of the first Islamic centuries. As recently as 1989, François Déroche could identify only fourteen manuscripts written in Arabic (excluding Qurʾans and Christian writings) that could be securely dated before AH 300. Of these, six came from the mosque-library of Kairouan in the modern nation of Tunisia. Since then, eighteen more manuscripts dated before 300 have come to light, seventeen of which come from Kairouan (listed in the Appendix). Not only has our evidentiary basis for studying Muslim scholars more than doubled, the majority of this ancient material derives from a single location. The importance of this shift in evidence has not been widely appreciated, and so this book focuses on the ways that this rich material evidence can form a framework of inquiry, grounding our reading of literary sources.

For example, Donner, following Fuat Sezgin and many others, gives us a list of "books" on history written by Muslims, including twenty-four authors who lived before Wahb b. Munabbih, putative author of the earliest dated literary manuscript.[35] However, analysis of the Kairouan manuscripts suggests that this list is all but meaningless. First, we have no material evidence of books (in the sense of authored texts) from such an early period. Further, even when we do find books (around AH 200), we continue to see fluid texts of mixed authorship for many generations. Second, we do have sparse evidence for some texts that antedate authored books, but these appear to be simple compilations of reports (*aḥādīth* or *akhbār*) with no ordering principle and little authorial control. Third,

[trans.], The New Edinburgh Islamic Surveys [Edinburgh: Edinburgh University Press, 2009], 1) who argues that these speculations have "a truly damaging effect," however, since such challenges force historians to reassess the value of their sources.

35 Donner, *Narratives*, 297–306. Wahb's text does not appear in Donner's list, perhaps because it has to do with pre-Islamic history.

Donner suggests that we can see "rough trends" in early historical scholarship from such a list of titles, yet again, the Kairouan manuscripts demonstrate that titles were fungible, often attached to a text long after its composition. Finally, Donner's list might give the impression of a scholarly culture based on written materials in the seventh century, when our evidence (as Donner himself admits) points rather to an oral culture with some written materials.

This is important because of the distinction I maintain between proto-scholars (individual savants who passed on knowledge in an informal manner) and scholars (who worked together in interconnected communities). As I discuss in Chapter 3, the Kairouan manuscripts allow us to prove the existence of a mature scholarly community just before the beginning of the third/ninth century. By this, I mean that scholars at that point had begun to write actual books, a notion that I restrict to a text written in a uniform style in a single effort and then passed on to other scholars verbatim. To have books therefore means to have a community that can maintain the discipline necessary for the faithful transmission of these texts. Further, these earliest books are both first- and second-order texts. First-order texts are those that attempt to clarify rules of ritual or practice, establishing a practical guide for Muslims to follow.[36] Second-order texts are of value only to a very specialized group of readers, because they are interested in the small details, interstitial categories, and controversies that arise after application of these first-order rules.[37] In other words, these are sophisticated texts that had moved beyond the simple collection of authoritative statements of the Prophet and other legal authorities, though this process of collection continued through the ninth century and beyond. However, if the appearance of this community is the beginning of one sociological process (the *ʿulamāʾ* as a significant social and religious force), it is the end of another, and so the question I attempt to answer in Chapters 1 and 2 of this book is: what was the sociological foundation from which that scholarly community arose? I am not the first to ask this question.

[36] For the earliest example of these first-order questions, see Brockopp, "The Minor Compendium of Ibn ʿAbd al-Ḥakam (d. 214/829) and Its Reception in the Early Mālikī School," *Islamic Law and Society* 12, no. 2 (2005), 149–181, at 164–174.

[37] For a definition of first-, second-, and third-order legal texts in light of the *Mudawwana* (a second-order text deriving from the middle third/ninth century), see Brockopp, "Saḥnūn's *Mudawwanah* and the Piety of the 'Sharīʿah-Minded'," in Kevin Reinhart and Robert Gleave (eds.), *Islamic Law in Theory: Studies on Jurisprudence in Honor of Bernard Weiss* (Leiden: E. J. Brill, 2014), 129–141, at 137–139.

Literary Evidence

During the ninth century, as the scholarly community matured, it sought to establish its own congruence with the history of Islam.[38] One of the earliest of these texts is the *Taʾrīkh* of Abd al-Malik b. Habib (d. 238/853). Already in the ninth century, it was impossible for Ibn Habib to imagine a history of Islam without a scholarly class, and his *Taʾrīkh* insists that every generation of Muslims was led by scholars. As we will see in Chapter 1, however, he is hard pressed to identify many of these scholars by name and gives very little evidence of their scholarly accomplishments. His text, however, was antecedent to a very productive genre in Islamic scholarly history, the biographical dictionary.[39] As this genre developed, single texts would include hundreds of short biographies (and many longer ones), listing the scholars of past generations and their major accomplishments. By the time this genre of writing reached its mature state, in the eleventh century, the *ʿulamāʾ* had been well established as key authority figures for centuries, deeply rooted in the tradition.

It is certainly true that these texts were first written down only centuries after the facts discussed in this book, and that their authors often had political and historical preferences that caused them to suppress or fabricate memory.[40] Also, it would be fair to say that literary sources are not always interested in historical truth, but sometimes preserve stories merely for their entertainment or hermeneutic value. Nonetheless, these texts remain a vital resource for our study for three reasons. First, and

[38] Donner, *Narratives of Islamic Origins*, 112ff. While I agree with Donner's general views about the legitimizing value of history writing, I subscribe to a sociological, rather than psychological, explanation.

[39] For an analytical summary of the genre, see R. Stephen Humphreys, *Islamic History: A Framework for Inquiry*, rev. ed. (Princeton: Princeton University Press, 1991), 187–207. For analysis, see Dwight Reynolds (ed.), *Interpreting the Self: Autobiography in the Arabic Literary Tradition* (Berkeley: University of California Press, 2001); Jawid Mojaddedi, *The Biographical Tradition in Sufism: The* ṭabaqāt *Genre from al-Sulamī to Jāmī* (Richmond, Surrey: Curzon, 2001); Michael Cooperson, *Classical Arabic Biography: The Heirs of the Prophets in the Age of al-Ma'mun* (Cambridge: Cambridge University Press, 2000) and idem, "Ibn Ḥanbal and Bishr al-Ḥāfī: A Case Study in Biographical Traditions," *Studia Islamica* 86 (1997), 71–101.

[40] In *Religious Scholars and the Umayyads*, Steven Judd gives many examples of these preferences (25–34), but holds that the overall bias of these texts is usefully different than the bias of chroniclers. This may be so, but Judd's book also exemplifies the pitfalls of too great a dependence on this one source. For example, he purports to describe "the Umayyad scholarly community" (14) as reflected in these sources when I believe that no organized community existed in this period, at least not the way that I am defining it.

perhaps most obviously, these texts are often our only source of information about many persons and events in early Islamic history. To abandon them because of their problematic nature is simply to consign much of this history to oblivion.[41] Second, all literary texts are not alike. Texts written for widely differing purposes (grammatical explication, legal exegesis) can "accidentally" contain important historical facts,[42] and manuscript analysis can reveal the additions and deletions of later generations as texts are copied. Third, literary texts do not come to us in isolation, but can be read in the context of other evidence. Because of the unique manuscript evidence from Kairouan, I draw primarily on literary sources from the Maliki tradition. Unlike prosopographical texts from other schools of law and theology, many of the second- and third-century figures mentioned in the Maliki biographical dictionaries are represented in the manuscript tradition, either as authors, scribes, students, or owners of manuscripts. Further, in the case of Ibn Habib and Abu l-Arab, we find their own texts among these manuscripts and, in the case of Abu l-Arab, his personal hand-written copies. Therefore, the manuscripts provide independent verification of some of the activities and acquaintances of these biographers.

Beyond the biographical dictionary, other literary texts occasionally offer insights as to the workings of scholars. These include accounts of the Prophet's life and that of his earliest companions (mostly concerned with political and military matters) and collections of traditions (*ḥadīth*). One might well imagine the original, oral nature of these stories as the Prophet's accomplishments, along with those of pre-Islamic Arab heroes such as Antar and Imru l-Qays, would have been remembered and performed wherever there were Arabs to hear them. Attempts have been made to reconstruct some of these early narratives, such as the *Life of the Prophet* by Ibn Ishaq (d. 150/767), from fragments preserved in literary texts written centuries later.[43] There are also political histories that give us detailed background for some of the names and expressions we see on coins and papyri and specialized histories of bureaucrats. For example, al-Jahshiyari (d. 331/942) wrote an important history of bureaucracy (*Kitāb al-wuzarāʾ wa l-kuttāb*) through the year 296/908. But the unique manuscript that preserves his text was written hundreds of years later.

[41] Patricia Crone, *Slaves on Horses: The Evolution of the Islamic Polity* (Cambridge: Cambridge University Press, 2003), 7; quoted in Donner, *Narratives*, 26.

[42] Donner, *Narratives*, 16–19.

[43] I address the problems of such reconstruction attempts in Chapter 2.

Likewise, early legal texts may preserve material that stems from even earlier periods, but with all of these, teasing out that earliest layer is difficult and controversial.

Many of these texts are based on an oral literature known as *ḥadīth*. In its simplest form, a *ḥadīth* is a narrative introduced by a chain of authorities, such as the following well-known *ḥadīth:*

> Scholars are the heirs of the prophets who have endowed them with knowledge as a legacy. He who has chosen knowledge has taken a generous share, and he who has taken a path towards the acquisition of knowledge, for him God will smooth a path to Paradise.[44]

In this book, I take a generally skeptical view of our ability to argue the authenticity of individual *ḥadīth*,[45] and my analysis does not depend on an ability to determine whether individuals in the chain of transmission fabricated or simply passed on words attributed to the Prophet. I do accept, however, that generations of proto-scholars and scholars engaged in the transmission of *ḥadīth*. Further, examination of early manuscripts helps us to isolate key nodes of activity that can help corroborate other evidence in reconstructing the earliest communities of Muslim scholars.

To summarize this overview of the sources, my study presumes that any history of early Muslim scholars must conform to what we know about early Islamic history based on documentary evidence. This gives us two boundaries that are fairly secure. In the earliest period (622–680 CE), we can affirm that there were no Islamic scholarly institutions and no Arabic books (save perhaps the Qurʾan).[46] There must have been,

[44] Gilliot, "'Ulama'," 10: 801. Arendt Wensinck, *Concordance et indices de la tradition musulmane*, 8 vols. (Leiden: E. J. Brill, 1936–1988), 4:321.

[45] I am impressed by the work of Harald Motzki and others in building a plausible case for the activity of certain proto-scholars, such as Ata b. Abi Rabah (d. 105/723), but Motzki is not always clear about the limited nature of his claims. In a response to Gledhill ("Motzki's Reliable Transmitter: A Short Answer to P. Gledhill," *Islamic Law and Society* 19, no. 2 [2012], 194–199), Motzki clarifies that the notion that we can recover "authentic" transmissions from Ata is subject to problems of transmission of variants, editorial influences, and "all the imponderables of the early 2nd cent. H., when written documentation of instruction was in its infancy" (196).

[46] By institutions I refer to the professional schools (*madrasas*) and positions of high authority (*qāḍī* and *muftī*) that fully manifested themselves in the ninth century and beyond. This is not to say that were no scholars during this early period, only that they must have acted and functioned differently because these institutions did not yet exist. At a workshop in June of 2016, Gudrun Kraemer pointed out to me that the Qurʾan does not necessarily fit my definition of a book, since it does not manifest a uniform style. As I argue in Chapter 1, however, while the Qurʾan may not have been originally composed as a book, it was made into one through a secondary scholarly process.

however, knowledge and awareness of scholars in the established religious traditions of Judaism, Christianity, and Zoroastrianism. History seems to suggest that this was a period of nearly constant warfare, both wars of conquest and various civil wars, but what little material evidence we have suggests an administration that was professional and effective. It is reasonable to expect, therefore, that our earliest scholars were engaged in the bureaucracy, yet evidence seems to suggest that they were individuals somewhat set apart from the vicissitudes of politics who had the leisure and inclination to devote time to the collection and passing on of memory on an oral basis to the next generation. The second boundary is met in 200/815 by which point we have overwhelming evidence of self-conscious scholarly communities. Chapters 1 and 2 lead up to that second boundary, while Chapters 3, 4, and 5 are devoted to explaining the history of those earliest communities.

AUTHORITY AND "CONNECTIVITY"

The above-quoted *ḥadīth*, "scholars are the heirs of the prophets," points to one central question for this book: that of authority and legitimation. The question is important because it is not at all obvious how a religion survives the death of the founding figure with his direct, charismatic authority. The early history of Islam is littered with the murdered bodies of pretenders to the Prophet's authority, including those of his son-in-law Ali and his grandson Husayn. The Umayyad princes, who eventually took power in Damascus in 661, seem to have ruled more like Byzantine emperors than like the Arab tribal leaders from whom they were descended. Meanwhile, other Arab leaders claimed holdings of the former Byzantine and Persian empires for their own, establishing virtually independent fiefdoms far from the grip of Damascus.

In reviewing the evidence, I find that Muslims survived the turmoil of their first century largely without the help of scholars. Only after the year 200/815 when scholars were relatively well established did they begin to play a legitimizing role, and soon thereafter it became impossible to imagine Islam without them. As I see it, the biographical dictionary was both the record and the device by which their scholarly authority was made known to others. This unique form of literature has been widely studied, and I make use of it in this book to contrast its interpretation of history with the evidence from the material sources. There is, however, another famous *ḥadīth* that is central to understanding the *ʿulamāʾ*, yet it points to a very different role for scholars: "Seek knowledge even if in China."[47]

Three aspects of this short phrase are worth noting. First, the command to seek (*uṭlubū*) is related to the Arabic word for student (*ṭālib*). Communities of scholars were not merely made of leaders, but also of followers, students who ensured the legacy of their masters by writing down their texts and passing on stories of their exemplary actions. A list of students is an essential part of any entry in a biographical dictionary, and ancient manuscripts preserve the names of many other students whose identity is otherwise lost to us.

Second, the notion of "knowledge" in this *ḥadīth* is clearly not something restricted to "Islamic" sources, such as Qur'an and *ḥadīth*, for then there would be no reason to travel to China for it. Rather, knowledge is a more universal concept, and the philosophers would explain that all knowledge is from God, who himself is the all-knowing, the source of the active intellect. This perception leads to the third point, connectivity.[48] Whatever else we may say about early Islamic history, it is full of movement. From the Prophet's night journey and *hijra* to the conquests, we see great movements of peoples in the seventh century. And this movement continues into the mercantilism of the eighth century. If we see scholars only as those who draw the lines of orthodoxy, then we miss their roles as travellers and boundary crossers who traverse great distances (both physically and conceptually) to seek knowledge. In the communities reflected in the Kairouan manuscripts, scholars, books, and ideas travel the shores of the Mediterranean just as easily as commodities, such that regional capitals in North Africa and Spain are closely connected to Damascus, Medina, and Baghdad and begin to rival them as centers of learning. For this reason, evidence from a library in North Africa can be highly informative of the Muslim scholarly project in general.

[47] This *ḥadīth* does not appear to be in our earliest collections, and some have questioned its authenticity; I do not have an opinion on this matter as the relevant point is its ubiquity during the period when scholarly communities were well established. That is, I am interested in it as a reflection of scholarly self-understanding, not as historical evidence for the existence of this practice during the lifetime of the Prophet.

[48] Peregrine Horden and Nicholas Purcell, *The Corrupting Sea: A Study of Mediterranean History* (Oxford: Blackwell, 2000), 123–171. My interpretation here was inspired by my residency at the National Endowment for the Humanities Institute in Barcelona in 2013, entitled "Networks and Knowledge: Synthesis and Innovation in the Muslim-Christian-Jewish Medieval Mediterranean."

To return to the definition I offered at the beginning of this introduction: scholarly knowledge is an intrinsic personal quality, a social phenomenon with tangible effects and also a divine gift. Historically, we see this first when individuals live an exemplary life by mirroring the life of the Prophet. Of course, there are many ways to do this, and later writers classify such individuals as mystics, ascetics, warriors, or scholars, but the key element is a personal decision to devote oneself to Muhammad's example, or at least to describe one's activities as devoted in this way. Over time, as generations become further removed from the sources of authority, it is mastery of the religious sources that becomes key. Initially, these sources are limited to knowledge of the Qurʾan and the Prophet's life story, but eventually the sources expand to include not only Qurʾan and *ḥadīth*, but also commentary on these, rules of grammar, modes of reasoning, and other products of the scholarly process. The spread of Muslims in the world also requires authority to be passed on through personal contact: traveling in search of knowledge, living with exemplary scholars, treating scholarly books as relics, and recreating simulacra of authoritative places (especially Medina) in new territories. I place divine authority last in terms of historical development, which is exactly opposite to the way that Iyad b. Musa imagines history. In his view, scholars are authoritative because God willed them to be so, a point he proves through careful interpretation of Qurʾanic texts. But historically the aura of divine authority arrives last, as scholars are late to crown their achievements with the inevitability of divine foreordainment. It is not the purpose of this book to argue what God actually does, but in terms of sociological effect, it is clear that by claiming the mantle of the Prophet, scholars wield real authority in Muslim societies, giving them the support to stand up against political and other powers.

I

Foundations, 622–680

In a book about the rise of the scholarly class in Islamic history, it may seem odd to begin in the early seventh century. After all, it is not until the end of the eighth century that the hallmarks of this institution become visible: a community of teachers and students who establish an independent institution of scholarship, setting themselves up as arbiters of correct religious action on both the individual and societal planes. Further, only in the ninth century do we have our first dated manuscript fragments that confirm the existence of this group. However, as I have studied these ninth-century fragments over the past two decades, it has become increasingly clear to me that they exhibit dependence on what must have been a long and complex history. Much of that history is hidden from us, but it need not remain entirely obscure. Building on both material and literary evidence, we can learn a great deal about the specific ways that the scholarly class arose, as well as some suggestions as to why they became the arbiters of Islamic orthopraxy.

In delving into this past, stories form a significant resource, often our only witness to important events. These stories come down to us through a complex process of oral and written transmission, leading to serious debates on their usefulness for any reconstruction of the scholarly past, especially for this nearly sixty-year period from 622 to 680. For example, Muslims themselves recall this period as one of almost constant warfare – not only the famous conquests that would see the fall of the Sasanid Empire and the absorption of much of the Byzantine, but also a series of deadly civil conflicts. As a result, narratives of early events can be distinctly partisan in nature; examples of both selective memory as well as wholesale fabrication are not hard to find. For modern historians, these differing accounts are useful because they allow us to discern interpretations of events (which vary widely) from basic factual matters (which all interpreters address).[1] However, this manipulation of data has led to a historiographical debate between "sanguine" scholars and skeptics. Skeptics doubt the possibility of extracting any useful information from narrative sources and put their faith in material evidence (coins, papyri) and non-Muslim historical accounts to ground an alternative telling of early Muslim history. Healthy skepticism is useful in questioning certain assumptions that modern historians make when reconstructing the past, especially a period that is held to be exemplary for later generations of Muslims. As discussed in the Introduction, however, I do not believe that literary sources should be abandoned, since reading them in the context of other forms of evidence yields important insights. I begin therefore with a pair of well-known stories that, upon further analysis, have surprising implications.

After the death of the Prophet Muhammad in 11/632 we are told that leadership of the community passed to his Companion and friend Abu Bakr b. Abi Quhafa. But Abu Bakr died soon afterwards and was succeeded by Umar b. al-Khattab, who had a much larger impact on the community. What is interesting is that Muslim historians, writing centuries after the fact, remember these early leaders as having great difficulty establishing rules that accorded with religious authority. For example, the story is told that Umar prescribed stoning as the proper punishment for cases of adultery, and that he was certain that there was a verse from the Qur'an to back him up. However, among all the Companions of the Prophet who had heard revelation from Muhammad's lips, no one else seemed to have remembered that verse. The story is recorded in the *Muwaṭṭa'* of Malik b. Anas (d. 179/795) with great drama:

Malik said, on the authority of Yahya b. Sa'id on the authority of Sa'id b. al-Musayyab whom he heard say: "When Umar b. al-Khattab came from Mina, he made his camel kneel at al-Abtah; coming together in an open space, he cast his cloak out and dropped to the ground. Then he raised his hands to the sky and said, "Oh God! My years have lengthened, my strength has weakened, and my flock is scattered. Gather me up to you having missed and neglected nothing." Then he came to Medina and preached to the residents, saying, "Oh, People! Paths (*sunan*) have been laid down for you. Obligations have been demanded of you. You have been left with a clear way unless you lead people astray to the right and left." He struck one hand upon the other and said: "You seem to have utterly

[1] Donner, *Narratives*, 26–27.

forgotten the stoning verse! People are saying: 'We cannot find two *ḥadd* punishments in God's book.' But the Messenger of God, may God bless him and grant him peace, stoned [in cases of adultery]; so we have stoned! By Him who holds my soul in His hand, had it not been that people would have said 'Umar b. al-Khattab added [a verse] to the Book of God Most High,' I would have written it: 'As for the man and the woman, stone them absolutely [*al-shaykh wa l-shaykha fa'rjumū-humā l-batta*].' Certainly, we recited that [as part of the Qur'an during the lifetime of the Prophet]."[2]

This story may well be apocryphal, but consider the fact that whatever fabrications may have occurred, those who passed on this story did not appear to have a problem with the representation of early Companions as having differed on which verses belonged in the Qur'an. Nor did they fabricate a community of scholarly experts who could have helped Umar resolve his conundrum. Further, the fact that the "missing" verse is recorded explicitly here demonstrates the community's continuing anxiety about the authenticity of revelation, even 150 years after the Prophet's death when the story was first written down.

It is quite reasonable that Umar faced many situations not anticipated either by the Prophet or the Qur'an, even though that assumption is in tension with the notion that Islam was perfected before Muhammad's death. The best known example of Umar's independence is a second well-known tale of Umar establishing the *dīwān*, an ordered ranking of membership in the community to help determine the just distribution of spoils from the wars of conquest that were proceeding apace.[3] On its face, this register would seem to contradict the idea of the *Umma* as a community that stressed the essential equality of Muslims. Our historians confirm that the notion was debated, but this particular theological concern did not arise. One version of the debate from al-Baladhuri (d. 279/892) reads as follows:

Muhammad b. Sa'd told me on the authority of al-Waqidi from A'idh b. Yahya from Abu l-Huwayrith from Jubayr b. al-Huwayrith b. Nuqaydh that Umar b. al-Khattab, [may God be] satis[fied with] him, took counsel with the Muslims regarding implementation of the register (*dīwān*).

[2] Mālik b. Anas, *Al-Muwaṭṭa'*, Aḥmad Rātib 'Armūsh (ed.), Recension of Yaḥyā b. Yaḥyā (Beirut: Dār al-Nafā'is, 2001), 592 (chapter on *ḥadd* punishments, *ḥadīth* no. 1501). As I discuss in Chapter 3, the *Muwaṭṭa'* was not an authored text, but has come down to us in several different versions. This same *ḥadīth*, for example, is also found in al-Shaybani's recension (Beirut: Dār al-Yarmūk, n.d., 200), with some slight differences, including an addition to the "missing" Qur'an verse.

[3] A. A. Duri, "Dīwān" in *Encyclopaedia of Islam*, 2nd ed. See also Gerd Puin's dissertation, *Der Dīwān von 'Umar ibn al-Ḫaṭṭāb: ein Beitrag zur frühislamischen Verwaltungsgeschichte* (Bonn: Rheinischen Friedrich-Wilhelms-Universität, 1970).

Ali b. Abi Talib suggested: "Each year, divvy up the wealth (*māl*) that you take in, but take nothing for yourself." Uthman said: "I believe that great wealth will make the people rich. But if you do not keep careful account, so that you know who has taken and who has not, I reckon there will be chaos." Al-Walid b. Hisham b. al-Mughira recalled: "I once went to Syria and saw its kings implementing a register to recruit an army. So implement a register and recruit an army!"

So [Umar] took their counsel and called upon Aqil b. Abi Talib, Makhrama b. Nawfal and Jubayr b. Mut'im, for they were spokesmen for the Quraysh, and said: "Register the people according to their rank, starting with the clan of Hashim, followed by Abu Bakr and his people, and then Umar and his people." When they looked at Umar he said: "By God, I wish it to be this way." So they began with those closest to the Prophet, God bless him and grant him peace: the closest, then the next closest, placing Umar where God himself had placed him.

Muhammad [Ibn Sa'd] told me on the authority of al-Waqidi from Usama b. Zayd b. Aslam from his father and his grandfather who said:

The clan of Adi came up to Umar and said: "You are the representative of the Prophet of God, God bless him and grant him peace, and the representative of Abu Bakr who himself was the representative (*khalīfa*) of the Prophet of God, God bless him and grant him peace. If you have placed yourself where these [worthies] have placed you, then it is the people (*qawm*) who have written down [the register]."[4]

I recount these well-known stories about Umar to help us draw the first boundary that I referred to in the Introduction. These stories indicate that early Muslim historians agreed that, after the death of Muhammad, the community seems to have lacked an authoritative method for establishing religious knowledge. In the first case, Umar finds no one to back up his memory of a verse from the Qur'an and so is forced to make a ruling that seems to contradict the text of the Qur'an.[5] Notably, he is willing to impose his ruling on the community, even though he is unwilling to impose his memory of a missing verse upon the Qur'an. In the second case, Umar gathers advisers around him, listens to their very different proposals (none of which were based on Qur'an or Prophetic precedent), and then comes up with his own decision, which itself is different from what his advisers had suggested. Again, the point is not what Umar actually did, but how he is remembered. Even two hundred years after these events, Muslim historians

[4] Aḥmad al-Balādhurī, *Futūḥ al-buldān*, 'Abdallāh Anīs al-Ṭabbā' and Umar Anīs al-Ṭabbā' (eds.) (Beirut: Mu'assasat al-Ma'ārif, 1987), 630–631 (ed. DeGoeje, 1882, 449–450). The 'Adī b. Ka'b was Umar's own clan, a minor branch of the Quraysh.

[5] I have no problem with the notion that Umar recognized the Qur'an as something that ought to be authoritative, even though the evidence suggests that there was still considerable variation in the text at this time. Nonetheless, I believe Wael Hallaq goes too far in claiming that Umar's "enforcement of Quranic laws point to the centrality of the Quran in the emerging state and society" (Hallaq, *Origins*, 33).

did not imagine anything like a cadre of authoritative people of knowledge (i.e., the *'ulamā'*) to have existed during this period, probably because there was no such group. We have no suggestion (in either material or early literary sources) of a formal community of Muslim scholars, nor were there madrasas, books of Islamic law, classification of the sciences, or any of the other social institutions we commonly associate with the *'ulamā'*. This does not mean that there were no advisers or no religious authorities, only that we should not expect such individuals to conform to the standards for an *'ālim* developed centuries later.

I underscore these points because of a tendency by modern authors to misrepresent the earliest period of Islam in one of two ways. On the one hand, apologists downplay the confusion of the early community on how to be a Muslim.[6] They regard the early community of the Prophet's Companions as *al-salaf al-ṣāliḥ*, a group blessed by their proximity to Muhammad and so participants in a "golden age" of correct practice. Such a view represents the past as an ideal example for Muslims to strive for – a worthy use of religious history but one that diminishes the actual challenges faced by this community. On the other hand, extreme skeptics doubt whether Muhammad existed at all and regard most literary sources as pious fictions.[7] Both views miss the fact that our early literary accounts do not present a unified view of Muslim history; rather, they preserve accounts that document significant disagreement about the meaning of important events.[8] As I suggested in the Introduction, these views could benefit from a better theoretical understanding of how new religions emerge, especially within the context of ancient civilizations and well-established religious traditions.

We do not need to travel back in time to know certain things about seventh-century Medina, because new religions continue to emerge all around us. Sociological studies of these new religious movements suggest that followers are not "brainwashed" automatons locked into "cults" but rather engaged participants who work with the charismatic leader to achieve their goals.[9] People attracted to new religious movements do not conform to

[6] Apologists are not the same as the "sanguine" scholars, described in the Introduction; rather, they hew to Donner's "descriptive approach" to Muslim history (Donner, *Narratives*, 5–8). I include here both popular authors, such as Karen Armstrong and Tariq Ramadan, as well as blogs and websites written for pious consumption.

[7] Donner, *Narratives*, 26, calls this the "radically skeptical argument."

[8] Ibid.

[9] Len Oakes, *Prophetic Charisma: The Psychology of Revolutionary Religious Personalities* (Syracuse: Syracuse University Press, 1997), 30–43.

a single personality profile, nor do they share some sort of sociopathology.[10] They vary widely in their commitment to the overall project of the leader. We see an echo of this in reports from the lifetime of the Prophet Muhammad, when believers were instructed over and again to bring any questions "before God and Muhammad."[11] Apparently, they needed reminders to do so because it was not obvious even to them where to find religious authority. To be sure, there are many stories that portray early followers asking Muhammad about the most mundane questions, but the sources also record tales of others in Mecca and Medina who ignored or rejected his rulings. Another insight from sociology is what happens after the death of the founder. In most cases, the variety of viewpoints among followers leads to a dissolution of the group; in the rare cases where the movement continues it often makes use of a different authority structure.[12] Again, the historical narratives fit these expectations, portraying the Bedouin Arabs as "apostates" who abandoned their new faith after Muhammad's death. Instructively, Abu Bakr brought them back into the community not through the religious teachings of a new prophet but through good old fashioned force of arms. Likewise, the stories of Umar strongly suggest that neither the Qurʾan nor the Prophet's example had yet been established as the premier arbiter of correct human action, not even 150 years after Muhammad's death when these tales were recorded. In other words, early leaders after Muhammad's death were faced with a stark choice: either they could continue the charismatic authority of the Prophet (and become prophets themselves) or they could hold the community together by other means (military action, tribal bonds, etc.).[13] Their choice not to play the prophet may have stemmed from

[10] Oakes reached this conclusion based on administration of the Adjective Checklist to over 100 members of emerging religious traditions in Australia and New Zealand (*Prophetic Charisma,* 125). The same cannot be said of charismatic leaders, however, who, according to research by Oakes and Heinz Kohut, have a tendency toward narcissism (ibid., 30–32).

[11] See, for example, articles 26 and 63 of the so-called "Constitution of Medina" in Michael Lecker, "Glimpses of Muhammad's Medinan decade" in Jonathan E. Brockopp (ed.), *The Cambridge Companion to Muḥammad* (New York: Cambridge University Press, 2010), 75–79.

[12] Max Weber, *Max Weber on Charisma and Institution Building*, S. N. Eisenstadt (ed.) (Chicago: University of Chicago Press, 1968), 55.

[13] My discussion here refers only to the fact that these early Caliphs did not see themselves as prophets in the mold of Muhammad, nor were they remembered as such. I am not saying that they claimed no religious authority. Again, Weber's categories (*Charisma,* 54–57) are useful for distinguishing the various ways that charismatic authority continues on after the Prophet's death. Regarding the Shiites, I follow Asma Afsaruddin in regarding early Alid claims to hereditary authority as anachronistic. Asma Afsaruddin,

their genuine belief in Muhammad's mission. But regardless of their motivations, their actions, I would argue, led to a separation of religious authority from political concerns. At least during this earliest period, there may well have been Qur'an reciters and individuals who catalogued Muhammad's every action, but such experts (if they existed) were of little value to Umar. What he needed was a bureaucracy, and that's exactly what his *dīwān* established when Umar named Aqil b. Abi Talib, Makhrama b. Nawfal, and Jubayr b. Mut'im as secretaries to run his register.

I freely admit that the story of Umar establishing his register, as it has come down to us, is nothing more than an imaginative reconstruction of early conversations – each character plays according to type: Ali the self-denying leader, Uthman in fear of "the people," Umar the willful leader.[14] Further, the origins of the bureaucracy are disputed. The tale cited above portrays al-Walid b. Hisham as citing a Byzantine precedent for the bureaucracy of the *dīwān*, while al-Jahshiyari (d. 331/942), who wrote a history of secretaries and wazirs, extends the idea back through Muhammad to an ultimately Persian provenance.[15] But the actual origins are less important for my purposes than the fact that these secretaries were experts of a kind, yet not the same as what we would later recognize

"Where Earth and Heaven Meet: Remembering Muḥammad as Head of State" in Brockopp (ed.), *Cambridge Companion to Muḥammad*, 178–195, at 190. On early Shiite scholars more generally, see Liyakat Takim, *The Heirs of the Prophet: Charisma and Religious Authority in Shi'ite Islam* (Albany: State University of New York Press, 2007) and Maria Dakake, *The Charismatic Community: Shi'ite Identity in Early Islam* (Albany: State University of New York Press, 2008).

[14] These types serve the purposes of later writers, such as the scholars who reported the first story in which Umar is presented as not having the least concern that the stoning punishment was wrong (after all, the Prophet himself did it), only whether it was in the Qur'an. The tale happens to fit nicely into the Malikis' overall argument that the practice of the people of Medina is a better guide to proper religious action – better than most *ḥadīth* and, in this case, better than exegesis of the Qur'an. See Brockopp, "Competing Theories of Authority in Early Mālikī Texts" in Bernard Weiss (ed.), *Studies in Islamic Legal Theory* (Leiden: E. J. Brill, 2001), 3–22.

[15] Al-Jahshiyari undoubtedly exaggerates the role and formality of both secretaries and of a bureaucracy during this period, but it is not unreasonable that Umar would require administrative assistance. *Kitāb al-wuzarā' wa l-kuttāb* traces the history of secretaries and viziers until 296/908. See also Wadād al-Qāḍī, "Early Islamic State Letters. The Question of Authenticity," in Averil Cameron and Lawrence I. Conrad (eds.), *The Byzantine and Early Islamic Near East, Vol. 1: Problems in the Literary Source Material* (Princeton: Darwin Press, 1992), 215–275; Robert Hoyland, "New Documentary Texts and the Early Islamic State," *Bulletin of the School of Oriental and African Studies* 69, no. 3 (2006), 395–416; and Jeremy Johns, "Archaeology and the History of Early Islam. The First Seventy Years," *Journal of the Economic and Social History of the Orient* 46, no. 4 (2003), 411–436.

as *ʿulamāʾ*. Umar's needs were those of statecraft – just punishment and just distribution of wealth – and it is reasonable to suggest that he established standards that would be broadly accepted as just. The pragmatic state-focused nature of this bureaucracy is important, because it is fundamentally opposed to key aspects of religious authority such as salvation and life after death. Finally, however the bureaucracy was established, we know it existed, because almost all of our material evidence for the first one hundred years is produced by it.

MATERIAL SOURCES AS A FOUNDATION FOR THE RISE OF THE *ʿULAMĀʾ* UP TO THE YEAR 680

At first glance, it may seem that the history of early Muslim scholarship must remain in shadow, since I have just suggested that material culture can inform us only about bureaucracy, not proto-scholars. Nor do historical accounts from outside the Muslim world tell us much about specific activities undertaken by any proto-scholars. Nonetheless, these sources do anchor our perception of this period in key ways. First, Islam was born into a world that was already made. Coins, methods of taxation, techniques of building had been established, and the bureaucrats smartly did not make sudden changes to a functioning system. Second, the languages of commerce and taxation were not Arabic, and to communicate with their subjects, the new Arab rulers had to make use of experts who knew Greek and Persian (as well as Coptic and other local languages). Only by the end of this early period do we see Arabic becoming more broadly legible. Third, the boundaries between whatever we might term "Islam" and the religious traditions of surrounding cultures were fluid. The earliest legends on coins (as well as religious formulae on papyri) contain statements that would be unobjectionable from a Christian, Jewish, or even Zoroastian point of view. The distinguishing statement from Abd al-Malik's famous "reformed" coin, that God sent Muhammad "with the guidance and the religion of truth to make it prevail over all religion," first appears after the period under consideration here, in the year 77/696–697, and it seems to mark a change in public perception. All of these points underline the same central fact: whatever identity Islam had before the appearance of this coin, it was a small minority movement surrounded by religious and cultural traditions with deep roots and great sophistication.

These facts have long been noted, but their implications for the rise of the *ʿulamāʾ* have not been fully appreciated. As discussed above, the way I am defining a scholar it is not enough simply to have knowledge; the scholar must also be recognized as authoritative. In the seventh century, the influence of any Muslim religious scholar would have been restricted to a very small group at best. For example, our earliest dated correspondence in Arabic, a papyrus from 22/643, was composed toward the end of Umar b. al-Khattab's reign (see Figure I.1 in the Introduction). It is a receipt for which Abdallah b. Jabir (Umar's commander in Upper Egypt) did not need the authority of any scholar or any religious text to determine just requisition; the needs of his army appear to have been justification enough. This short receipt is prefaced with a generic inscription "In the name of God" both in Greek and in Arabic.[16] It is succinct and orderly, with date and names of the parties. This document is not simply translated, however, and Abdallah b. Jabir appears to have employed two scribes; regardless, he had access to bureaucratic knowledge that was authoritative and appears to have been religiously inflected, but that bears no obvious connection to Islam.[17] Similarly, our early coins also seem to indicate continued dependence on a bureaucracy whose authority did not rest upon recognizable Islamic foundations. The earliest coins perfectly mimic those of the previous regime, and the simple Arabic inscription "*jayyid*" (valid) can be read as an appeal that nothing (much) had changed.[18]

To summarize: the small amount of material evidence that we possess for this period runs a parallel path with the story of Umar establishing his *dīwān*. We can infer the existence of "people of knowledge" during this earliest period, but only in the sense of individuals who had the knowledge and expertise required to run a state. Any state needs certain people of knowledge to run its bureaucracy, but these people serve at the pleasure of the state and derive their authority from it. Once the state no longer has need of their services, they are dismissed. That said, it is hazardous to speak of social institutions like "state" and "bureaucracy" during the beginning of this period, though by the time of Muʿawiya a bureaucracy does seem to have been established.[19]

16 Demiri and Römer, *Texts from the Early Islamic Period of Egypt*, 9. The Arabic adds *al-raḥmām al-raḥīm*.

17 Ibid., xii, 8.

18 Gaube, *Arabosasanidische Numismatik*, 18–37. See also Michael Bates, "History, Geography, and Numismatics in the First Century of Islamic Coinage," *Revue Suisse de Numismatique* 65 (1986), 231–263.

19 Hoyland, "New Documentary Texts," 398–407. I recognize, of course, that later historians had just as difficult a time imagining the Medinan caliphs without a bureaucracy as later legal scholars, who could not imagine Islam without an *ʿulamāʾ*. Al-Jahshiyari painstakingly attempts to reconstruct all the secretaries who served the Prophet and each of the early Caliphs. Notably, his book begins with a description of the Sasanid state, which also leaned heavily on a learned bureaucracy. Similar to my argument about the rise of the *ʿulamāʾ*, however, I think it would be wiser to term these individuals proto-

Bureaucrats and *ʿulamāʾ* share some areas of expertise, notably literacy in Arabic, and there are also numerous examples in historical texts of individual bureaucrats who served as members of the *ʿulamāʾ*, and vice versa. This has led some modern scholars to suggest that the *ʿulamāʾ* emerged from the ranks of the bureaucrats.[20] This is an intriguing thesis, and one that is certainly possible, but I cannot agree with it for four reasons: the expectations of our theoretical model, historical memory, the evidence of early legal categorization, and our first Qurʾan manuscripts. According to Weber, a functioning bureaucracy can help explain the rise of a successful Arab state, but would not further the interests of an Islamic religion. In fact, Weber characterized the bureaucratic state as the antithesis of religious authority, which itself is based on the almost anti-nomian authority of the charismatic leader.[21] Weber's model suggests, therefore, that religious leaders would have their roots outside of a state structure.[22]

The second reason for preferring separate origins for scholars and bureaucrats is the fact that Muslim historians treat these groups separately. Abd al-Malik b. Habib in his *History* follows a path familiar to Eusebius and other Christian writers, prefacing his biographies of scholars with a history of the world, beginning with creation.[23] His list of the earliest religious scholars is directly preceded by several *ḥadīth* from the Prophet, ending with this one on the authority of Abu Hurayra.

> [The Prophet] said: "The Hour will not arise until knowledge (*ʿilm*) fades away and *al-harj* increases." They said: "Oh prophet of God, what is *al-harj*?" He said: "killing (*al-qatl*)."[24]

secretaries, since they did not fully embody the development of the bureaucratic state that we see under the early Abbasids, for example.

20 Joseph Lowry, *Early Islamic Legal Theory: The Risāla of Muḥammad ibn Idrīs al-Shāfiʿī* (Leiden: E. J. Brill, 2007), 366–368. Lowry calls this the "functionalist" view of Islamic legal development, one shared by Wael Hallaq, Joseph Schacht, and others. There is a risk, however, of over-generalizing. Both Schacht and Hallaq recognized a role for "pious specialists" whose "practice was idealized and opposed to the realities of the actual administration" (Schacht, *An Introduction to Islamic Law* [Oxford: Clarendon, 1964], 27; see also 49. Compare Hallaq, *Origins*, 63).

21 Weber, *Charisma*, 51–52.

22 Weber, of course, was not the last word on religious leadership, and his critics suggested that he made too much of the "outsider" status of the charismatic individual. Nonetheless, his view of bureaucracy is less controversial, and the different function of these institutions in society should be taken into account.

23 ʿAbd al-Malik b. Ḥabīb. *Kitāb al-Taʾrīj (La historia)*, Jorge Aguadé (ed.) (Madrid: Consejo Superior de Investigaciones Científicas, 1991).

24 Ibid., 156.

In other words, Ibn Habib considers knowledge, mediated by both the Qur'an and the Prophet Muhammad, to be the primary source of scholarly authority, and its loss will lead to violence and death at the eschaton.[25] It seems to me, then, that Muslim historical memory understands scholars to arise as a direct result of the saving knowledge that God sends into the world, not a fulfilment of the pragmatic needs of a state.

As for my final reasons, these are based on the material evidence of our earliest literary manuscripts and our earliest Qur'an manuscripts. The Kairouan collection preserves a copy of a law text by al-Majishun (d. 164/780–781; number 13 in the Appendix), and many libraries preserve ancient copies of the *Muwaṭṭa'* by Malik b. Anas (d. 179/795). Both of these texts follow an organizational scheme that appears to have been both widespread and well established by the early Abbasid period. The origins of this scheme are disputed, but it evidently does not follow Jewish or Christian precedents, nor does it appear to be based on the bureaucratic needs of the state. In contrast, some of our earliest Qur'ans must have been expensive and so may well have been produced for wealthy individuals, such as local governors, but the Arabic script suggests that the specialists who produced these impressive manuscripts were not from the state chancery.

It must be admitted, though, that the dating of the earliest Qur'an manuscripts is controversial, and so it seems safest to place the majority of these in the late seventh century. I will therefore deal with them fully in Chapter 2. However, recent scholarship has claimed that a few manuscripts may have been produced before 680 and so could be seen as primary evidence of scholarly activity in this earliest period. These are exciting finds, but their preliminary nature recommends a cautious approach.[26] I will limit myself here to two observations. First, there is now some evidence that during the period after Muhammad's death there were multiple, slightly differing versions of the Qur'an.[27] If true, this would support the notion of individual proto-scholars as opposed to an organized scholarly structure deriving from the bureaucracy. Second, a comparison of the script of seventh-century bureaucratic writings with the script of these earliest Qur'an fragments suggests a separate, parallel development in the

25 This at least seems to be Ibn Habib's reasoning; there are other possible interpretations.

26 See the extensive discussion in Déroche, *Qur'ans*, 11–14. For a recent example, see the instructive controversy surrounding a fragment discovered in Birmingham, England (Maev Kennedy, "Qur'an Verses Dating from Seventh Century Go on View in Birmingham," *The Guardian*, October 2, 2015).

27 The key piece of evidence here is Sana I, a palimpsest (erased text found underneath another version of the Qur'an). See the overview in Sinai, "Consonantal Skeleton," 275–276.

handwriting of two distinct groups.[28] In the late seventh century, and perhaps earlier, it appears that the training regimen for those who wished to write out the Qur'an differed from that required by those who wished to record tax payments. This is meagre evidence, and my reconstruction is speculative, but it does support my contention that the text of the Qur'an is a historical document from the first half of the seventh century. I am not suggesting that the order of chapters and the consonantal structure (*rasm*) was completely closed by 650, but I am saying that variants discovered thus far are fairly limited. This is important because even the most ardent skeptic ought to consider views expressed in the Qur'an to reflect perceptions of early seventh-century devotees.[29] It is also helpful for the purposes of my inquiry, since not only does the Qur'an have a great deal to say about knowledge (*'ilm*), it even uses the classical Arabic word for scholars (*'ulamā'*). Even more intriguing, it seems to suggest a very different origin for our religious experts than that promoted by historians such as Ibn Habib.

THE TEXT OF THE QUR'AN AS DOCUMENTARY EVIDENCE FOR SCHOLARS IN EARLY SEVENTH-CENTURY MEDINA

The Qur'an refers often to knowledge, both as a quality of God and as a positive aspect of human existence, given freely to God's prophets.[30] Building on this foundation, apologetic literature from both the pre-modern and modern period imagines that scholars and scholarship have been part of the Islamic story from the earliest period. These interpretations of the Qur'an cannot help but color our sense of the text, but they should not exclude the Qur'an as a possible source for understanding the earliest community of Muslims. For example, most Qur'anic references to people possessing knowledge are quite generic, and not obviously referring to specific groups of individuals. In Sura 30, people who have knowledge and faith are contrasted with transgressors (*mujrimūn*) on judgment day (Q 30:55–56). In Sura 16, God give signs to people who think (*qawm yatafakkarūn*, verse 11) or people who reason (*qawm ya'qilūn*, verse 12) or people who remember (*qawm yadhdhakkarūn*, verse 13). In other words, a major part of God's activity in the Qur'an is to teach people, to give them knowledge. Also in this sura, however, is a sad refrain: *akthar al-nās lā ya'lamūn* – "most people do not know" (Q 16: 38; cf. 16:75, 101). This repeats the Qur'an's anthropology

28 Gruendler, *Development*, 137. See Figures 2.3 and 2.4 and discussion in Chapter 2.
29 With the caveat, of course, that the *rasm* could support multiple readings.
30 Rosenthal, *Knowledge Triumphant*, 19–32.

that people resist knowledge and forget what they do know; therefore, God sends books, reminders, and prophets to teach them.

This general discussion of the need for knowledge and learning obviously forms an excellent context for the rise of professional scholars in Islamic history, but the Qur'an makes only very occasional reference to such teachers in Arabia. For example, Sura 16:43 tells the ignorant hearer to consult "the people of remembrance" (*ahl al-dhikr*). As I will discuss below, Qadi Iyad b. Musa al-Yahsubi (d. 544/1149) sees this as referring to the scholarly class that was familiar to him in the twelfth century, yet the context of the verse suggests otherwise. The Sura begins with a list of God's bounties: livestock, horses, sun, and rain; these are signs for a people who think, reason, or remember (16:11–13). The topic then turns to judgment day, when God is most knowing (*'alīm*) of people and their wrongdoing (verse 28). It is in the context of people complaining on judgment day that they were not warned that verse 43 comes in:

> Before you, we sent men whom we inspired – ask the people of remembrance if you do not know – with explanations and warnings, and we sent down the remembrance to you to explain to the people that which was sent down to them, perhaps they will ponder it. (Q 16:43–44)

When this verse is read within the broader context of the Sura, it is evident that the "people of remembrance" are authorities who may be consulted about the history of God's activity in the world, specifically about the history of previous prophets. The fact that the hearers of the Qur'an are instructed to ask them means that they must have been local residents, readily available. But also worth noting is the fact that they appear to be a separate group outside the audience directly addressed by these passages.

Some later interpreters take this split as prima facie evidence for the existence of both religious scholars as well as Muslims who need instruction. For example, Qadi Iyad uses this verse to prove that there were always people ignorant of the right way to do things; he calls these individuals *muqallids*, those who ascribe authority to others.

> This is the lot of the *muqallid* to struggle for [knowledge of] his faith. The one with more knowledge does not abandon the *muqallid* nor does he put him off, even if he is occupied with learning. Rather, [the *muqallid*] asks him right then about that which he does not understand, until he understands it. This is exactly what God Most High said: "Ask the people of remembrance if you do not know." (Q 16:43)[31]

[31] 'Iyāḍ b. Mūsā, *Tartīb al-madārik*, 'Abd al-Qādir al-Saḥrawī et al. (eds.), 8 vols. (Rabat: Wizārat al-Awqāf, 1982), 1:60. The word *muqallid* is found nowhere in the Qur'an.

Iyad continues in his argument to point out that the Prophet sent out individuals to teach others the basics of faith. To back this up he repurposes Q 9:122. Read within the context of the surrounding verses, it appears to be referring to a division of labor in battle, but when parsed differently, it can be read as giving divine imprimatur to the *'ulamā'*: "From every group among you there are individuals who have become learned in the ways of faith, warning their people when they return to them."[32] In Iyad's time, the verb *yatafaqqahū*, which I have rendered as "have become learned," would resonate even more powerfully with Iyad's sense of scholarly mission, since by his time the same verbal root referred to scholars of Islamic law (*fuqahā'*), and this verb had come to mean "become learned in the arts of jurisprudence (*fiqh*)." The verb "warn" is likewise a loaded term, since it is associated in the Qur'an with the specific duties of prophets to warn individuals against the hellfire that awaits them as a consequence of their sins. By the ninth century, scholars had taken on this characteristic as their own special province, warning rulers when they overstepped the boundaries of the sharia.[33]

Interpreters like Iyad take these verses as proof that a recognized group of scholars existed in the Prophet's lifetime. Expanding on Ibn Habib's formulation, Iyad simply asserts that these individuals were "the *fuqahā'* of the Companions of the Prophet of God – God bless him and grant him peace – who gathered knowledge from him and learned the occasions of revelation for the commands and the prohibitions" all from the Prophet directly.[34] Sura 4:59 is then used to solidify the position of these scholars: "Oh you who believe: obey God and obey the messenger and those among you who possess authority (*al-amr*)." The notion of authority in this verse is ambiguous, and a variety of groups (military commanders, Shii Imams, and scholars) have used it to justify their right to command others.[35]

32 Ibid., 1:61.

33 This creative exegesis is quite common, and authors of this literature point to verses which seem to declare the *'ulamā'* to be among God's servants (Q 35:28) and mention of "those given knowledge" as raised by God by degrees (52:11). See discussion in Louise Marlowe, "Scholars" in *The Encyclopaedia of the Qur'ān*, ed. Jane Dammen McAuliffe et al. (Leiden: E. J. Brill, 2001–2005); also Gilliot, "'Ulamā'."

34 'Iyāḍ, *Tartīb*, 1:61. As we will see below, Iyad blames the following generations for abandoning this teaching and introducing dissent.

35 Marlowe, "Scholars." For a thorough review of the pre-modern and modern exegetical literature on this verse, see Asma Afsaruddin, "Obedience to Political Authority: An Evolutionary Concept" in M. A. Muqtedar Khan (ed.), *Islamic Democratic Discourse: Theory, Debates, and Philosophical Perspectives* (London: Lexington Books, 2006), 37–60.

Iyad and other compilers of biographical dictionaries, however, see it as license for requiring the obedience of their students and others.

It is perfectly reasonable that Ibn Habib, Qadi Iyad, and other historians treat the past as a mirror of their present. But this activity forces them to suppress evidence or to engage in selective memory. For example, nowhere in their accounts is there a mention of the influence of non-Muslims on the development of the Muslim concept of scholarship, even though (as I will discuss below) some narrative sources claim that the Prophet himself ordered Zayd b. Thabit and others to study at a *bayt al-midras* in Medina. Given the presence of active Christian and Jewish scholarly communities in the Near East during this period, we should at least consider the possibility that the "people of knowledge" referred to by the Qur'an are not Muslim scholars but Jewish and Christian scholars.[36]

For example, let us subject Qur'an 16:43 to a more detailed analysis.

وَمَآ أَرۡسَلۡنَا مِن قَبۡلِكَ إِلَّا رِجَالٗا
نُّوحِيٓ إِلَيۡهِمۡۚ فَسۡـَٔلُوٓاْ أَهۡلَ
ٱلذِّكۡرِ إِن كُنتُمۡ لَا تَعۡلَمُونَ ٤٣

Before you (male, singular), we sent men whom we inspired – ask (plural command) the people of remembrance if you (plural) do not know –

بِٱلۡبَيِّنَٰتِ وَٱلزُّبُرِۗ وَأَنزَلۡنَآ إِلَيۡكَ
ٱلذِّكۡرَ لِتُبَيِّنَ لِلنَّاسِ مَا نُزِّلَ
إِلَيۡهِمۡ وَلَعَلَّهُمۡ يَتَفَكَّرُونَ ٤٤

with explanations and warnings, and we sent down the remembrance (al -dhikr) to you (male, singular) to explain to the people that which was sent down to them, perhaps they will ponder it. (Q 16:43–44)

As the Arabic makes clear, the phrase "ask the people of remembrance if you do not know" is an aside, addressed to a plural audience, whereas the rest of the excerpt speaks to a single male. Further, we note that the "people of remembrance" are to be asked about men whom God inspired "with explanations and warnings (*bi-l-bayyināt wa-l-zubur*)." Elsewhere in the Qur'an, *bayyināt* are not simply explanations, but manifest proofs or even revelation

[36] For one example of a classical exegete who prefers this interpretation for Q 16:43, see al-Ṭabarī, *Jāmiʿ al-bayān fī taʾwīl al-Qurʾān*, 13 vols. (Beirut: Dār al-Kutub al-ʿIlmiyya, 1999), 7:587.

(Q 24:1, 2:87); likewise, the word translated here as warnings (*zubur*) is a Qur'anic term for scripture (as in Q 54:43), related to *al-zabūr*, the Psalms of David (Q 21:105).[37] In other words, people of remembrance appear to be experts on the Hebrew scriptures.[38] These findings may seem surprising, but they accord with the one Qur'anic verse that explicitly mentions the *'ulamā'*.[39]

> It is certainly a sending down (revelation) from the Lord of the worlds
> A trustworthy spirit has come down with it
> Upon your (male, singular) heart, so that you may be among the warners
> In a clear Arabic tongue
> It was already in the warnings of the first ones (*la-fī zubur al-awwalīn)*
> Or did they not have a sign that the *'ulamā'* of the people of Israel would know?
> Even though we revealed it to one of the gentiles?
> So he recited it to them so that they would believe in it. (Q 26:192–199)[40]

Far from being out of place, it seems that this connection between *'ulamā'* and "the people of Israel" would have been familiar to the audience of the Qur'an, since another Qur'anic verse encourages the listeners to be "masters" *(kūnū rabbāniyyīn)* in the teaching of scripture and study (Q 3:79). While the term *rabbānī* can have a variety of meanings,[41] its two other appearances in the Qur'an clearly refer to rabbis.[42]

The Qur'an makes many references to Jews and disputes openly with them on several points, but because of the elliptical nature of the text, it is

[37] Arie Schippers, "Psalms," in *The Encyclopedia of the Qur'ān*. See the same phrase, *bi-l-bayyināt wa-l-zubur*, in Q 3:184 and 35:25.

[38] Al-Ṭabarī (*Jāmi' al-bayān*, 7:587) identifies them both as experts on the Torah as well as experts on the Torah and Gospel who converted to Islam.

[39] Note the parallel in Q 10:94 "ask [male singular] those who have been reading scripture (*al-kitāb*) before you." Q 35:28 also employs the word *'ulamā'*, but here it is used as an adjective – God's servants who have the characteristic of knowledge – rather than as a named group. The context, however, is also the discerning of God's signs.

[40] My interpretation of the Arabic is slightly different from that in other translations.

[41] Marlowe, "Scholars," where she writes: "For the term *rabbānī*, the classical commentators record several interpretations, most of which emphasize the pursuit of religious knowledge." Cf. al-Ṭabarī, *Jāmi' al-bayān*, 3:323–327. In a recent article, Wael Hallaq ignores the connection to Judaism and translates this term as referring to educators, guides, and "leaders of the *umma*" ("Qur'ānic Constitutionalism and Moral Governmentality: Further Notes on the Founding Principles of Islamic Society and Polity," *Comparative Islamic Studies* 8, nos. 1–2 [2012], 1–51, at 24). Hallaq is right that this is al-Tabari's preference, but he misreads Mujahid's comment that the "*rabbānī* are higher than the *aḥbār*." This latter term is understood by Hallaq to refer to a hierarchy among the Muslim *'ulamā'* when it makes more sense to follow the Qur'an's own use of the term as referring to rabbis (Q 9:31).

[42] Gordon Newby, *A History of the Jews of Arabia: From Ancient Times to Their Eclipse under Islam* (Columbia: University of South Carolina Press, 1988), 57.

hard to place verses within a specific historical or geographical context. We can, however, draw some general conclusions about the presence of Jewish communities in Arabia from non-Muslim historical sources. First, given the widespread presence of Jewish communities throughout the Near East, it is plausible that there were Arab Jewish tribes in the *Ḥijāz* and that they had some form of religious authority figures.[43] It does not seem likely, however, that great sages, such as those who compiled the Talmuds, lived in the area, or that the *bayt al-midras* (house of study) in Medina mentioned in literary texts could be anything on the order of the great schools of Sura and Pumbedita in Iraq (or the Christian scriptoria of Alexandria). If it existed, it could only be a far more humble school perhaps with a small collection of texts and individuals who could teach the basics of reading and writing. Given our general knowledge of caravan routes and the high mobility of people in this period, it seems quite likely that any Medinan Jews were in communication with the more significant communities of Iraq and Palestine.[44]

To summarize my analysis of the Qur'anic text, material evidence, and non-Muslim historical sources, I find no evidence of Muslim scholars during the lifetime of the Prophet. I do find, however, a general tendency to associate knowledge with religious authority, and also an awareness of people who possess such knowledge in adjacent religious communities. While it is possible that these "*ʿulamāʾ* of the people of Israel" resided in Iraq or Palestine, it is also plausible that a Jewish community existed in west central Arabia in the seventh century. This connection is important, because when we turn from the Qur'an to examination of the historical texts, we find that many Companions identified as among what Qadi Iyad calls the "people of *fiqh*" are remembered as having had significant interaction with Jewish communities.

43 Ibid., 20–21, where Newby mentions an inscription from Harran that puts Jews in Arabia as early as the sixth century BCE. Michael Lecker has devoted much of his work to wresting the history of these communities from the Muslim literary sources. See, for example, his *Muslims, Jews, and Pagans: Studies on Early Islamic Medina* (Leiden: E. J. Brill, 1995). I am quite impressed with the plausibility of his reconstructions. However, Lecker's strongest evidence is for property ownership, economic activity, and political alliances; it does little to inform us of the religious or intellectual life of this community.

44 We have no direct evidence of such connections, but the rabbis of the *Mishnah* (compiled in the third century CE in Palestine) were in communication with Arab Jews and commented on their specific, and somewhat variant, practices.

THE FIRST GENERATION OF PROTO-SCHOLARS: A SPECULATIVE RECONSTRUCTION

Literary sources provide much information on early "scholars;" indeed, if it were not for Muslim literary sources, we would know nothing at all about most scholarly activities in this early period. But in contrast with the Qur'an, these sources were written down centuries after the events they purport to represent. Further, many of these stories appear to be theological in nature, that is, stories whose primary purpose is the elucidation of God's saving activity, not necessarily the transmission of historical information. This does not mean, however, that stories about this earliest generation of Muslims are useless. On the contrary, early interest in recording information about this generation offers modern historians a wealth of detail, some of which runs afoul of later notions of piety.[45] Based on a judicious reading of these sources in light of my analysis of the Qur'an and other contemporary evidence, it is possible to piece together a plausible history of proto-scholars in this generation. Of course, this reconstruction is tentative and open to revision.

All early proto-scholars are considered "Companions of the Prophet Muhammad." The names of these people, who had the good fortune of knowing the Prophet personally, were recorded in lists, possibly the earliest form of historical knowledge easily memorized and perhaps even written down. As mentioned above, lists of Companions were said to have been used by the Caliph Umar b. al-Khattab to determine the proper distribution of war spoils. Some of these lists, such as those preserved by the early historians Ibn Ishaq, al-Waqidi, and others, include individuals who traveled with the Prophet on his *hijra* from Mecca to Medina. Others are lists of those who fought with the Prophet at Badr. From these simple lists a literary genre grew that sought to gather all known information about these early Companions and compile it, culminating in books such as the thirteenth-century scholar Ibn al-Athir's *'Usd al-ghāba fī maʿrifat al-ṣaḥāba*, which reaches seven volumes in the printed version. These texts are full of information about these Companions and their activities. Naturally, any historical reconstruction based on these materials must remain speculative, but some useful observations may be made.

[45] Michael Lecker calls similar details "pearls in a vast sea" and uses them to establish topographical information on Medina during the time of the Prophet. Lecker, "Glimpses," 68.

First, there is an interesting tendency to conflate the categories of *ʿulamāʾ* and *ṣaḥāba*, that is, to suggest that everyone who knew Muhammad must also have possessed authoritative religious knowledge. In his *Ṭabaqāt ʿUlamāʾ Ifrīqīya* (list of African scholars), Abu l-Arab al-Tamimi (d. 333/945) is keen to demonstrate that North Africa is no marginal province, but rather destined to play a significant role in Muslim history. He opens his book with numerous *ḥadīth* from the Prophet Muhammad extolling the virtues of Africa:

[Abu l-Arab] Muhammad b. Ahmad b. Tamim said: Ahmad b. Abi Sulayman and Habib – who was the head of the court of complaints under Sahnun – and Isa b. Miskin all reported to me, saying: Sahnun told us, on the authority of Abdallah Ibn Wahb on the authority of Abd al-Rahman b. Ziyad on the authority of Abu Abd al-Rahman al-Hubuli, who said that the Prophet of God – God's blessings and peace be upon him – said: On the day of resurrection there will arise a people from my community from Africa; their faces will be strongly illuminated, like the light of the moon when it is full.[46]

This *ḥadīth* is followed by several tales about the Prophet's Companions, culminating in a list of fifteen who went to Africa at some point.[47] Other historians compiled similar lists for all the areas of the newly Muslim world[48] as if to sacralize these territories with the presence of those who had at least seen Muhammad in their lifetimes. Some historians, however, had a more stringent set of criteria for considering Companions to be *ʿulamāʾ*. For example, the *Taʾrīkh* of Abd al-Malik b. Habib (d. 238/853) mentions only seven Companions of the prophet who were "the *fuqahāʾ* of the Companions": three caliphs – Abu Bakr, Umar b. al-Khattab, and Ali b. Abi Talib – and four others – Abdallah b. Masʿud, Muʿadh b. Jabal, Ubayy b. Kaʿb, and Zayd b. Thabit.[49] Ibn Habib then clarifies that not all

[46] Abu l-ʿArab, *Kitāb Ṭabaqāt ʿUlamāʾ Ifrīqīya*, Mohammed ben Cheneb (ed.) (Beirut: Dār al-kitāb al-Lubnānī, n.d.), 1. Following the convention of his manuscript sources, Mohammed ben Cheneb published Abu 'l-Arab's text together with two other works: the continuation by his student Muḥammad b. al-Ḥārith b. Asad al-Khushanī (d. 371/981), also called *Kitāb Ṭabaqāt ʿUlamāʾ Ifrīqīya*, and a second work by Abu l-ʿArab, *Kitāb Ṭabaqāt ʿUlamāʾ Tūnis*. The first book runs from pp. 1–125, the second from 127–241, and the third from 243–256. Hereafter, I will cite all three simply as Ben Cheneb, *Ṭabaqāt*.

[47] Ben Cheneb, *Ṭabaqāt*, 16–17.

[48] See, for example, al-Suyūṭī, *Ḥusn al-Muḥāḍara*, 2 vols. (Beirut: Dār al-Kutub al-ʿIlmiyya, 1997), 1:132–209, where he counts 354 Companions among those who participated in the conquest or who resided in Egypt at some point in their lives, including eighty of the Prophet's Companions who helped determine the *qibla* of Amr's mosque.

[49] Ibn Ḥabīb, *Kitāb al-Taʾrij*, 156.

of these scholars were really *fuqahā'* or *'ulamā'*, and that the most learned in jurisprudence (*al-afqah*) of the seven were Ali and Mu'adh b. Jabal.[50] For the next generation, Ibn Habib names only two, Abdallah b. Abbas (d. 68/686–688) and Abdallah b. Umar (d. 79/793), and clarifies that Ibn Abbas was the more impressive of the two:

> The two of them were the most learned (*afqah*) of this generation, but they preferred Abdallah b. Abbas over Abdallah b. Umar for [his] insight (*fiqh*) and breadth of knowledge. They used to call him "the sea of knowledge." Ata used to say: "I never saw a more noble *majlis* [teaching session] than the *majlis* of Ibn Abbas: the jurists (*ahl al-fiqh*) would be with him, asking him questions, the masters of tradition (*aṣḥāb al-ḥadīth*) would be with him, asking him questions, the Qur'an interpreters (*aṣḥāb al-tafsīr*) would be with him, asking him questions, and the grammarians (*aṣḥāb al-naḥw*) would be with him asking him questions, all of them he would answer, as if entering a deep sea."[51]

In this account, Ata b. Abi Rabah (d. 114–115/732–733) not only lionizes Ibn Abbas, but also provides him with groups of scholars, neatly divided into academic disciplines. As I will discuss in the subsequent chapter, however, there is little evidence that such sophisticated scholarly groupings existed in Ata's lifetime, much less during the life of Ibn Abbas. Yet despite this tendency to exaggerate, Ibn Habib still names only four non-caliphal Companions as *fuqahā'*. A contemporary of Ibn Habib writing from the opposite end of the Muslim world is even more limited in his accounting: according to Ali b. al-Madini (d. 234/849): "The knowledge of the Companions of the Prophet concerning the prescriptions of the law fell to three [Companions], by whom it was acquired: Ibn Mas'ud, Zayd b. Thabit and Ibn Abbas."[52]

Lists such as these are quite common in the historical sources, and they raise many questions. First, of the three names that Ali b. al-Madini acknowledges, one of these (Ibn Abbas) is someone that Ibn Habib assigns to the next generation. In fact, these same sources tell us that Ibn Abbas was a boy of no more than thirteen when the Prophet died, whereas Ibn Mas'ud was a long-standing Companion who served the Prophet in various important capacities during his lifetime. Second, the lists are teleological, oriented toward the spread of religious knowledge to later generations. This helps to explain the prominence of Ibn Abbas, an

[50] Ibid., 157.
[51] Ibid., 158–159.
[52] Ibn al-Jawzi, *Talqīḥ fuhūm ahl* al-*athar fī 'uyūn* al-*ta'rīkh wa 'l-siyar* as quoted in Gilliot, "'Ulamā'."

importance ascendant of the Abbasid caliphs, but leaves open the question of what role, if any, scholars may have played in the Prophet's lifetime. Finally, the other figures on Ibn Habib's list have biographies that preserve evidence of a more intriguing possibility, one that connects with the Qur'an's reference to "people possessing knowledge," mentioned above.

Representations of the Earliest *fuqahā'* Up to 632

Of the various individuals in these lists, I want to focus on four who are held to have played a significant role during the Prophet's lifetime: Abdallah b. Mas'ud (d. 32 or 33/652–654), Mu'adh b. Jabal (d. 18/640), Ubayy b. Ka'b (d. between 19/640 and 35/656), and Zayd b. Thabit (d. 42/662–663 to 56/675–676). I am leaving aside Abu Bakr, Umar b. al-Khattab, and Ali b. Abi Talib, because they are too well-represented in the sources, and so the process of separating out the various polemical positions of their biographers is too large of a task for this study.[53] As for Abdallah b. Abbas (d. 68/686–688) and Abdallah b. Umar (d. 79/693), I will address them in the following chapter. Again, my interest here is in how Muslim historians represent these individuals, which I believe can offer us important clues to the history of religious scholars.

In their own way, all four of these figures are controversial. Ibn Mas'ud, an important early Companion of the Prophet, is said to have rejected Uthman's compilation of the Qur'an, preferring his own, different ordering of suras. Zayd b. Thabit and Ubayy b. Ka'b were also involved in the compilation of Uthman's codex, an event I will discuss below. Interestingly, Ibn Mas'ud is the only one of these four who emigrated with the Prophet from Mecca; the others are all Medinan Companions. The historians record numerous stories about these individuals during the Prophet's lifetime, but none is quoted more often than a disputed *ḥadīth* about Mu'adh b. Jabal. Toward the end of his life, Muhammad is said to have appointed Mu'adh b. Jabal to Yemen as a judge. Before sending him, the Prophet asked:

"How will you form your judgments?" Mu'adh said, "I will judge according to the Book of God." He asked, "What if you find no solution in the Book of God?" He replied, "Then [I will judge] by the *sunna* of God's Prophet – God's blessings

[53] See, for example, Linda Kern, *The Riddle of 'Umar b. al-Khaṭṭāb in Bukhārī's* Kitāb al-Jāmi' al-Ṣaḥīḥ *(and the Question of the Routinization of Prophetic Charisma)*, unpublished Ph.D. thesis, Harvard University (1996).

and peace be upon him." He asked, "And what if you do not find it in the *sunna* of the Prophet – God's blessings and peace be upon him?" He replied, "Then I will formulate my own judgment (*ajtahidu ra'yī*)." He said, "Praise be to God who has granted success to the messenger of His prophet – God's blessings and peace be upon him."[54]

Because it seems to offer an early version of the four-source theory of Islamic jurisprudence, this tradition has been often quoted and analyzed. Its obvious anachronisms[55] did not prevent major *ḥadīth* collectors from judging it to be *ṣaḥīḥ* or "sound." Such *ḥadīth* are prime evidence not for the notion that early judges followed a commitment to judging by God's book and the Prophet's example, but rather quite the opposite, that when later scholars imagined how early judges functioned, they did not place them in the complex world of an actual court, but made them out to be representatives of ideal court process. What interests me, however, is why of all people Muʿadh b. Jabal would be chosen for this representation instead of one of the more famous of the Prophet's Companions or one of the heroes of the early conquests. The answer, I believe, is twofold. First, Muʿadh may actually have played a role as a judge of sorts[56] and, second, this pious *ḥadīth* was put into circulation to counterbalance certain other aspects of both his biography and that of other Companions.

Along with Zayd b. Thabit and Ubayy b. Kaʿb, Muʿadh b. Jabal is remembered as one of the Prophet's scribes. This characteristic is important, since we would expect scholarly authority to be connected to both the religious power of the Prophet (and the Qur'an) and also the unusual authority of the written language, and these three figures, according to the sources, were among the few Muslims who were literate. All three were

[54] Al-Tirmidhī, *al-Jāmiʿ al-Ṣaḥīḥ wa-huwa Sunan al-Tirmidhī*, 5 vols. (Beirut: Dār al-Kutub al-ʿIlmiyya, 2000), 3:616 (*kitāb al-aḥkām*, 7); see also Wensinck, *Concordance*, 1:390. Whether or not such a discussion actually took place is irrelevant for my argument here. The point is that the tradition represents it as having taken place, just as it remembers competing stories about authority. See also G. Trompeau and M. Bernand, "Ḳiyās" in *Encyclopaedia of Islam*, 2nd ed., and references there.

[55] First, Muʿadh could hardly have been able to judge by using the Qur'an when according to Muslim historians, the Prophet continued to receive revelation until his death and the Qur'an was not written down during his lifetime. It is possible, of course, that something else is meant by the "Book of God" here, but that raises other questions. Second, it is rather odd to see the Prophet pronouncing blessings upon himself, a clear indication of this *ḥadīth* first being attributed to a later authority and only later extended to make Muhammad the source. Third, most historians agree that early qadis were not, in fact, judges in Islamic courts but government functionaries (Hallaq, *Origins*, 34–40).

[56] See Michael Lecker, "Judaism among the Kinda and the Ridda of the Kinda," *Journal of the American Oriental Society* 115, no. 4 (1995), 635–650, at 638–639.

also Ansari, that is, they came from Medina.[57] What is surprising is that the Qur'an also makes a connection of literacy to Medina, particularly to the Jewish community there. After all, it is Medinan Jews who are called "people of the book" and described as knowledgeable about the prophets of old.

It is not particularly important for my argument whether these Jewish communities actually existed or not, only how the historians represented them. As for their existence, though, it seems to me that we have two possibilities: either the historians held Jewish scholarship in high esteem when they were recording these stories in the ninth and tenth centuries or they did not. If they did, then perhaps they enhanced (or fabricated) these associations to boost the reputations of these early Companions. If they did not hold Jewish scholarship in high esteem (as seems to have been the case), then they preserved these stories in spite of the embarrassing connections.[58] Either way, the accounts have survived, including this description of a *bayt al-midras* (house of study) in Medina where these three Companions, along with many others, appear to have studied writing. For Zayd b. Thabit, this may have included the writing of Hebrew (or perhaps Aramaic). Zayd's words are recorded thus:

> The Messenger of God ordered me to study for him the script of the Jews, and he said to me: "I do not trust the Jews with regard to my correspondence" [i.e., correspondence with the Jews, written in their script]. Not even half a month passed until I learned it and I used to write for him to the Jews, and when they wrote to him, I read their letter.[59]

The distrustful attitude expressed here toward Jews reveals a tortured relationship with Judaism in the Muslim historical sources as both a threat and a source of wisdom.[60] This duality is extended to the persons

[57] Michael Lecker, "Zayd b. Thābit, 'A Jew with Two Sidelocks': Judaism and Literacy in Pre-Islamic Medina (Yathrib)," *Journal of Near Eastern Studies* 56, no. 4 (Oct. 1997), 259–273.

[58] I would caution that these "Jewish" groups likely practiced an aberrant form of the religion that might share only a few characteristics with what we would recognize as Judaism today.

[59] Translation from al-Baladhuri by Michael Lecker, "Zayd B. Thābit," 267. See Lecker's discussion of this story and variants. Gordon Newby (*History of the Jews*, 22) takes one of these variants as evidence that the Jews spoke a dialect of Arabic, not that Zayd learned Hebrew in two weeks. See also Newby, "Observations about an Early Judaeo-Arabic," *Jewish Quarterly Review*, New Series, 61, no. 3 (Jan. 1971), 212–221.

[60] This relationship has its parallel in Christianity. See the extraordinary polemic against Jews dated to the seventh century in Patrick Andrist, "Questions ouvertes autour des *Dialogica polymorpha antiiudaica*," in Constantine Zuckerman (ed.), *Constructing the Seventh Century*, 9–26, and Dmitry Afinogenov, Patrick Andrist, and Vincent Déroche,

of Zayd, Ubayy, and Muʿadh, as all three Medinans are prized for their literacy and knowledge and given premier positions of intimacy with both the Prophet and the Qurʾan. At the same time, their personal connections to Judaism are a potential source of embarrassment and scorn.[61]

In conclusion, this brief review of scholarly activities during the lifetime of the Prophet finds no evidence of a group of organized Muslim scholars – experts in Qurʾan interpretation, theology, or law – during the life of the Prophet. At most, Muhammad depended on individual Companions for practical matters of correspondence and perhaps the writing down of the Qurʾan. Even if the tale of Muʿadh being sent to the Yemen is historically accurate, it still does not suggest the existence of anything like a caste of scholars who have an independent authority based on knowledge. At most, we find individuals serving as adjuncts and extensions of Muhammad's own authority. The connection of many of these individuals with Judaism or Jewish learning is intriguing and seems to confirm the Qurʾan's own reference to some of the "children of Israel" as scholars. Indeed, there is no reason to suppose that the Qurʾan's references to "people possessing knowledge" or to "scholars" (*ʿulamāʾ*) presumes belief in Islam. After all, the Qurʾan is quite universal in its

"La recension γ des *Dialogica polymorpha antiiudaica* et sa version slavonne, *Disputatio in Hierosolymis sub Sophronio Patriarcha*: une première approche" in Zuckerman (ed.), *Constructing the Seventh Century*, 27–103.

61 Lecker, "Ḥudhayfa b. Al-Yamān and ʿAmmār B. Yāsir, Jewish Converts to Islam," *Quaderni di Studi Arabi* 11 (1993), 149–162, at 152. Whether these negative accounts reflect seventh- or tenth-century views is hard to determine.
Provocative as always, Patricia Crone went so far as to refer to these people as "Muslim Rabbis" (*Slaves on Horses*, 5–6). She makes reference there to an unpublished paper by Michael Cook, "Monotheist Sages. A Study in Muslims and Jewish Attitude towards Oral Tradition in the Early Islamic Period." In a private communication in January 2014, Cook told me that he published only part of that paper, and not the part relevant to the notion of "monotheist sages."
Unlike Crone (and perhaps Cook), I am not suggesting that early Muslim *ʿulamāʾ* were rabbis, were directly influenced by rabbis, or even that they "borrowed" authority structures from Judaism. Rather, I am suggesting that the Jews of Arabia formed a significant background for early Muslim understanding of Qurʾanic references to knowledge and to "people possessing knowledge." Moreover, Judaism seems to be the clearest antecedent for early ideas of Islamic religious leadership after the death of the Prophet. The heart of religious leadership in Judaism concerns knowledge of the texts, of the calendar, of religious law for the fulfillment of duties. At least for post-temple Judaism there are no longer specific rites associated with a special class of priests. This is quite in contrast both with local polytheistic practices as well as with contemporary Christianity and Zoroastrianism. In these traditions, knowledge is important, but so also is the performance of specific rites (divining the future, saying mass, performing the fire rituals) by individuals who possess a charisma of office.

determination of humankind as largely ignorant and in need of teaching. What references there are to individuals with knowledge fit well the Qur'an's description of God as sending prophets into the world to teach the ignorant. These prophets, of course, include Christian and Jewish figures as well as Arabian ones, and so it should not be surprising that statements such as Sura 16:43 ordering the hearer to consult "the people of the remembrance" and 26:197 mentioning "the *ʿulamāʾ* of the people of Israel," should refer to non-Muslim individuals.[62]

This impression is reinforced through analysis of early Islamic history, which records the efforts of individual Companions of the Prophet to study with these possessors of knowledge, especially the Jews of Medina. While we may dismiss later claims that Muhammad stole his scripture from the Jews (or that he was an errant Christian bishop) as anti-Muslim polemic, Muslim sources record ample evidence that knowledge possessed by these Jewish peoples was highly valued. This is seen both in the stories of Companions who studied at the *bayt al-midras* and also with knowledge gained from early Jewish converts to Islam. It is useful to remember that the lines between Judaism and Islam during the life of the Prophet may not have been very clear – certainly not as clear as they are today. Just as early Christianity took a century to distinguish itself from Judaism (and early Buddhism from Hindu traditions), so also the forms of Judaism and Islam that would have been found in Medina probably looked very much alike in this period. Both groups were Arabs and spoke Arabic. Further, Jewish messianic movements were widespread during this period, a notion that Muhammad appears to have made use of. In the political situation of our age, much has been made of Muhammad's "break with the Jews," slaughter of Qurayza tribe members, and Umar's expulsion of Jews from Arabia, but these tales explain only one side of the story, and in many cases, the tales themselves are contested. In terms of the rise of the Muslim scholar, and the place of that scholar within the Islamic tradition, there is no better forerunner than the place of scholars and scholarship within Judaism, a tradition apparently well-known both to Muhammad and to his followers.

Proto-scholars during the Medinan Caliphate, 632–656

After Muhammad's death we no longer have even the Qur'an as documentary evidence, and through the Medinan caliphate we have almost no

62 Again, as discussed above, this interpretation is found in the mainstream exegetical tradition.

physical evidence whatsoever, other than a few scraps of papyrus. From non-Muslim literary accounts (and of course the Muslim historians themselves), we know that both the Persian Empire and much of the Byzantine Empire (importantly Syria and Egypt) fell to bands of Arabs, coming from the desert oases.[63] The internal politics of these Arabs, however, are known to us only from the Muslim literary accounts, which tell us that confusion reigned in determining the succession to Muhammad. Abu Bakr's short caliphate (632–634) was marked by the "wars of apostasy," where tribes with personal and political loyalties to Muhammad had to be forcibly brought back into submission (*islām*). Umar's ten years (634–644) saw the beginnings of an unprecedented expansion that brought both vast riches into Medina and also dissent. His murder at the hands of a Persian Christian slave is taken as emblematic of the dangers of such expansion. Uthman, in contrast, took significant steps to control this expansion, both appointing family members to positions of power and also reducing dissent in scripture and religious practice. For these actions he was vilified by Muslim historians and murdered by disaffected Muslims, some of whom were also Companions of the Prophet.

As mentioned above, Umar is held to have established a chancery that administered the *dīwān* and managed correspondence. The individual secretaries recorded by al-Baladhuri, al-Jahshiyari, and others, however, do not come into the lists of proto-scholars compiled by Ibn Habib, Ali b. al-Madini, Abu l-Arab, or Iyad b. Musa. These proto-scholars, rather, are remembered as having performed various other services. For example, in his history of scholars, Abu l-Arab al-Tamimi (d. 333/944) records an interesting dispute between Umar b. al-Khattab and al-Abbas, the Prophet's uncle, during Umar's caliphate.[64] Umar, it seems, wanted to expand the Mosque of Mecca onto land owned by al-Abbas. The two called upon Ubayy b. Kaʿb to serve as arbiter. What is interesting about this story is that this exemplary "scholar," one of the "*fuqahāʾ* of the Prophet of God," resolves the dispute not through interpretation of a Qurʾan verse or recollection of an appropriate *ḥadīth* of the Prophet, but by telling a story of David, Solomon, and the building of the temple in

63 An excellent summary is found in Brock, "Syriac Views," 9–21. See also Hoyland, *Seeing Islam*, and Mikhail, *From Byzantine to Islamic*.

64 Ben Cheneb, *Ṭabaqāt*, 107. The tale is remembered in the context of advice given to the Aghlabid Amir Ziyadat Allah who wanted to expand the mosque of Kairouan. It is, therefore, an interesting nesting of literary authority.

Jerusalem.[65] It is a narrative from Jewish history, related by an *anṣārī* Companion who studied at the *bayt al-midras* in Medina, that resolves a dispute between two of the Prophet's most illustrious Companions. Whether authentic or not, this old story recommends at least a cautious approach to presumptions that early Muslim belief was markedly different from Arabian Judaism.

Many attempts have been made to identify specific connections between Muslim, Christian, and Jewish scholars during the early period, and all have failed to convince.[66] Again, as I have stated before, I believe the fundamental problem is that we simply have too little information on either Muslim or Jewish communities of this time. Still, we have come a long way since Abraham Geiger and Ignaz Goldziher, and these advances ought to be noted. First, scholars are moving away from the discrete religious tradition model toward a more productive description of a common religious milieu. Just as Maimonides' philosophy partakes of a common vocabulary shared by Muslim, Jewish, and Christian thinkers,[67] so also the Qur'an appears to share certain legal concerns with the Christian-Jewish text *Didascalia Apostolorum*.[68] As Sidney Griffith has pointed out, however, this does not mean that Muhammad was in direct communication with Christian-Jewish communities, or even that these communities existed in seventh-century Arabia.[69] Second, the influence of converts among the Prophet's Companions and other early authorities has been analyzed in detail, most recently by John Nawas, who concludes that non-Arab converts did not have an outsized influence on scholarly development.[70] As Motzki rightly points out, this connection continues to

65 Ben Cheneb, *Ṭabaqāt*, 108–109. The manuscript is damaged here, but the outlines of the narrative are quite clear, and Ubayy rules in al-Abbas' favor.

66 See, for examples, Patricia Crone, *Roman, Provincial and Islamic Law* (Cambridge: Cambridge University Press, 1987); W. Heffening, "Zum Aufbau der islamischen Rechtswerke," in W. Heffening and W. Kirfel (eds.), *Studien zur Geschichte und Kultur des nahen und fernen Ostens* (Leiden: E. J. Brill, 1935), 101–118.

67 David Burrell, *Knowing the Unknowable God: Ibn Sina, Maimonides, Aquinas* (South Bend: University of Notre Dame Press, 1992).

68 Zellentin, *The Qur'ān's Legal Culture*. My thanks to Chase Robinson for this reference.

69 Griffith, review of *The Qur'ān's Legal Culture* in *Theological Studies* 76, no. 1 (2015), 172–173, at 173.

70 John Nawas, 'The Birth of an Elite: mawālī and Arab 'ulamā'', *Jerusalem Studies in Arabic and Islam* 31 (2006), 74–91; this is a slightly expanded version of his chapter "A Profile of the mawālī 'ulamā'", in Monique Bernards and John Nawas (eds.), *Patronate and Patronage in Early and Classical Islam* (Leiden: E. J. Brill, 2005), 454–480. My thanks to Chase Robinson for these references. Nawas's conclusions are limited by the fact that he is subjecting literary sources to statistical analysis.

be sought out because of a prejudice that "the high level of Islamic culture cannot be the product of people living at the fringe of the advanced civilizations of the ancient world."[71] But as I will demonstrate in Chapter 3, scholarly communities were not at all unified, even in the third/ninth century. Alongside mature scholarly texts, we still have evidence of a continuing oral tradition in the ninth century based on the example of charismatic individuals who play a role similar to that of Jewish sages.

Again, however, associations with Judaism were not always regarded as positive. During the collection of the Qur'an under Uthman, Ibn Mas'ud is remembered as leveling a remarkable slur against Zayd b. Thabit, saying variously that Zayd was still in the womb of an unbeliever when Ibn Mas'ud was already reciting the Qur'an, or that he was a Jewish boy playing in Medina when Ibn Mas'ud had already memorized seventy suras.[72] Both Ibn Mas'ud and Ubayy b. Ka'b are remembered as serving with Zayd on the committee to establish Uthman's codex and also retaining their own, differing readings of the text. The stories of the collection of the Qur'an, of course, are a nearly hopeless morass of competing authoritative tales. For my purposes, however, precise dating of the event(s) does not matter because (1) the process clearly happened at some point (the Qur'an is evidently a series of oral texts subjected to a conservative editing process) and (2) the attempt and partial failure of the project fits well into other evidence that bureaucracy and scholarship followed separate paths in this period. As described above, no pre-compilation Qur'anic manuscripts have yet been found, and radiocarbon dating suggests a seventh-century provenance for the earliest manuscripts. Therefore, I will accept a date of 650 as plausible.[73]

The compilation of the Qur'an was an event at the intersection of literacy and religious authority, so is not surprising that exemplary proto-scholars, such as Ibn Mas'ud, Ubayy, and Zayd, should be centrally involved. These individuals were among the few who straddled the bifurcated worlds of bureaucratic and charismatic authority, having served as the Prophet's own secretaries. But it is important to note that Uthman is represented as having neither the political nor the religious standing to establish even these most illustrious of the Prophet's scholarly

[71] Harald Motzki, 'The Role of Non-Arab Converts in the Development of Early Islamic Law," *Islamic Law and Society* 6 (1999), 293–317, at 295.

[72] Lecker, "Zayd b. Thābit," 259–262. Another version puts a similar slur in the mouth of Ubayy b. Ka'b.

[73] For an overview, see Sinai, "Consonantal Skeleton," 273–276.

Companions as an authoritative community.[74] It may be that the split between bureaucracy and religious authority was already too entrenched by Uthman's reign for the Qur'an compilation project to succeed. Yet neither was it a complete failure because the vast majority of early Qur'an fragments show a remarkable level of congruence.

The lack of a central, authoritative scholarly community, however, does not mean that proto-scholars were ineffective or without influence, only that this authority was limited. It seems reasonable to suggest that just as Ubayy's reading of the Qur'an was said to be popular in Syria, while Ibn Mas'ud's reading was popular in Kufa, other proto-scholars also had their local partisans. We may see later devotees of Ibn Abbas and Abdallah b. Umar as indications of these small circles of authority, along with partisans of Ali b. Abi Talib and his family. In other words, one may speculate that the failure of Uthman's Qur'an project exacerbated, if it did not cause, a decentralized form of religious authority. At the same time, papyri from Egypt demonstrate the continued existence and effectiveness of a bureaucratic state.[75] As I will discuss in the next section, I believe that this split between pragmatic state bureaucracy and individual religious authorities only grew under Mu'awiya, at which time the documentary evidence can be read as bearing witness to this separation.

The narrative accounts of the Qur'an's compilation are worth our attention for one further detail, the fact that they describe a process that is the hallmark of a particular form of scholarship. Regardless of when the compilation actually took place, accounts agree that (1) materials were gathered from a wide variety of sources, (2) material was authenticated, (3) a fair copy was produced, and (4) this copy was transmitted verbatim (albeit without certain vowel and consonant marks). This is a common method for transmuting oral knowledge to written form, and it is also a process that for the next 150 years would be applied only to the Qur'an. The importance of this fact can scarcely be overstated, though Gregor Schoeler is one of the few to understand its implications.[76] Simply put, the compiling of the Qur'an into a written text is the imposition of a

[74] In my view, this suggests, in turn, the modest nature of the Jewish *bayt al-midras* in Medina. Had it been a house of learning with a significant reputation, we might expect Uthman's project to have turned out differently.

[75] A useful overview is found in Rāġib, "Premiers documents."

[76] Schoeler, "Die Frage der schriftlichen oder mündlichen Überlieferung der Wissenschaften im Islam," *Der Islam* 62 (1985), 201–230. See also Schoeler, *Genesis*, 1, where he proclaims the Qur'an to be "the very first work of Arabic Literature" even though it "needed some twenty-five years to become an actual 'book', an actual 'literary work'."

new notion of scholarship onto scripture. While books were known – especially after the conquests of Egypt, Palestine, Syria, and Persia in the 640s – there were no other books in Arabic. Not only this, no similar attempt would be made to write Arabic books until *ḥadīth* collections and histories began to be compiled in the mid-eighth century – and even then (as I will discuss in Chapter 3), we have no evidence for the ability to control and protect the correct transmission of these writings until around the year 800.[77]

The production of a written Arabic book in the seventh century is remarkable, but even more remarkable is the fact that the integrity of the text was maintained, verbatim, from the seventh century until the present. This extraordinary treatment is, I would argue, strong evidence for the existence of a community of literate individuals devoted to the practice of preserving the Qurʾan as a sacred text. Further, the great number and variety of early Qurʾan manuscript fragments suggests a connection to wealth, perhaps even royal patronage, and large-format Qurʾans in particular indicate connections between proto-scholar and administrative power even while the ranks of secretaries and Qurʾan scribes seem to have been distinct. Finally, consistency of orthography and decoration indicates some sort of professional community. [78] Nonetheless, I do not believe that ritual devotion to careful reproduction of the Qurʾan is evidence for a community of scholars during this period. Only later do we see Qurʾanic verses appearing publicly, first in coins and architecture and eventually on tombstones and correspondence. This suggests that early Qurʾan scribes were working as individuals or in small groups and had relatively little influence or authority in the broader society.

The Medinan caliphate, therefore, is both a period of great triumph and also great loss. While the Islamic world was extended through an extraordinary series of military successes and diplomacy,[79] the loss of the Prophet and the loss of knowledge of early Companions left a tremendous gulf of

[77] The history of the Arabic book in Christianity, however, is not so clear. As I will discuss below, our earliest dated Christian Arabic manuscripts are just as old as our earliest dated Muslim manuscripts, and there is good reason to suspect that Arabic books were first composed by Christians.

[78] For a fascinating insight into a trace of this work visible in a palimpsest, see Asma Hilali, "Le palimpseste de Ṣanʿāʾ et la canonisation du Coran: nouveaux éléments," *Cahiers du Centre Gustave Glotz* 21 (2010), 443–448.

[79] See evidence for an embassy to China in 651 in D. D. Leslie, Yang Daye, and A. Youssef, *Islam in Traditional China: A Bibliographical Guide* (Sankt Augustin: Monumenta Serica Institute, 2006), 33.

religious knowledge and authority. Uthman's supposed compilation of the Qur'an can be seen as a response to this loss, but a failed one. This lack of religious authority, however, did not stop the need for a trained corps of literate secretaries. While not exactly scholarly communities, such chanceries had to develop an expertise of sorts and, on a pragmatic basis, made decisions that would determine some legal practices for centuries.

656–680: the Establishment of Muʿawiya in Damascus

From the point of view of the history of scholarship, Uthman's appointment of his cousin Muʿawiya as governor of Damascus in 650 appears to have further isolated proto-scholars from the halls of power. Some literary accounts seem to suggest that the wealth and power of these provincial governors (Muʿawiya in Syria, Amr in Egypt) overshadowed that of the Medinan caliph, who was dependent on these far wealthier governors for transmitting tax revenues and grain to the capital. Alone among these governors, Muʿawiya ruled not from an Arabic/Islamic garrison town (Fustat in Egypt, Kufa in Iraq), but from an ancient city with its own history. Muʿawiya also had the fortune of governing a large Arab (though not yet Muslim) population in Syria, again in contrast with other provinces. Wisely, he adapted to an already functioning bureaucracy, minting coins that retained many features of the Byzantine coins that preceded it, and maintaining the local bureaucracy of Greek-speaking scribes. Muʿawiya's name, in fact, is the first to be found on early coins,[80] and evidence from early papyri demonstrates an active bureaucratic correspondence in Greek and Arabic.[81] Even the surviving architecture of the period demonstrates a union of Byzantine structures with Arabic/Islamic ideals. Muʿawiya's thirty-year rule in Damascus, therefore, was marked by pragmatism and a fruitful blending of Arab and Byzantine cultures. He supported no grand religious projects on the order of magnitude of his cousin's collection of the Qur'an, but rather implemented policies that gradually strengthened and centralized his rule.

For our purposes, the civil wars of 656–661 were important only for their disruption of the flow of history. While Ali b. Abi Talib was held by

80 J. Walker, *A Catalogue of the Muhammadan Coins in the British Museum. Volume I: Arab-Sassanian Coins* (London: British Museum, 1941), 25–26.

81 Rāġib, "Premiers documents." Only after Muʿawiya's reign would some documents be written solely in Arabic. I am, here, fully in agreement with Hoyland's argument that we should read the evidence in light of Abd al-Malik's bureaucratic reforms, which could not have risen *ex nihilo* (Hoyland, "New Documentary Texts," 401).

later generations to be a key exemplar of religious scholarship – and of course the first of the Imams for Shiism – there is little evidence that he advanced the development of scholarship: perhaps his reign was simply too short to make a significant impact. Muʿawiya, of course, secured his power base by outfoxing Ali b. Abi Talib at the negotiations after the battle of Siffin, but this did not end the Alid challenge to his reign. Generally, the Alid movement is remembered as a kind of political and (until Karbala) military resistance to the status quo. More recently, scholars have explored the religious dimension of Alid claims as an extension of the Prophet's charismatic authority.[82] But a significant aspect of this authority may have been scholarly in the sense of authoritative interpretations of Qurʾan and Muhammad's *sunna*.[83] Nonetheless, while it seems reasonable that Ali and some of his progeny served as significant learned authorities among a small community, we should not exaggerate their influence.

Muʿawiya's effective separation of the state from religious affairs[84] might have resulted in a polity that would eventually have become a vassal state of the Byzantine Empire.[85] Had Muʿawiya been successful in conquering Constantinople,[86] for example, the absorptive powers of the Christian church might well have succeeded in classifying Islam as nothing more than a Christian heresy, one that could be gradually brought back into the fold of orthodoxy. However that may be, literary sources suggest that Muʿawiya's relative disinterest in religious affairs meant that he had little impact on the private sphere. We are told, for example, that the last of the Prophet's intimate Companions, Zayd b. Haritha, Zayd b. Thabit, Abdallah b. Masud, and Muhammad's wife Aʾishah bint Abi Bakr, were sought out by the follower generation, who asked them questions about proper religious practice. It also seems that popular storytellers regaled listeners with tales of the Prophet's exploits during this period, and some literate individuals may have written down

[82] See, for examples, Takim, *Heirs of the Prophet*, and Dakake, *Charismatic Community*. Ali is held to have had his own, slightly variant, copy of the Qurʾan.

[83] Still an emerging concept, as Hallaq makes clear in *Origins*, 46–47.

[84] Abd al-Aziz Duri, *Early Islamic Institutions: Administration and Taxation from the Caliphate to the Umayyads and ʿAbbāsids* (New York: Tauris, 2011), 22–23.

[85] There is some evidence that Byzantium already thought of Egypt in this way, at least in the 640s (Booth, "Muslim Conquest," 640).

[86] An event that may need redating according to Mark Jankowiak's new reading of Byzantine sources, "The First Arab Siege of Constantinople," in Zuckerman (ed.), *Constructing the Seventh Century*, 237–320.

the first rough accounts of his life story.[87] Scholarship on sacred history, prophetic sayings, and Qur'an interpretation, therefore, may have become a private affair. Unsupported by the government, it was carried out by pious individuals who were not professionals and who made their living by other means. As mentioned above, these separate trajectories for bureaucracy and scholarship may have been established as early as Abu Bakr's reign; attempts to bring them back together were never wholly successful.

In 680, Muʿawiya's appointment of his son, Yazid, to the throne led to two insurrections: one by Muhammad's grandson Husayn in Karbala and a second by the son of a famous Companion, Abdallah b. al-Zubayr, in Mecca and Medina. As I will discuss in Chapter 2, these insurrections are significant since both appear to have used religious claims to justify their existence. In a way, they may have led to the Umayyad state's abandonment of Muʿawiya's neutral policies and adoption of religious claims of their own. While these actions did not result in the establishment of the *ʿulamāʾ* by the state, they do reflect a growing influence of Muslim actors.

CONCLUSIONS

My reconstruction here is an attempt to make sense out of scant data, using both sociology as well as observation of contemporary emerging religious traditions as a guide. All new religions, Islam included, begin as minority traditions responding to ideas embedded in local cultural contexts. Richard Bulliet estimates that the population of Iran and Syria around the year 750 was less than 10 percent Muslim, which extrapolates down to a few percent or less for the period under consideration in this chapter.[88] These numbers are made even smaller by the fact that these regions were sparsely populated to begin with and that such Muslims as may have existed were not unified in their conception of what it meant to be a Muslim. The story of Arabic is similar, but not quite the same; it seems that in the seventh century there were many more Arabic speakers than there were Muslims, but even so, Arabic as a written tradition paled

[87] Written versions of this largely oral material appear in early manuscript fragments; see Nabia Abbott, *Studies in Arabic Literary Papyri. Volume 1: Historical Texts* (Chicago: University of Chicago Press, 1957), 65–99 and my discussion in Chapter 3.

[88] Richard Bulliet, *Conversion to Islam in the Medieval Period: An Essay in Quantitative History* (Cambridge, MA: Harvard University Press, 1979); see the graphs on pp. 23 and 109.

in comparison with those of Greek, Middle Persian, and Coptic within the broader context of Near Eastern history. The distinction between an illiterate, private population versus a literate, public elite is one that will be important for understanding evidence in Chapter 2. The minority positions of both Arabic and Islam form one solid boundary for the interpretation of our evidence: whatever proto-scholars existed in the seventh century CE, their authority could not have extended beyond their local circle of influence, a minority within a minority.

The second boundary, however, prevents us from dismissing these proto-scholars altogether. Evidence from ninth-century manuscripts preserves fairly sophisticated eighth-century texts that themselves are predicated upon years of oral transmissions. Further, these eighth-century scholars depended upon a chain of charismatic authority to justify their arguments, seeing the early generation of Companions as exemplary. This does not mean that statements attributed to Abdallah b. Abbas or Zayd b. Thabit are true, only that we must account for the fact that, within a century, they have become authoritative. The simplest solution is to accept the accounts of the literary sources to a limited extent, understanding that whatever status these men may have had in the seventh century was magnified significantly by later writers.

Extreme positions are the hardest to defend: either that these individuals were always considered to be authoritative or that they never existed. In the first case, Muslim historians themselves undermine their stature when they describe this period as one of conflicting authorities – a description that accords with the expectations of sociological theory. In the second case, the fact that these individuals are named in some of our earliest manuscripts reduces the window for fabrication to a very small opening; it is far easier to manipulate memory than to create it from scratch. This leaves us with a broad middle ground, one in which I have tentatively suggested: (1) that our first proto-scholars were drawn from the small literate class, one that had close ties to Jewish communities and (2) that, after Muhammad's death, these religious experts had a fraught relationship with the state. While some may have consulted with political leaders from time to time, the majority seem to have established their authority among small circles of disciples, devoted to the study of the Qurʾan and the preservation of details of Muhammad's life.

My suggestions are speculative, but I believe they make sense of the data. Our material evidence from this period is scant, and the quantity and quality of the evidence will improve in later chapters. I have developed this model, in part, with this late seventh-century evidence in mind, particularly the public works of Abd al-Malik b. Marwan and a private tombstone memorializing one Abbasa, daughter of Jurayj; both of these are discussed in Chapter 2. In contrast to the paucity of material sources for the mid-seventh century, the literary evidence is rich and full of detail. These details, however, are often contradictory, pointing to multiple centers of authority from a very early period. In many ways, understanding seventh-century Islam as a minority tradition makes it easier to accept the basic outline of Muslim history as factual: that Muhammad was considered a Prophet, that he died in the first half of the seventh century, and that he had Companions who outlived him and who passed on his story to others. Plausibility is challenged only when we try to define precisely the notions of "Muslim" or "Islam" or when we forget that while the first caliphs may well have been Muslim, they ruled over a territory and a bureaucracy that was not.

As a final note, it may be helpful to consider the importance of history in justifying a religious tradition.[89] Just as ninth-century Muslims looked back upon two centuries of Muslim history to justify the truth of Islam, so also seventh-century Muslims saw their religion as part of a long history of God's revelatory action in a world largely shared with Jews and Christians. The Qurʾan itself recognizes this fact in urging followers to consult "the people of the remembrance" (Q 16:43) and "the *ʿulamāʾ* of the people of Israel" (Q 26:197). Seventh-century Muslims, therefore, also enjoyed a storied past, but it was one in which the connection to Jewish and Christian religious stories was an essential part of their identity.

[89] Jonathan Brockopp, "Theorizing Charismatic Authority in Early Islamic Law," *Comparative Islamic Studies* 1, no. 2 (2005), 129–158.

2

Integration of the Proto-Scholar, 680–750

The seventy-year period covered in this chapter is one of the most momentous in Islamic history as we move from an emerging empire in Damascus, through conquest and civil war, and end at the triumph of the Abbasid movement. Historians, writing centuries later, tell us that in the 680s the situation was grave: few were alive who had known the Prophet personally, and the empire was in revolt. Berbers in North Africa and Persians in Khurasan were rejecting Arab rule, while serious insurrections were mounted in Medina and Kufa. The historians ascribe religious meaning to these revolts, but what little contemporaneous evidence we have confirms that the identity of the leadership was in question. As mentioned in the Introduction, coins from as late as 689 CE still had fire altars on them in old Sasanid territories, while coins minted in the old Byzantine lands still had crosses. Arabic appears here, but it is joined to Pahlavi and Greek inscriptions. Early bureaucratic correspondence on papyri from Egypt confirms that local languages (Greek and Coptic) continued to be used, alongside Arabic. But as discussed in Chapter 1, material evidence for the Arabic/Islamic world in the seventh century is thin. We still have very little documentation of any kind, and what we have is often not religious in nature. We are dependent on literary sources to fill in significant gaps.

By the end of the Umayyad period material sources are more plentiful and tell a very different story. We have many more papyri, including a cache of documents from the Egyptian governor Qurra b. Sharik (ruled 709–715).[1] Coins have lost their iconography altogether and now display

[1] This collection is one of the most important finds for the history of early Islamic Egypt. The majority is in Vienna, though a portion of the collection is in Heidelberg and the

only Arabic inscriptions; on the other hand, we also have significant architectural monuments dated to this period – both sacred and secular – that evoke wealth and power. We can say with great confidence that by the late seventh century, an Arab empire was established and that it grew in power and influence during the period covered in this chapter. That said, we should not mistake the empire's power as a marker for the rise of Islam as a religion. As mentioned previously, Bulliet's estimate suggests that by 750, less than 10 percent of the population in Syria and Iran was Muslim, and it is reasonable to presume that this proportion was similar throughout the Near East.[2] In other words, Muslims and Arabs were on the ascent, but still formed a small ruling elite over a vastly non-Muslim population, even while the definition of Muslim and Arab was changing.

In Chapter 1, I concluded that any religious experts that existed before 680 must be considered "proto-scholars" because while they may have had some expertise and circumscribed authority, there is no evidence of training or organization. The period under consideration here seems to have been a time of transition when proto-scholars become more integrated into society, marked by the first elements of training. Most modern historians of Muslim scholars agree,[3] and some have argued forcefully for more attention to be paid to the Umayyad period.[4] However, these writers are dependent almost exclusively on literary sources, and as a result they tend to over-emphasize the organized nature of scholarship during this period, writing of "schools" and "books" when we have no evidence that these existed, at least not in any formal sense.[5]

University of Chicago; see Nabia Abbott's useful introduction in *The Kurrah Papyri from Aphrodito in the Oriental Institute*, Studies in Ancient Oriental Civilization 15 (Chicago: University of Chicago Press, 1938). I am grateful to Professor Andrea Jördens and Dr. Lajos Berkes for facilitating my work on the Heidelberg papyrus collection in June 2015.

2 Bulliet, *Conversion to Islam*; in various chapters, Bulliet outlines the difficulties of making estimates for different parts of the Muslim world at this time. Already in the first reviews, significant questions about Bulliet's methodology were raised; see, for example, the review by Hugh Kennedy in *International Journal of Middle East Studies* 13, no. 2 (May 1981), 250–252. For a recent overview of conversion in Egypt in the early Islamic period, see Mikhail, *From Byzantine to Islamic*, 51–78.

3 Hallaq, for example, writes that "the rudiments of legal scholarship" developed "between 700 and 740 AD" (*Origins*, 63); see also Schacht, *Introduction*, 23–31.

4 Judd, *Religious Scholars and the Umayyads*, 11–13.

5 Schacht's caveat from fifty years ago bears repeating when he says that the term "ancient schools ... implies neither any definite organization nor a strict uniformity of doctrine within each school, nor any formal teaching, nor again any official status, nor even the existence of a body of law" (*Introduction*, 28). Patricia Crone similarly defines these early schools as "congeries of scholars who lived in the same city, often making a livelihood as merchants and shopkeepers and discussing law in their spare time"; like Schacht, she dates

As I will discuss in Chapter 3, only at the end of the eighth century do we have our first solid evidence of an actual community of scholars. Before 750, the material evidence suggests that we only have individual teachers who are taking the subjects of *ḥadīth* collection, Qur'an interpretation, theology, law, and history seriously.

To illustrate the lack formal scholarly training in this period, consider this story of the Umayyad Caliph, Umar b. Abd al-Aziz (d. 101/720), receiving advice from al-Hasan al-Basri (d. 110/728), claimed by many as an early theologian, Sufi, and ascetic, and from Mutarrif b. Abdallah (d. 95/713–714), a lesser known ascetic also from Basra. It is recorded for us by Abdallah b. Abd al-Hakam (d. 214/829), an Egyptian scholar whose work I will discuss in later chapters:

Salim al-Aftas said: Umar b. Abd al-Aziz was among the best dressed and best-cologned people. When he was greeted with the rank of Amir al-Mu'minin [and thereby discovered that he had been elected Caliph], he put his head between his knees and sobbed. The people said: "He is crying for joy at [being elected] caliph."

Then he raised his head, rubbed his eyes and said: "Oh God, enrich me with intelligence (*'aql*) that will benefit me, and make the one whom I receive more important than the one who withdraws from me." Then he called the barber who cut his hair; subsequently he called for writing materials (*dawāh wa-qirṭās*) and wrote with his own hand:

> From the servant of God, Umar b. Abd al-Aziz to al-Hasan b. Abi l-Hasan al-Basri, and to Mutarrif b. Abdallah b. al-Shikhkhir: Peace be upon you both! I praise God – there is no other god than He – for the both of you, and I ask that He bless Muhammad, His servant and messenger. To the point:
>
> I commend the awe of God to you both. Even if one says it much, one acts upon it little. When my letter reaches you, admonish me and do not flatter me. Peace!

So al-Hasan b. Abi l-Hasan al-Basri replied to him:

> To Umar b. Abd al-Aziz. Peace be upon you! I praise God – there is no other god than He – for you. To the point:
>
> This world is the abode of dread. Adam – peace be upon him – descended upon it as a punishment. Despise its honors, and honor the one who despises it. For it impoverishes the one who has intercourse with it; and every day someone is killed (*qatīl*) in it. O commander of the faithful, be like the convalescent patient with his wound: patiently endure the strength of the medicine if you fear the length of the tribulation!"

them to about 720, but says they may have existed earlier (*Roman, Provincial and Islamic Law*, 20). For discussion, see Brockopp "The Formation of Islamic Law: The Egyptian School, 750–900," *Annales Islamologiques* 45 (2011), 123–140, at 123–124.

Mutarrif b. Abdallah b. al-Shikhkhir wrote:

> To the Servant of God Umar, Commander of the Faithful from Mutarrif b. Abdallah: Peace be upon you, O Commander of the Faithful, God's Mercy and His blessings. I praise God – there is no other god than He – for you. To the point:
>
> Let your fraternization be with God and your concentration be upon Him. For a people who consort with God and concentrate on Him – so that they are with Him altogether – are a stronger community than those who have greater numbers. Those who fear that which kills their hearts die to the world. They leave it behind, since they know it will leave them behind. They become enemies to that which other people resign themselves. God placed us (viz. the righteous) [on the earth] and you are among them. But [the righteous] have become few. Peace![6]

The result of this exchange of letters, Ibn Abd al-Hakam informs us, is that Umar b. Abd al-Aziz sold all his belongings and donated thousands of dinars to "the path of God."[7] In this exchange, and indeed in the whole *Sīra* of Umar b. Abd al-Aziz, the role of the scholar has changed dramatically, at least in the memory of the historians. During the life of the Prophet and shortly after his death, such scholars as we found served the pragmatic needs of the Prophet and the early state. Those who could write were employed as secretaries, and Zayd b. Thabit was sent to learn "the script of the Jews" to help with these functions; Muʿadh b. Jabal was to use his knowledge of "God's book" and Muhammad's practice to govern the Yemen. After the Prophet's death, Umar b. al-Khattab continued this pragmatic usage, appointing administrators to run his *dīwān*, and asking Ubayy b. Kaʿb to arbitrate in a dispute with al-Abbas. For his part, Uthman gathered Ubayy and other literate Muslims together to compile the Qurʾan. To be sure, Uthman's Qurʾan project seems to have solidified a growing separation of proto-scholars from state administration, but in these earlier cases, proto-scholars are depicted as working closely with

[6] *Sīrat ʿUmar b. ʿAbd al-Azīz*, Aḥmad ʿUbayd (ed.) (Cairo: al-Maktaba al-ʿArabiyya, 1927), 123–124. Both the Arabic word "*sīra*" and the English "biography" can give the wrong impression of the nature of this text, which is really a collection of exemplary stories about Umar and not a true biography. Suleiman Mourad, *Early Islam between Myth and History: Al-Ḥasan Al-Baṣrī (d. 110H/728CE) and the Formation of His Legacy in Classical Islamic Scholarship* (Leiden: E. J. Brill, 2006), devotes chapter 3 of his book, pp. 121ff., to the overall exchange between al-Hasan and Umar b. Abd al-Aziz. He refers to this specific exchange, but does not quote it.

[7] *Sīrat ʿUmar*, 124. The "path of God" is often understood as warfare, but given the asceticism of the two interlocutors, it may have been in support of mendicants.

temporal authority. In contrast, Umar b. Abd al-Aziz writes to religious persons who appear to be far from the court, and they offer advice that is singularly impractical. The last thing a good governor should do is abandon the world. Oddly, Umar b. Abd al-Aziz takes their advice, and elsewhere in Ibn Abd al-Hakam's account he appears to be a scholar of sorts himself, engaging in theological debates and sending learned men off to North Africa to begin teaching there.[8]

But as with all our literary sources, there is every reason to be cautious about the historicity of these reports. First, Suleiman Mourad has undertaken an extensive study of al-Hasan al-Basri's texts and has determined that many of them are false attributions, actually written down centuries after the death of this sage.[9] As Mourad points out, al-Hasan al-Basri is depicted here as an independent savant, but in fact he was also Umar's governor in Basra. As Mourad argues,

> To have the exchange of letters be between al-Ḥasan al-Baṣrī and ʿUmar II carries great authority and extends a powerful and persuasive message, since it emphasizes the statesman's and scholar's joint eagerness to maintain religious duties, obligations, and proper observance. To have that exchange be between ʿUmar II and his governor of Baṣra ... does not underscore the virtuous exchange of advice and counsel between the scholar and the statesman.[10]

Second, we have no direct witnesses to scholarly activity in this period.[11] Our very earliest scholarly manuscripts are fragments, the dating of which is highly speculative; even Nabia Abbott, who tends toward sanguine assessments, cannot place them earlier than 780 (well after the period considered in this chapter). This has not prevented many scholars from attempting to reconstruct "books" by "authors" such as Ibn Ishaq (d. 150/767), Wahb b. Munabbih (d. 110/728 or 114/732), or even Ibn Abbas (d. 68/687–688).[12] As I will discuss below, these worthy efforts raise more questions than they resolve, and they are often based on a mistaken notion of the development of Muslim scholarship. In Chapter 3, I will argue that no texts can be reconstructed with any confidence until

[8] Ben Cheneb, *Ṭabaqāt*, 20–21.

[9] Mourad, *Early Islam*, 128. For a counter-argument, see Hallaq, *Origins*, 71–72.

[10] Mourad, *Early Islam*, 123; in other cases, Mourad demonstrates that the same text is attributed to various exemplary individuals, such as al-Hasan, Umar b. Abd al-Aziz, and even Ali b. Abi Talib.

[11] Even Hallaq (*Origins*, 72), admits that none of the writings ascribed to scholars from this period has survived.

[12] Fuat Sezgin, *Geschichte des arabischen Schrifttums*, 9 vols. (Leiden: E. J. Brill, 1967–1984), 1:27; Donner, *Narratives*, 297–306.

the 770s, with actual books coming a few decades later. Further, when we survey these earliest possible texts, we still see distinctive oral elements that seem at odds with the notion of books written by putative scholars, such as Ibn Abbas and al-Hasan al-Basri.

Mourad's conclusions, that this account has been manipulated and that texts attributed to al-Hasan al-Basri are pious forgeries, therefore seem reasonable, but there is still some value in these stories. Note, for example, that in Ibn Abd al-Hakam's account, al-Hasan and Mutarrif write with authority but do not derive that authority from expected places. Neither of these scholars is remembered as quoting Qur'an or Muhammad's practice in responding to the commander, even though the sentiments they express could have been supported with passages from these sources. Nor do they invoke the authority of a scholarly community, either in the sense of a tradition of learning and teaching or in the sense of a lineage of knowledge. Al-Hasan and Mutarrif depend, rather, on aphorisms, a form of learning that appears to have had a long history in Arabic-speaking circles (and elsewhere), and they recommend individual acts of self-abnegation based simply on their personal authority. In sum, even though Ibn Abd al-Hakam is writing at a point when scholarly communities were established, his historical text accidentally preserves characteristics of earlier scholars who were quite different from what he must have known in late eighth- and early ninth-century Egypt.

Literary texts, therefore, can offer useful information, but they need to be interpreted within the context of what is sociologically possible and what our material evidence indicates. No matter what some modern historians may claim, reconstructing "books" from quotations attributed to these proto-scholars is a fraught task, both because we cannot discern between the thoughts of proto-scholars and the memory of later scholars who transmitted and edited their thoughts and also because it posits and then recreates an anachronistic notion of a community of scholars devoted to book transmission. The fact that we have no manuscripts of literary Arabic datable to this period could be due to the destructive powers of weather, insects, and time, but it is also very possible that there were no manuscripts to destroy. Again, however, this does not mean there was no writing at all, since both proto-scholars and their students may have used notes. Therefore, reconstructive efforts are not entirely worthless, but before I turn to a detailed analysis of these efforts, it is helpful to secure some key pieces of information that can be gleaned through analysis of material remains.

THE EVIDENTIARY BASIS OF UMAYYAD HISTORY, 680–750

Unlike Chapter 1, we now have a wealth of material evidence to consider: coins with longer and more detailed inscriptions, an extensive collection of both bureaucratic papyri and also Qur'anic manuscripts, and epigraphy, now including architecture. This evidence is vital for understanding the expanding Umayyad empire, which was increasing in wealth and sophistication, but it also gives us key information about the rise of the religious scholar. To begin, we note details that already emerged in the last chapter: Byzantine and Persian influences remain very important, and Arabic is gradually becoming established as an instrument for written communication. To this, however, we can add an important shift in the public use of religious language. In the earliest period, we found no public mention of Muhammad or the Qur'an, and what religious language was used fit well within a broader monotheistic context. Now, however, we note both an increase in the frequency of religious claims and also a subtle repositioning, centered on the figure of Muhammad.

For example, more than eighty years ago in Aswan, Egypt, an ancient tombstone was discovered that memorialized the life of one Abbasa bt. Jurayj b. Sanad. This tombstone has already been analyzed several different times, but its short inscription bears repeating here:

> In the name of God, the Merciful, the Compassionate. The greatest calamity of the People of Islam is their being bereft of the Prophet Muhammad, may God bless him and grant him peace. This is the tomb of ʿAbbāsa, daughter of Jurayj, son of Sanad. May the compassion, forgiveness and satisfaction of God be upon her. She died on Monday, fourteen days having elapsed from Dhu l-qaʿda, of the year seventy-one, confessing that there is no god, but God alone, He has no partner, and that Muhammad is His servant and His apostle, may God bless him and grant him peace.[13]

This inscription is of unparalleled importance; it is the earliest datable mention of Islam, of a "people of Islam," and of a clear use of the two-

[13] Hassan Mohammed El-Hawary, "The Second Oldest Islamic Monument Known, Dated A.H. 71 (A.D. 691). From the Time of the Omayyad Calif 'Abd-el-Malik ibn Marwān," *Journal of the Royal Asiatic Society of Great Britain and Ireland* 2 (Apr. 1932), 289–293, at 290–291. I have slightly modified al-Hawary's translation, which is to be preferred over that of Leor Halevi, "The Paradox of Islamization: Tombstone Inscriptions, Qur'ānic Recitations, and the Problem of Religious Change," *History of Religions* 44, no. 2 (Nov. 2004), 120–152, at 125–126. See also Gruendler, *Development*, 17.

article confession of faith as a means of conversion from Christianity. This last point is made plain by the Christian names of Abbasa's father and grandfather,[14] as well as by the grammatical construction: "she died ... confessing that ..." The two slight additions to what later would become the standard confession of faith also seem useful for the purposes of discerning between Islam and Christianity.[15] What most interests me here, however, are not these important points, but rather the social context of these words on a tombstone. It is not coincidence that these words match later attestations of religious formulae: someone had to have instructed the stone carver what to inscribe on this tombstone; further, someone had to have instructed Abbasa in the basics of the religious beliefs and practices of the "people of Islam." Thus, this simple tombstone gives us an indirect indication of the existence of a private religious expert in upper Egypt before the year 71 (691 CE). It seems reasonable to suggest that such experts were common in Muslim communities of this period, instructing individuals in aspects of the faith (conversion, burial rites) that have no impact on the state. Their authority was religious, perhaps deriving from that of Muhammad himself, whose death is regarded as "the greatest calamity."

In my view, Abbasa's tombstone is an indirect witness to two key processes in the development of scholarly communities: a devotion to the memory of the Prophet Muhammad and an early focus on private ritual. Again, I am suggesting that, apart from the development of state interests at this time, individuals were pursuing private, informal study of the Qurʾan and of Muhammad's life.[16] The first process is the collection of *ḥadīth*, including stories about Muhammad's life and example, since there is good evidence to believe that these efforts were underway and perhaps beginning to be formalized in the Umayyad period.[17] The second process is the organization of *ḥadīth* and other dicta into distinct areas of law. Many attempts

[14] There is some question about the pointing of these names; see El-Hawary, "Second Oldest," 292. Sanad is a Coptic name, while Jurayj is a diminutive of George.

[15] These are the phrases "*waḥdahu*" (He alone) and "*lā sharīka lahu*" (He has no partners), both of which emphasize God's unity and lack of "partners." The occurrence of these phrases in other Umayyad era epigraphy may have served the same function.

[16] As I have argued elsewhere (Brockopp, "Interpreting Material Evidence"), it is important that we do not get caught up in a teleological assessment of the religious activities of these early communities, seeing their Islam as somehow incomplete or aberrant.

[17] Hallaq, *Origins*, 63–64. I do not go so far as Judd (*Religious Scholars and the Umayyads*), however, in seeing the production of formal texts devoted to *ḥadīth* during this period. As I will discuss later in this chapter, our earliest scraps of evidence suggest a devotion to the Prophet Muhammad within the context of Jewish prophets; in Chapter 3,

have been made to explain the order of *fiqh* chapters, which generally begin with matters of ritual but differ substantially thereafter in the earliest texts.[18] Despite these differences, however, the very concept of chapters does seem to go back to the Umayyad period, and one possibility is that the order preserves a rough chronology, with the first chapters reflecting those matters (prayer, ritual, burial) that early communities most closely identified with religion, and further chapters (business transactions, slavery, land tenure) gradually added as the notion of religious law expanded.

Abbasa's tomb therefore gives us a useful *terminus ad quem*, a date after which we know that there were proto-scholars instructing Muslims in matters of faith. There is no reason to presume that these individuals were professionals who underwent a course of training and devoted most of their time to study, or that their influence was wider spread; it is more likely that they had other primary roles in society and that instruction and learning were more of an avocation. However, as we use this tombstone to interpret other material evidence from this same period it is possible that they were beginning to play a more public role within the small Muslim communities of the period. For example, remarkably similar language about Muhammad is found both on the Dome of the Rock (72/691–692) and also on Umayyad coins after the "reform" of 77/696–697, where Muhammad is also called "*rasūl Allāh* (God's messenger)" and where it is also averred that "There is no god but God alone; he has no partner" (see Figure 2.1).[19] It is possible that with these remarkable public statements by political authorities, we are seeing a rising influence of religious proto-scholars among the Umayyad Caliphs.

Because I see these proto-scholars as small, disorganized groups of individual savants, not well connected to the state, my view is opposed to that of the sanguine historians described in the Introduction. Following a sociology of emerging religious traditions, I presume that a new religious tradition takes many decades to achieve its full expression, only gradually gaining new members as it distinguishes itself from other, more established, religious traditions. But neither would many skeptics accept my interpretation of the evidence. At the outset, however, let me clarify that the basic premise of the skeptics is one that I share: any account of early Islamic history must make sense of the material evidence that

I argue that the evidence confirms that even well after the Umayyad period, *ḥadīth* collections are still being written in informal texts.

18 Heffening, "Aufbau."

19 As I discuss below, the statement on these coins was anticipated by Pahlavi inscriptions.

Figure 2.1: Gold dinar of caliph Abd al-Malik, 77/696–697,

survives; further, witnesses from neighboring cultures must also be taken into account.[20] Where we part ways is in the preferential treatment they give these important sources, and the way they exclude evidence that does not fit their interpretive scheme. Robert Hoyland, for example, is so exercised by the obviously Islamic formulae on Abbasa's tombstone that he suggests that when the stone carver inscribed "in the year seventy-one" he actually meant the year 171,[21] even though we have no evidence of any other tombstone where the word "one hundred" was omitted.[22] At least Hoyland, to his credit, attempts to account for the tombstone, while other skeptics ignore it, a necessary move for those who are convinced that "Muḥammad is not a historical figure"[23] or that "historical Islam began at the earliest in the middle of the eighth century."[24] Elsewhere, I have discussed the problems of these positions, arguing that they reflect a serious misunderstanding both of the nature of material evidence and also of the different roles for public and private religion.[25] Here, I will

[20] Yehuda D. Nevo and Judith Koren, *Crossroads to Islam: The Origins of the Arab Religion and the Arab State* (Amherst, NY: Prometheus Books, 2003), 9.

[21] Robert Hoyland, "The Content and Context of Early Arabic Inscriptions," *Jerusalem Studies in Arabic and Islam* 21 (1997), 77–102, at 87.

[22] Nor is "one hundred" ever omitted from papyri, so far as I know. Due to the existence of dual dating in papyri (with dates given according to both the *hijrī* and also Christian calendars), such a habit of omission (were it to exist) would be noticeable.

[23] Nevo and Koren, *Crossroads*, 11; quoted with approval by Karl-Heinz Ohlig, "Foreword: Islam's 'Hidden' Origins" in Ohlig and Puin (eds.), *Hidden Origins*, 8.

[24] Luxenberg, "New Interpretation," 141.

[25] Brockopp, "Interpreting Material Evidence."

restrict myself to analysis of this material as it pertains to the gradual transformation of the proto-scholar from a private to a more public figure.

Far from being unusual for the late seventh century, the phrases on Abbasa's tombstone resonate closely with contemporary material evidence, suggesting that 71/691 was a turning point when private religious authorities increasingly gained the ear of the state. For example, on Abbasa's tombstone appears the phrase "There is no god but God alone; He has no partner." This is mentioned as part of Abbasa's confession of faith, similar to, but not precisely the same as, statements found in the Qur'an.[26] However, this precise wording is found on coins from 72/691–692 and afterwards and four times in the mosaics of the Dome of the Rock (completed in the same year).

These similar phrases have very different effect in their various contexts. In the case of the tombstone, they mark Abbasa as different from her father and grandfather, a powerful, transformative effect, but one that is still largely in the private sphere. In the case of the coins (and similarly the Dome of the Rock), the phrases are also discriminating, distinguishing this new religious view from others. On the coins, this is accompanied by an implied threat that God sent Muhammad (and by extension his representatives) "with the guidance and the religion of truth to make it prevail over all religion." Here, religious authority is put to a very different purpose where the goal is not so much the private edification of persons as it is the public interests of the State. This is an important shift, but we should be wary about presuming too much about the State's understanding of Islam.

As I will discuss in subsequent chapters, early ninth-century manuscripts provide us with a *terminus post quem* for formal scholarly interest in Muhammad's life and example,[27] but they and my observations about the nature of seventh-century evidence only limit the scope of the skeptical argument, they do not fully undercut it. The fact is, apart from the claim in Abbasa's tomb, and in coins and architecture (that Muhammad is a prophet and that God is one, not three), many aspects of early Islam do look like contemporaneous forms of Christianity. This is especially obvious in the case of architecture, since the Umayyad mosque in Damascus,

[26] The fact that Abbasa's tombstone has no quotations from the Qur'an is an important part of Halevi's argument for considering it to be authentic (Halevi, "Paradox," 127).

[27] As discussed below, a *Sīra* attributed to Wahb b. Munabbih dates from the early ninth century. Also, Nabia Abbott has published undated fragments from a book celebrating Muhammad's battles that she dates to the late second/eighth century; see her *Studies*, 1: 65–79.

for example, did not replace the Cathedral of St. John until 706 – even Muslim historians tell us that Christians continued to worship there together with Muslims in the earliest period.[28] The first wholly new construction of religious architecture, the Dome of the Rock in Jerusalem, was not only built by Byzantine architects, it is built on the site of Solomon's temple, a spot sacred to Jews and Christians alike. It is, in fact, not a mosque at all, since it surrounds an enormous outcropping of limestone; a significant congregation of Muslims cannot pray inside of it. While Christoph Luxenberg is mistaken about the meaning of the word *muḥammad* that is inscribed inside the dome,[29] he is right to point out that much of the polemic in the frieze need not be understood as anti-Christian; it could certainly fit in the realm of intra-Christian debates over the nature of Jesus Christ.

Luxenberg's claim that the Umayyads were actually promoting a form of early Christianity, therefore, is not entirely off-base, but it gains its shock value from a presumption that Islam in the seventh century *ought* to be substantially different from other religious traditions. But this presumption is misguided. Our evidence points to a gradual definition and differentiation of Islam from Judaism and Christianity, a finding that has important implications for the role of the scholars. Whereas Judaism appeared to play the primary role as a "mirroring self-object" during Muhammad's lifetime,[30] Christians were the majority population outside of Medina, and it seems that Christianity takes over this role in the Umayyad period.

Religious formulae on coins are important signs of change, but alone they can tell us almost nothing about the identity, training, or professional activities of proto-scholars. The most we can surmise from this evidence is that the public perception of Islam was changing and that proto-scholars were playing a role in this change. Conversion to Islam may have been increasing, and Abbasa could have been one of many converts from this period, but given the fact that Muslims still remained a small minority in most places, it is the positive public perception of Islam that is more

28 Nancy Khalek, *Damascus after the Muslim Conquest: Text and Image in Early Islam* (Oxford: Oxford University Press, 2011).

29 Luxenberg, "New Interpretation."

30 I adapt this terminology from Heinz Kohut, who employs it as part of the identity formation of an individual (*The Analysis of the Self: A Systematic Approach to the Psychoanalytic Treatment of Narcissistic Personality Disorders* [Chicago: University of Chicago Press, 1971]). Despite its psychological baggage, I find this term more accurate than the broader notion of "other."

Figure 2.2: Pre-reform drachma from 32/652 (COC27636),

important. Because coins are conservative in nature, they are ideal markers of public perception. In a multireligious environment where Muslims are a small minority, significant changes in the appearance of a coin could result in the lack of confidence in the currency. This conservative nature explains the observed trajectory in these coins. Again, our earliest coins have only short Arabic phrases added to Byzantine and Sassanid coins (Figure 2.2) that are physically quite similar to pre-Islamic coins, complete with crosses, fire altars, and other symbols of authority.[31]

The Arabic phrases that first appear here ("In the name of God" and "praise belongs to God") are unobjectionable from a Christian, Jewish, or even Zoroastrian perspective and therefore would have caused no concerns about the value of the currency.

The name Muhammad first appears alone in Arabic on a few eastern coins from 38 and 52 (of the Yazdgird era, so 670 and 684 CE),[32] and in 70/689 the statement Muhammad is the messenger of God first appears in Pahlavi script. In 72/691–692 (five years before the Umayyad "coin reform") another coin appears that includes this statement plus the Pahlavi equivalent of "There is no God, but God."[33] It is possible that the

[31] Gaube, *Arabosasanidische Numismatik*, 18–37.
[32] Ibid., 36.
[33] Malek Mochiri, "A Pahlavi Forerunner of the Umayyad Reformed Coinage," *Journal of the Royal Asiatic Society of Great Britain and Ireland* 2 (1981), 168–172. For discussion,

coins that have survived are only a selection of what was minted, but based on this evidence, it appears that coin inscriptions from the former Byzantine territories followed a separate trajectory from those in the former Sasanid lands, and that the western coins (see Figure 2.1) are responding to changes that first appeared in the east.[34] Further, as with Abbasa's tombstone, we may speculate that proto-scholars are playing a role, both in determining the wording of these formulae and in promoting their appearance. Finally, there must be some perceived advantage to putting these statements on the coins, one that outweighs the disadvantages of making a change in the first place.

The answer to this riddle, I suggest, lies in both a dissatisfaction with the Umayyad caliphate and the claims made by rivals (the Alids and the Zubayrids, according to historical texts) to represent the increasingly influential "people of Islam." Whereas Muʿawiya developed a pragmatic and effective bureaucratic state in Damascus, the Alids and Zubayrids may have appealed to a different form of authority, one that required the services of proto-scholars.[35] It seems reasonable to suggest that Abd al-Malik b. Marwan responded to the effectiveness of this move first by building the impressive Dome of the Rock and then by reforming the coinage.[36] Not only does this line of argument make good sense out of the material evidence, it also dovetails nicely with an important finding by Beatrice Gruendler regarding early Qurʾan manuscripts.

see Volker Popp, "The Early History of Islam, Following Inscriptional and Numismatic Testimony," in Ohlig and Puin (eds.), *Hidden Origins*, 17–124, at 65–66. See further A. S. Eshragh, "An Interesting Arab-Sasanian Dirhem," *Oriental Numismatic Society Newsletter* 178 (2004), 45–46; Stefan Heidemann, "The Evolving Representation of the Early Islamic Empire and Its Religion on Coin Imagery," in Angelika Neuwirth et al. (eds.), *The Qurʾān in Context* (Leiden: E. J. Brill, 2010), 149–195; Stuart D. Sears, "The Sasanian Style Coins of 'Muhammad' and Some Related Coins," *Yarmouk Numismatics* 7 (1997), 7–17.

34 Crone makes a similar point in *God's Caliph*, 25; she does not, however, make the connection to the polemical use of public religion that I am arguing here. For a fascinating discussion of coin evidence as a basis for political history, see Robinson, *ʿAbd al-Malik*, 35–36.

35 Robert Hoyland makes a similar argument, adding the evidence of Christian historians: "That the revolt of Ibn al-Zubayr had religious implications is confirmed by a contemporary Christian source, which says of him that 'he had come out of zeal for the house of God and he was full of threats against the Westerners, claiming that they were transgressors of the law'" ("New Documentary Texts," 397). Crone also points out that Ibn al-Zubayr was known as *khalīfat al-Raḥmān* (*God's Caliph*, 12).

36 I am suggesting therefore that he is responding to changes in the religious landscape, not causing them as Popp and Luxenberg argue. Robinson sums it up nicely: "the Marwanids seem to have learned a Zubayrid lesson" (*ʿAbd al-Malik*, 39).

Before addressing Gruendler's argument, however, it is important to establish that the earliest Qur'an manuscripts are in fact from the late seventh century. In Chapter 1, I argued that the text of the Qur'an reflects early seventh-century views, but here I am referring to the physical witnesses to that text. Our earliest example of a complete, dated manuscript of the Qur'an does not appear to be earlier than the fourth/tenth century, and our earliest dated substantial fragment is from before 229/844.[37] There are, however, very many undated fragments of Qur'an manuscripts, some of which may derive from the first/seventh century, based on the quality of the writing materials, the rudimentary nature of the early scripts, and the many small orthographic differences in comparison with later manuscripts.[38] Recent attempts have also been made to use radiocarbon dating,[39] including spectacular claims of Qur'ans dating to the lifetime of Muhammad himself,[40] but not only does radiocarbon dating give us a large range of possible dates, it also can date only the death of the animal (in the case of parchment). When the text of the Qur'an was written on that skin is not possible to determine from this method.[41] Moreoever, Déroche has submitted firmly dated manuscript samples for radiocarbon dating, revealing problematic discrepancies.[42] Taken individually, these methods of dating manuscripts are preliminary at best, but cumulatively they provide strong evidence, corroborated by the fact that the late seventh century is also when we find our first datable phrases from the Qur'an in the Dome of the Rock, followed closely by inscriptions in Mecca, dated to 80/699, that contain quotations from Q 38:26 and 4:87.[43]

37 Déroche, "Les manuscrits arabes," 345. The date on this manuscript is a secondary remark, written after the initial composition, possibly decades after.

38 Déroche, *Qur'ans of the Umayyads*; idem, "Manuscripts of the Qur'ān" in *Encyclopaedia of the Qur'ān*; Sinai, "Consonantal Skeleton;" see also Hans-Casper Graf von Bothmer, "Masterworks of Islamic Book Art: Koranic Calligraphy and Illumination in the Manuscripts Found in The Great Mosque in Sanaa," in W. Daum (ed.), *Yemen: 3000 Years of Art and Civilization in Arabia Felix* (Innsbruck: Pinguin-Verlag, 1987), 178–181.

39 Yasin Dutton, "An Umayyad Fragment of the Qur'an and its Dating," *Journal of Qur'anic Studies* 9, no. 2 (2007), 57–87; Behnam Sadeghi and U. Bergmann, "The Codex of a Companion of the Prophet and the Qur'an of the Prophet," *Arabica* 57 (2010), 343–436. Cf. Déroche, *Qur'ans*, 11–14.

40 Sinai, "Consonantal Skeleton," 276, n. 21; Déroche, *Qur'ans*, 13.

41 Déroche, *Qur'ans*, 11–14.

42 Ibid., 12–13.

43 Gruendler, *Development*, 18.

In recent years, there has been a sharp increase in scholarship on early Qurʾans, much of it summarized and subjected to detailed critical analysis in François Déroche's *Qurʾans of the Umayyads*. Déroche's book contains extensive descriptions and forty-four photographic plates of early Qurʾan manuscripts. I used that book as a guide during a research trip to Paris and Dublin in summer of 2015, yet I was not prepared for the variety and beauty of these early Qurʾans. For example, the sheer size of Is1404 in the Chester Beatty library in Dublin is astonishing, with each page measuring 47×38 cm. Déroche estimates that the complete manuscript consisted of 410 folios,[44] meaning that a herd of 205 animals was needed for its production. On the basis of this and similar manuscripts, Déroche argues that

> Both the Sanaa copy and the Dublin manuscript CBL Is1404 were produced during the first decades of the eighth century, under Umayyad rule and probably in some official context. The cost of these copies has risen dramatically when compared with former *muṣḥaf*s like the Fustat codex. The reflection on the appearance of the sacred book had been applied to both the general outer appearance (the *muṣḥaf* must be a large book) and to the presentation of the text (the *muṣḥaf* must be a beautiful book). A genuine culture of the book had developed – at least in some milieux.[45]

Déroche titled this chapter of his book "Imperial Scriptoria?" While he backs away from the suggestion that an Arabic scriptorium existed in the Umayyad period,[46] the connection he wants to make is worth exploring. By using the term "scriptoria," Déroche is hearkening back to Byzantine institutions of learning that continued to produce Christian texts long after the Arab conquests. Indeed, the production of large and beautiful Qurʾans during this period was very likely a response to similarly large and beautiful copies of the Bible produced in Byzantine scriptoria.[47] In this light, it is instructive to note that all of our early Qurʾans, like Bibles, are codices (sheets of parchments folded and stitched together through the fold in book form) and not scrolls (sheets stitched end-to-end) as was common for Torahs as well as papyrus documents.[48]

[44] Déroche, *Qurʾans*, 109
[45] Ibid., 118.
[46] Ibid., 133.
[47] Ibid., 117. A monumental Gospel was produced outside Damascus a few decades earlier, on December 24, 633; see Brock, "Syriac Views," 9. Von Bothmer came to similar conclusions concerning MS Sana'a DAM 20–33.1 (twenty-five folios) in "Architekturbilder im Koran: eine Prachthandschrift der Umayyadenzeit aus dem Yemen," *Pantheon* 45 (1987), 4–20.
[48] In private conversation, however, in December 2015, Barry Flood told me of the existence of scroll Qurʾans originally from Damascus. I have not been able to verify this information.

The Chester Beatty manuscript (Is1404) is evidently the pinnacle of a long history of Qur'an production. Its decorative flourishes (in red, yellow, blue, and green ink overlaying outlines in black) denote wealth and power. In his analysis of the script, Déroche finds a movement toward a *scriptio plena* that resolves some of the ambiguities found in earlier manuscripts. Admittedly, this evolutionary scheme from a *scriptio defectiva* (which Déroche calls the "old style") to a *scriptio plena* (termed the "modern style") is a matter of judgment.[49] But after examining the evidence for myself, I am ready to agree that earlier Qur'ans were not as closely associated with the centers of wealth and power as these late Umayyad Qur'ans. The famous San'a Palimpsest (a unique example of an older version of the Qur'an erased so that the expensive parchment could be reused for a new version) appears to be a transition document, with some signs of official sponsorship but without the regularity of late-Umayyad Qur'ans.[50] Moreover, the use of a *scriptio plena*, including marks to distinguish consonants, in bureaucratic papyri suggests that familiarity with this form of writing Arabic would have affected Qur'an manuscripts at a later stage, even while Qur'an scribes and secretaries continued to use different forms of Arabic script.

If the quantity and quality of Qur'an manuscripts datable to the Umayyad era is surprising, the number of papyri datable to this period is staggering. Leading the way is a cache of papyrus documents from Aphrodito that includes perhaps an entire library of documents from the Egyptian governor Qurra b. Sharik (r. 709–714 CE) who served under the Umayyad Caliph al-Walid b. Marwan. This cache is currently dispersed in several libraries around the world but is nonetheless one of the most well-studied collections. The fact that many of these documents are dated gives us unparalleled confidence in reconstructing the role of the chancery in this period of Umayyad administration. In her 1938 study of papyri fragments that had come to the University of Chicago's Oriental Institute, Nabia Abbott noted that they help to expose an "unwarranted underestimation of the spread of writing among the Arabs in general."[51] Indeed, the wide-ranging nature of the collection and the use of clear, fluent Arabic by scribes (some of whom must have been bilingual) gives the impression of a growing and literate reading public.

This impression is underscored by examination of undated papyrus fragments, of which hundreds remain untranslated and even

[49] Déroche, *Qur'ans*, 43.
[50] Ibid., 48–56.
[51] Abbott, *The Kurrah Papyri*, 10.

uncatalogued.[52] Many of these have been wrongly placed in the ninth century, and further research may help us to date these texts more accurately.[53] Alongside important documents from the chancery, then, we also find personal letters and other fragments that bolster Abbott's impression about literacy.[54] It is unclear, however, what these papyri might tell us about the rise of the Muslim scholar. On the one hand, it is evident that by the early eighth century, Arabic is being widely used, and a large literate population is a prerequisite for a class of scholars. On the other hand, we still have no material evidence of books; there are literary fragments on papyrus, but, as I will discuss in Chapter 3, these cannot be dated any earlier than the end of the eighth century. Nonetheless, a comparison of dated papyri and early Qurʾan fragments is revealing.

Because early manuscript fragments of the Qurʾan are not explicitly dated, Beatrice Gruendler does not subject them to detailed analysis in her survey of Arabic paleography.[55] However, she does note that early Qurʾans are "essentially epigraphic" in their scripts, while chancery documents are "a highly developed cursive." Further, she points out that "the divergence *between* the two cited groups [Qurʾans and chancery letters] is broader than *within* them."[56] In other words, Gruendler is arguing that there is not a single, linear development of Arabic paleography, but rather parallel developments. This finding, based solely on analysis of morphological differences in writing the Arabic script, has a far greater implication than Gruendler allows. For paleographers, her conclusions are a corrective of Grohmann and a setback for scholarship, since she is arguing that dated materials from the chancery cannot be used to date early Qurʾan fragments, but historians may take the same evidence and draw an entirely different conclusion. The consistency of writing within the chancery implies a larger social world behind the scribe who actually penned a specific document. Consistency means standards set by an authority and taught to other scribes; it implies a structure of discipline. Similarly, consistency within the production of early

52 For a recent overview, see Petra Sijpesteijn, "Arabic Papyri and Other Documents from Current Excavations in Egypt, with an Appendix of Arabic Papyri and Some Written Objects in Egyptian Collections," *Bardiyyat, Newsletter of the international Society for Arabic Papyrology* 2 (2007), 10–23; the vast majority of early papyri stems from Egypt, although a few are known from Nessana and other locations.

53 Eva Mira Grob, *Documentary Arabic Private and Business Letters on Papyrus: Form and Function, Content and Context* (New York: De Gruyter, 2010), 4–7.

54 Khaled Mohamed Mahmoud Younes, *Joy and Sorrow in Early Muslim Egypt: Arabic Papyrus Letters, Text and Content*. Ph.D. dissertation, Leiden University (2013), https://openaccess.leidenuniv.nl/handle/1887/21541.

55 Gruendler, *Development*, 135.

56 Ibid., 137, emphasis in original.

Qur'an's implies a separate discipline and structure serving different ends. In other words, parallel developments in writing Arabic are consistent with the notion of distinct groups of individuals, both literate, but one using their skills for the service of the state and the other for the writing of Qur'ans.[57] A look at examples is revealing.

As illustrated by this single sheet of papyrus (Figure 2.3), bureaucratic letters are short and to the point. The writing is neat, but not labored, and a cursive style lends itself to the quick and efficient production of these documents. In contrast, the "epigraphic" style found in the earliest Qur'an fragments (such as Figure 2.4) is harder to produce – it requires time and patience to keep the letters properly spaced, similar in many ways to the patient calligraphy required to produce Torah scrolls. Slow, deliberate writing of a Qur'an is consistent with a pious practice of devotion to a holy book. It is reasonable to suppose that experts in this form of writing would also be especially devoted to the lessons of its contents.[58]

The fact that the Arabic written in early Qur'an manuscripts uses neither dots to distinguish certain consonants nor vowel markings does not necessarily prove their archaic nature, since consonantal markings are found already in mid-seventh century bureaucratic papyri (see Figure I.1). Rather, they underline the separate development of bureaucratic and Qur'anic script as well as the fact that the Qur'an remained an oral text that depended on the written text primarily as a mnemonic device. If I am correct that they developed their skills outside of Umayyad bureaucracy, early Qur'an scribes may have been some of our earliest proto-scholars, writing, studying, and utilizing the Qur'an for religious purposes that were largely private.[59]

[57] The distinction I am drawing here between bureaucratic scribes writing tax receipts and pious proto-scholars writing holy texts is one of Weberian types. It is meant for analysis and need not necessarily to conform perfectly to reality. It is entirely possible that some individuals did both, such as appears to have been the case in the early period with Zayd b. Thabit. Nonetheless, the distinction is important because while a functioning bureaucracy can help explain the rise of a successful Arab state, it does little to elucidate the rise of an Islamic religion.

[58] Again, there are exceptions and possibly interactions between these two groups. In the Qurra papyri located in Heidelberg, for example, are large format letters (P. Heid. arab 1 and 3) written in a monumental script – the orthography is still markedly different from early Qur'ans, however. See the photographic reproductions in Jāsir Abū Ṣafiyya, *Bardiyyāt Qurra b. Sharīk al-ʿAbsī* (Riyadh: King Faysal Institute for Islamic Research and Studies, 2004), 326 and 328. My thanks to Lajos Berkes for this reference.

[59] See here the provocative suggestions by Estelle Whelan that Medina may have had a school of Qur'an copyists and also developed the first grammarians ("Forgotten Witness: Evidence for the Early Codification of the Qur'ān," *Journal of the American Oriental Society* 118, no. 1 [1998], 1–14, at 12–13). My thanks to Asma Afsaruddin for this reference.

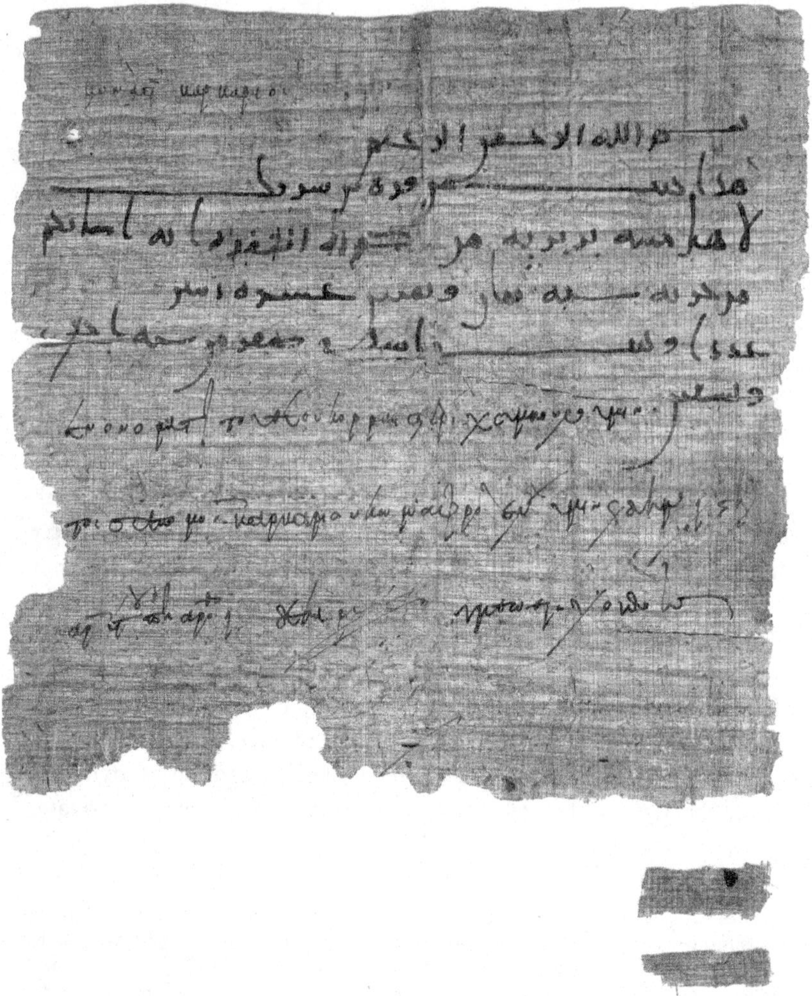

Figure 2.3: Bilingual (Arabic/Greek) tax memo, dated 90/709 (P. Heid. Inv. Arab 13r)

This then would help to explain the fact that Qurʾanic instructions on warfare, slavery, inheritance, and other public (and semipublic) legal matters were not widely applied in the Umayyad period, if at all. Umar was not alone in making a ruling in opposition to the plain text of the

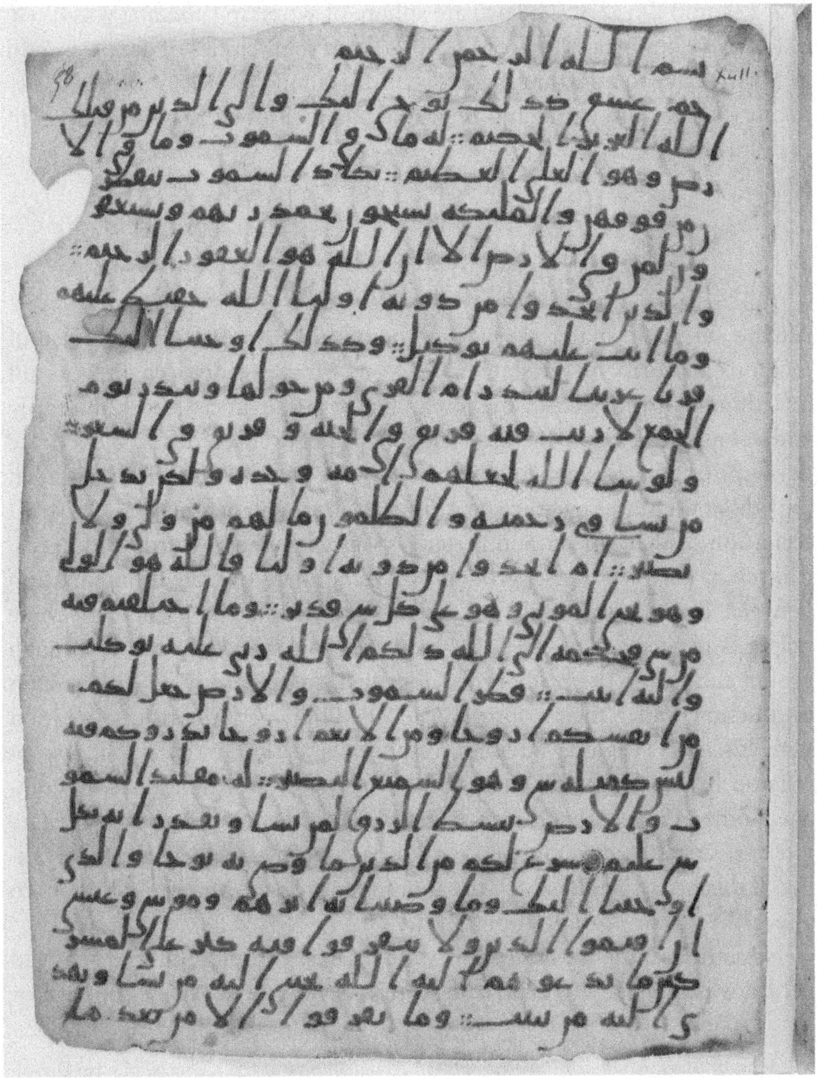

Figure 2.4: Early Umayyad Qur'an, beginning at Sura 42 (Arabe 328a, fol. 58r), part of the Codex Parisino-Petropolitanus, Bibliothèque nationale de France.

Qur'an; later scholars such as Malik b. Anas (d. 179/795) expressed shock at the idea that Qur'anic injunctions on slavery would be applied literally. "It is not fitting (*lā yanbaghī*)," he wrote "for a free man to marry a slave when he can afford a free wife" in direct contradiction of

Q 2:221 and 24:32.[60] The private sphere of worship (*ʿibadāt*) was likely much more important to proto-scholars and their circles of devotees, and it is instructive to note that there is little dissent in the Muslim world today about the rites of fasting and pilgrimage, activities extremely detailed in the Qurʾan.

PROTO-SCHOLARS IN THE UMAYYAD PERIOD: A SPECULATIVE RECONSTRUCTION

All the surviving material evidence points to a limited symbolic use of religious authority by the state under Muʿawiya, perhaps as a direct result of Uthman's overreach in this area. The state advanced, both militarily and economically, not on the basis of Prophetic precedents, but on the development of an efficient bureaucracy. Religious authority continued outside of the state structure on a private, moral plane, focusing on ritual recitation of the Qurʾan and memory of the Prophet's words and deeds. The split between these groups is exemplified by the differentiation between bureaucratic and Qurʾanic scripts. While the number of these religious devotees was small, they apparently formed a cohesive enough group such that the Zubayrids appealed to them by reforming coin production under their control. Abd al-Malik, perhaps in consultation with his own religious advisers, responded to this initial public use of religion by building the Dome of the Rock and reforming his own coinage. Some of our early Qurʾan fragments also seem to be a result of state interest, since their production would have been an expensive undertaking. If this is so, then it is perhaps another part of an Umayyad program to appeal to this important population.

Nonetheless, the nature of this state interest throughout the Umayyad period was limited.[61] We have no material evidence of systematic legal or

[60] Mālik b. Anas, *Kitāb al-Muwaṭṭaʾ*, Ḥasan Abdallāh Sharaf (ed.), 2 vols. (Cairo: Dār al-Rayān li-l-Turāth, 1988), 1:365. In a useful little online article, Yasin Dutton summarizes many of the ways that the jurists eventually developed to deal with inconsistencies and seeming contradictions in the Qurʾan ("The Sources of Islamic Law: An Overview" www.muhajabah.com/docstorage/dutton.htm, accessed Aug. 8, 2013). My research suggests, however, that early jurists did not make use of these elaborate devices and were less concerned to go against the Qurʾan.

[61] The symbolic use of public religious authority is also seen clearly in architectural survivals from this period, including major mosques in Damascus, Aleppo, Amman, and elsewhere. At the same time, however, the famous desert hunting lodges of the Umayyad princes, with their frescoes devoted to the hunt and other bodily pleasures, suggest a desire to escape from religious authority.

theological projects at this time,[62] nor did the Umayyad state establish an official priesthood along the lines of that maintained by the Byzantine Empire. The result of this limited engagement was twofold. On the one hand, private proto-scholars continued their activities apart from a growing state bureaucracy. On the other hand, commercial and international law developed on the basis of the pragmatic needs of the state. This distinction is mirrored by the relative unity of tenth-century legal texts on matters of private ritual (times and forms of prayer, fasting in Ramadan) compared with wide disagreement on public matters of land tenure, inheritance, business transactions, and the status of slaves. As we see in Abbasa's tombstone and also in the stories of advice given to Umar b. Abd al-Aziz, proto-scholars may have advised both public and private individuals in matters of faith and moral behavior, but they had little to offer in the way of practical advice to a ruler.

While the fundamental presumptions are different, my outline actually agrees with the claims of early Muslim legal historians in several ways. As we saw in Chapter 1, Qadi Iyad b. Musa simply asserted that scholars were to be found among the Prophet's companions, and that the Prophet taught them "according to their capacity for knowledge and familiarity with the meanings of words, the illumination of hearts, and the opening of breasts. They were the most knowledgeable of the Imams without dispute."[63] Iyad contends, however, that this first generation was only interested in the fundamentals of the faith and did not delve deeper into the finer points – after all, they only addressed the life that they knew. Change occurred, however, in the generations addressed in this chapter, those of the "followers" and of the "followers of the followers." According to Iyad,

> Events multiplied and cases came forward; decisions (*fatāwā*) on these [cases] diverged. The community gathered these statements and committed their insights to memory. They studied where they differed and where they agreed, though they were wary of publicizing these matters and of dissent deviating from precision. So they worked to gather the sunna and clarify the foundations. [The experts] were asked, and they answered, and thus the foundations (*qawāʿid*) were laid.[64]

There are many points of interest in this account, but worth noting first is the fact that Iyad writes as if the early community of believers was

[62] Literary sources, of course, mention several such projects, such as the collection of *ḥadīth* by al-Zuhri (Judd, *Religious Scholars and the Umayyads*, 53–59).

[63] ʿIyāḍ, *Tartīb*, 1:61.

[64] Ibid., 1:61–62.

unified. After a "golden age," when the Prophet taught his community directly, Iyad does acknowledge disagreement and dissent, but he imagines a process of "gathering" a unified sunna out of this diversity. Of course, we have no evidence that there was any organized inquiry into scholarly matters, either during the Prophet's lifetime or among the first generations after the Prophet. We also have much evidence of political and social instability, but these play no role in Iyad's reconstruction. Nor does he acknowledge any role for Christian or Jewish scholars; indeed, it seems that non-Muslims hardly existed in Iyad's mind. On the other hand, two aspects of Iyad's account do seem to follow the evidence. First, he does not suppose this scholarship is based on written materials, but only on oral transmission of knowledge, with important judgments "committed to memory." Second, he acknowledges the role of geographic dispersion as a productive factor:

> [As they dispersed to] the various quarters of the earth, the unity (*ijmāʾ*) of the Muslims ran up against the traditions of local fashion. They traded with them and studied their doctines (*madhāhib*) as had no one before, recognizing the superiority of that which came previously, though they surpassed it and added to its knowledge.[65]

Iyad's description of proto-scholars as individual savants spread throughout the world, studying the doctrines of Jews and Christians and expanding on them, fits well with my own understanding. Nor do I think it unlikely that they both continued to recite the Qurʾan and also repeated the stories of the Prophet. I only disagree that these were collected in any sort of systematic or unified fashion.[66] It is evident that in 680 the identity of the early Islamic movement was still quite open, and it could certainly have developed in a variety of ways. At that point it was not at all clear that Arabic should become the common language of the Empire, or that the Empire would survive. Islam itself was still in formation, and its survival was also not certain in the face of much larger numbers of Christians, and of other ancient religious traditions that had a far more systematic theology. In fact, we know that Islam did survive, and it seems that while the state had a role in ensuring that survival,[67]

[65] Ibid., 1:63.

[66] Judd, in contrast, argues that al-Zuhri had a "book of 400 *ḥadīth* reports" (*Religious Scholars and the Umayyads*, 56).

[67] Judd makes this argument most forcefully, but Schacht also claimed that "it was the Umayyads and their governors who were responsible for developing a number of the essential features of Islamic worship and ritual, of which they had found only

a group of recognized teachers also passed on stories of salvation, one of which was that of Muhammad. But if these scholars existed, and their stories were passed on to later generations, then it would seem reasonable that we could reconstruct their teachings. But this, I'm afraid, is possible only to a very limited extent.

BOOK CULTURE AND EARLY WRITING

In contrast with direct evidence for the use of Arabic in currency, bureaucracy, funerary inscriptions, amulets, weights, and Qur'ans, we have no direct evidence for proto-scholars writing anything during this period. In fact, the earliest dated fragments of literary Arabic come a full two centuries after the death of the Prophet. We have undated papyrus scraps from several texts that, Nabia Abbott argued, can be ascribed to the very early Abbasid period,[68] but even assuming that this dating is correct, these were still produced well past the period under consideration here; I will address these texts in Chapter 3. Further, the strongly oral nature of early texts recommends caution when dealing with claims that proto-scholars in the Umayyad period authored books.

Part of the problem has to do with the word *kitāb* in Arabic, which in the modern world usually means "book" but actually has a much broader semantic meaning field. As others have pointed out, the term *kitāb* is ambiguous.[69] In the Qur'an, *kitāb* means "scripture," either the Qur'an specifically (e.g., Q 2:2) or scripture in general (as in the expression *ahl al-kitāb*), while other early sources use the term to mean "document" or "treaty."[70] So when we read in later accounts that such-and-such a proto-scholar wrote a *kitāb*, we should not presume that this means a book in

rudimentary elements" (*Introduction*, 23). Robinson points out that the Zubayrids added to this program, especially regarding the sanctuary in Mecca (*'Abd al-Malik*, 38).

68 Abbott, *Studies*, 1:65 and 1:80 and 2:123.

69 Schacht, *Introduction to Islamic Law*, 42; Raif Georges Khoury, "L'Apport spécialement important de la papyrology dans la transmission et la codification des plus anciennes versions des *Mille et une nuits* et d'autres livres des deux premiers siècles islamiques" in Petra Sijpesteijn and Lennart Sundelin (eds.), *Papyrology and the History of Early Islamic Egypt* (Leiden: E. J. Brill, 2004), 63–95, at 69–70.

70 The covenant between the Meccan emigrants and the Medinans was called a *kitāb*; see Ibn Hishām, *Sīrat sayyidinā Muḥammad Rasūl Allāh*, F. Wüstenfeld (ed.) (Göttingen: Dieterichsche Universitäts-Buchhandlung, 1859), 340; Alfred Guillaume (trans.), *The Life of Muhammad According to Ibn Ishaq* (Karachi: Oxford University Press, 1978), 231. For the Qur'an's use of "*kitāb*" in 24:33, see Brockopp, *Early Mālikī Law: Ibn 'Abd al-Ḥakam and his* Major Compendium of Jurisprudence, Studies in Islamic Law and Society 14 (Leiden: E. J. Brill, 2000), 166–168.

the sense of a literary text produced in a single redactional effort passed on intact to later generations. None of our earliest manuscript witnesses to texts written in the early Abbasid period conform to this meaning of book, and so it is hard to imagine that such books were written in the Umayyad period.[71] I use each of these terms in a technical sense. A manuscript is a primary witness to a text; generally written on papyrus in this period (though parchment, coins, ostraca, and inscriptions are also available), it offers us a snapshot in time, what one person in a particular place happened to write down. A text, in contrast, is a composition by an author; it may be transmitted orally or in written form, and those forms may reflect the original authorial intent or they may stray significantly. A book, however, is a text that is produced in a single redactional effort in such a way that the author controls its production; further, through some means of coercion or institutionalization, subsequent copies reflect the composition of the original author.

To write a book, an author has to have a unified idea, an approach to the material that is carried out from beginning to end. Once this task is accomplished, the author must consider the work complete – it must not be in a continual stage of revision; this is what I mean by a single redactional effort. Finally, the book must be published, which in this period does not mean printing, but rather a method of transmission that maintains the fidelity of the author's original intent. To accomplish this, an institution of learning must be established that is either self-policing or that has some other coercive force attached to it.[72] By saying that there were no books in the first two hundred years of Islamic history, I do not mean that there was no learning, or that there were no experts or fields of knowledge.[73] I am only suggesting that the activities contained within the

[71] Motzki offers a useful summation of the problems of authorship in "The Author and his Work in the Islamic Literature of the First Centuries: The Case of ʿAbd al-Razzāq's *Muṣannaf*," *Jerusalem Studies in Arabic and Islam* 28 (2003), 171–201, at 171–176. As for Gregor Schoeler's extensive work on this issue, I engage it fully in Chapter 3.

[72] As I will discuss in Chapter 3, such an institution certainly existed in Egypt at the beginning of the third/ninth century, and it may have existed elsewhere as well.

[73] In this, I agree with Norman Calder, though I push the dates for written materials, and books, much earlier than he did. Still, Calder's description of the oral aspect of teaching is worth repeating: "It is not necessary to believe that [eighth-century] scholars actually wrote law-books, or even random lists of authority statements. They may, of course, have initiated this task but they are more likely to have been (like Mālik and his immediate predecessors in Madina) human repositories of a juristic tradition, mediators of a law which was, originally, orally passed on and locally relevant. The evidence of the *Mudawwana* suggests that the emergence of written material within this tradition cannot have been much earlier than 200, and that its earliest form was broad collections of

category of learning were different at a time when there were no Arabic books. Again, to say that there were no books is not to say that there was no writing, but when our literary sources refer to the *kitāb* of a proto-scholar, then, we have the following possibilities: (1) this person did not write a book, but did write a text of some sort; (2) this person did not write a text, but did give lectures which were compiled by students; (3) this person did not write a text, and the transmitter of this claim is either mistaken or is referring to a pious forgery. I will address each of these possibilities in turn.

First, it is entirely possible that proto-scholars committed some forms of knowledge to writing. While al-Ghazali suggested that writing Arabic was considered limited to the Qur'an in this early period, the large number of bureaucratic papyri argue otherwise. Further, the increasing use of Arabic on coinage suggests a growing literate public. Just because some of these early writings appear to be pious forgeries (such as the *Risāla* of al-Hasan al-Basri)[74] does not mean that they all are. And careful analysis of early *ḥadīth* collections has produced some evidence of both oral and written transmission. Still, in these cases it is not clear that a proto-scholar wrote out a text, since it may be his students who took notes at a lecture. For example, Ibn Habib tells us that Ibn Abbas was called "sea of knowledge (*baḥru l-ʿilm)*" and had a *majlis* where the "people of *fiqh*" would come to ask him questions.[75] There is no mention of writing here, only an oral method of knowledge transmission very close to rabbinical examples.

Second, it is possible that proto-scholars did not commit knowledge to writing or even that they were opposed to writing down of knowledge because of a distrust of the written word and a greater faith in the master-student relationship. In other words, perhaps we have no texts from this period because there was no need for texts: personal experience with a master was far more authoritative. If this is true, then on the one hand students from far away may have been motivated to write down the teachings of a master not so much as a mnemonic device but as a trophy, a sign that they were, in fact, in the presence of this master. On the other

authority statements" (*Studies in Early Muslim Jurisprudence* [Oxford: Clarendon, 1993], 16–17). Christopher Melchert follows Calder's reconstruction in "The Early History of Islamic Law," in Herbert Berg (ed.), *Method and Theory in the Study of Islamic Origins* (Leiden: E. J. Brill, 2003), 293–324, at 307.

[74] Mourad, *Early Islam.*

[75] Ibn Ḥabīb, *Kitāb al-Ta'rīj*,159. Curiously, Ibn Habib's wording seems to suggest the existence of "people of *fiqh*" who were not themselves companions.

hand, later generations, quite used to the notion that scholars wrote books, would have had difficulty imagining these early authorities having left no written account of their thoughts and insights. Therefore, they in a sense wrote books for them, based perhaps on a general notion of the proto-scholars' ideas and predilections. This, then, is the third possibility, that of pious forgeries, a term that I prefer to pseudepigrapha. The point of such a text was not to pass off one's work as that of someone else, but rather to honor the esteemed scholar of the past. The end result, however, is the same. Even though the lack of surviving manuscripts from the Umayyad period is not evidence that scholarship did not exist, it does put the nature of that scholarship into serious question, and it vastly multiplies the difficulties for the researcher.

With these three possibilities in mind, we are now able to address the claim, made by numerous researchers, to be able to reconstruct books supposedly written by Muslim scholars during the Umayyad period. Again, as mentioned above, Fred Donner offers a list of dozens of "books" supposedly written by Muslim historians before the year 800, based on lists found in literary accounts.[76] The first works on his list are attributed to Abdallah b. Abbas (d. 68/686–688) whom Ibn Habib also represented as one of the premier scholars from the generation after Muhammad's closest companions. Ibn Abbas is often cited by later scholars, both in chains of transmission for *ḥadīth* going back to the Prophet Muhammad and also as a legal authority in his own right. Other Umayyad scholars, whose "books" have been reconstructed include Urwah b. al-Zubayr (d. 93-4/711–713), Wahb b. Munabbih, and Ibn Ishaq. In undertaking these reconstructions, researchers have followed two distinct methodologies: (1) building a lost text on the basis of quotations found in later literary sources and (2) combining manuscript evidence with literary sources. I will address the second of these here because it appears to be the more promising.

Wahb b. Munabbih's *History of [King] David* (Figure 2.5) is the earliest literary manuscript with a secure dating, having been written down some time before *dhū l-qaʿda* 229 (July of 844).[77] That date is well beyond the period addressed in this chapter, but of all the Arabic manuscripts securely dated to the third/ninth century, this is the only one that

[76] Donner, *Narratives*, 297–306.

[77] Raif Georges Khoury, *Wahb b. Munabbih*, 2 vols. (Wiesbaden: Harrassowitz, 1972), 1:16. As Khoury notes, the date is written by a second hand, not the original scribe, a fact that Khoury is unable to explain. It does not lend confidence to the dating claim, but this point is not relevant to my discussion here.

Figure 2.5: *History of [King] David* (P. Heid. Inv. Arab. 23, fol. 1r),

purports to be a book deriving from a figure who flourished in the Umayyad period;[78] therefore it would seem to have the best claim to

[78] We also have early collections of *ḥadīth*, with chains of transmission that go back to seventh-century figures, but modern scholars generally understand these to be based on oral, not written, transmission.

authenticity. Wahb b. Munabbih was a proto-scholar who looms large in the literary memory of Islam;[79] a Yemenite of Persian heritage,[80] he is said to have died between 725 and 737. Born at the end of Uthman's reign, he was, according to Raif Georges Khoury, "the very model of an exemplary scholar of his time."[81] As the supposed author of dozens of "books" it hardly seems surprising that one of his texts survived. As it turns out, however, the manuscript of Wahb b. Munabbih's *History* is an object lesson in the dangers of attempting to reconstruct ancient texts, especially on the basis of single manuscripts. For example, consider the context of these papyrus fragments: the *History* is one of only six manuscripts in Arabic with a proven date before the year 250/864, joining three Qur'an fragments, one fragment of the Gospel of John in Arabic, and a fragment of the *Mudawwana* by Sahnun (d. 240/854).[82] The fact that these particular manuscripts have survived the past 1,150 years is, of course, complete coincidence, and from them we can draw no conclusions about the relative importance of any field of study in the third/ninth century. Still, it is worth reflecting on a few interesting characteristics of this group.

First, five of the six manuscripts purport to preserve texts written many decades before the composition date of the manuscript, and this presents particular problems of authenticity.[83] With the Qur'ans, I argued above that the fact that such a large proportion of our earliest dated Arabic manuscripts consists of Qur'ans, along with the significant number of ancient undated fragments, helps instill confidence about the authenticity of this text. Likewise, while we cannot know if the Gospel of John was translated earlier than 245/860 into Arabic, we can compare this translation with older versions in Greek. The composition date of Wahb's *History of King David*, however, is much harder to discern, since there is no corroborating evidence, either in Arabic or in other languages, that

[79] Khoury, *Wahb b. Munabbih*, 1:1.

[80] Khoury notes that the question of Wahb being Jewish is a more recent one, Raif Georges Khoury, "Wahb b. Munabbih" in *Encyclopaedia of Islam*, 2nd ed. Alfred-Louis de Prémare speculates that he could be of Jacobite Christian heritage, "Wahb b. Munabbih, une figure singulière du premier islam," *Annales: histoire, sciences sociales* 60 (2005), 531–548, at 541. My thanks to anonymous Reader B for this reference.

[81] "das Urbild des vortrefflichen Gelehrten seiner Zeit," Khoury, *Wahb b. Munabbih*, 1:194.

[82] Déroche, "Les manuscrits arabes," 345–346.

[83] The exception is Sahnun's text, which I will discuss in Chapter 3. I have been able to personally assess two of these manuscripts, the Heidelberg papyrus of Wahb's text and the Kairouan fragment of Sahnun's *Mudawwana*.

precedes the date of the manuscript.[84] It is possible that the text was in fact composed before AH 110 (the date of Wahb's death) or it could have been a pious forgery, written as late as AH 229. Second, Wahb's *History* also has no corroborating evidence *after* the date of the manuscript; in the case of the other five manuscripts, they are all simply the oldest dated copy of a text that has many other, later witnesses, allowing us to engage in comparative analysis and note whether stylistic or substantive changes are made to the text over time. The papyrus fragments of Wahb's *History*, however, form the unique witness to this text. It is true that Khoury uses quotations attributed to Wahb b. Munabbih found in later texts to complete the heavily damaged papyri, but these are not themselves witnesses to an authored composition, since they could easily derive from oral transmission, or from another source altogether. To be clear, Khoury bases his use of the quotations to reconstruct the text on the presumption that both quotations and papyrus share a common antecedent. This is one of the first two possibilities mentioned above – notes from Wahb's lectures were collected (either by Wahb or by his students) and these found their way into both this papyrus fragment and also the quotations in later literary sources. But no evidence excludes the third possibility: that the text was composed not in the early eighth century but in the early ninth, and only attributed to Wahb as a sign of pious respect. The difference of one century is small but important for our goal of dating the rise of scholarly communities.

A third characteristic of this group of early Arabic manuscripts is worth noting, and that is the appearance of the Gospel of John among them. This fact is a good reminder both that Arabic was as much a Christian as a Muslim language in the early ninth century and also that works are being translated into Arabic from surrounding cultures.[85] Again, historical texts tell us of dozens of books in philosophy, geography, and other areas that were translated into Arabic, beginning already in the eighth century, though we have no direct manuscript evidence of this activity.[86] With these observations in mind, it is interesting to note how little of the

[84] A possible exception to this claim is the material shared with *Midrash Shmuel* as I discuss below.

[85] Abbott (*Studies*, 1:48) dates the writing of Christian texts in Arabic "to about A.D. 700 at the latest."

[86] Déroche discounts the claims of early manuscripts on medicine and philosophy ("Les manuscrits arabes," 350). For an overview of the translation movement see Dimitri Gutas, *Greek Thought, Arabic Culture: The Graeco-Arabic Translation Movement in Baghdad and Early 'Abbasad Society (2nd–4th/8th–10th c.)* (New York: Routledge, 1998).

contents of Wahb's *History* mark it as a particularly Muslim text. Other than a handful of Qur'an citations and a few references to individual Muslim authorities (such as Ibn Abbas and Qatada) the *History of King David* could easily be a translation of a Christian, or Jewish, text. In both subject matter and order of presentation, it reads like a paraphrase of 2 Samuel in Arabic, with the addition of a few fabulous stories, such as that of the three slingshot stones that speak to David on his way to face Goliath.[87] In other words, even if this text were a book written by Wahb b. Munabbih, it does little to prove that Wahb was a Muslim scholar.[88]

Finally, despite the enormous work went into the conservation and reconstruction of this important papyrus fragment, I cannot agree with Khoury that these papyrus leaves are the "only remaining fragments from all the *books* of Wahb or his nephew."[89] I say this despite the fact that this text has some of the characteristics of a book, according to my definition. For example, internal evidence reveals an organized composition with a single style of writing from beginning to end. However, we cannot know that this presents the text's original form, putatively from before AH 110 or its final form when this manuscript was written. It is possible, for example, that Wahb or some other scholar simply added Qur'an references, or the wonder tales, to an already existing narrative frame. Further, the lack of later manuscripts suggests that this text was not widely circulated, nor do we have any evidence that the requisite institutions to ensure faithful reproduction of a text existed in Wahb's lifetime. All we can say with certainty is that this text was written down and circulated in the first part of the third/ninth century. Composition by Wahb b. Munabbih is possible, though there is much evidence against it.[90]

87 Khoury, *Wahb b. Munabbih*, 52. Note specific references cited by Nabia Abbott in her review, in *Journal of Near Eastern Studies* 36, no. 2 (Apr. 1977), 103–112, at 105.

88 Appended to this papyrus is a second fragment, physically similar to the first, that contains episodes from the Prophet Muhammad's life, but Khoury is cautious about the dating of this fragment (Khoury, *Wahb b. Munabbih*, 1:16–17). My examination in June 2015, suggests that the two texts were definitely composed at the same time; see discussion in Chapter 4.

89 "Auf jeden Fall scheinen diese Papyrusblätter, vielleicht schon zu jener Zeit, die einzig vorhandenen vom ganzen Buche Wahbs oder seines Neffen gewesen zu sein." Ibid., 1:17 (emphasis added). Elsewhere, even stronger, Khoury writes: "There can no longer be any doubt about the books attributed to the author. Their contents were transmitted orally, taught or set down in writing, partly at least in his own lifetime, and later by particular members of his family" (Khoury, "Wahb b. Munabbih").

90 As Khoury himself admits on pp. 185–188. Michael Pregill is even more skeptical of any authorship by Wahb. See his "Isrāʾīliyāt, Myth, and Pseudepigraphy: Wahb. B. Munabbih and the Early Islamic Versions of the Fall of Adam and Eve," *Jerusalem*

If it is so difficult to reconstruct one of Wahb's "books," *even from the most ancient dated literary manuscript*, we should be much less confident about reconstructing texts attributed to other scholars from the late Umayyad period based on late manuscripts or supposed quotations scattered through later literary texts. Yet scholars continue to engage in the attempt, led, in my view, by an overly sanguine view of the rapidity with which Muslim scholarly communities came into being. Ibn Abbas, for example, is said to have written a *Tafsīr* of the Qur'an that Fuat Sezgin suggests could be reconstructed by taking putative citations of Ibn Abbas from later exegetical literature, such as the commentary by Abu Jarir al-Tabari (d. 310/923).[91] The voluminous works of al-Tabari have already been mined for the reconstruction of the *Kitāb al-Mubtada'* (Book of Beginnings) by Ibn Ishaq,[92] and Gregor Schoeler has followed a similar methodology in reconstructing the accounts of Urwah b. al-Zubayr.[93] These are painstaking scholarly projects that include some brilliant insights into the nature of early Muslim society. But the continual discussion of "books" and the focus on individual "authors" gives us a false impression of scholarship during this period.

By imposing their own sense of order and boundaries (manufacturing a narrative arc; deciding where one text begins and another ends), modern scholars may be creating a false perception of what these proto-scholars

Studies in Arabic and Islam 34 (2008), 215–284, at 238–240. My thanks to anonymous reviewer B for this reference.

[91] Sezgin, *Geschichte*, I:27, does allow an oral aspect to the transmission: "Es muß noch geklärt werden, welche der Qur'ānkommentare, die seine Schüler von ihm überliefern, von ihm selbst geschrieben und welche nach seinen Vorlesungen von seinen Schülern schriftlich fixiert werden." See, however, Andrew Rippin, "*Tafsīr Ibn 'Abbās* and Criteria for Dating Early *tafsīr* Texts" *Jerusalem Studies in Arabic and Islam* 18 (1994), 38–83. Recently, Herbert Berg performed a monumental analysis of hundreds of citations of Ibn Abbas in al-Tabari's work in an attempt to determine whether or not these citations could reasonably be said to reflect Ibn Abbas's work. Looking solely at the style of exegesis, not at the content of the individual reports, Berg concludes that the notion of reconstructing lost works in this way is fatally flawed (*Development of Exegesis*, 228). While Berg's methodology is also flawed, his attempt is a valiant and instructive effort. See my review in *Islamic Law and Society* 12 (2005), 419–422.

[92] Gordon Newby, *The Making of the Last Prophet. A Reconstruction of the Earliest Biography of Muhammad* (Columbia: University of South Carolina Press, 1989).

[93] Schoeler, however, looks at individual *ḥadīths*, assessing the subtle shifts of content visible in various early transmissions. Gregor Schoeler, "Foundations for a New Biography of Muḥammad: The Production and Evaluation of the Corpus of Traditions from 'Urwah b. al-Zubayr," in Berg (ed.), *Method and Theory*, 21–28. See also Gregor Schoeler, *Charakter und Authentie der muslimischen Überlieferung über das Leben Mohammeds* (Berlin: de Gruyter, 1996).

actually achieved. For example, in Gordon Newby's reconstruction of Ibn Ishaq's *Book of Beginnings*, he includes a chapter on King David, which begins with the words "Wahb b. Munabbih said."[94] In fact, much of the material here is also found in the *History of King David*, attributed to Wahb, including the story of the three speaking stones.[95] Should we conclude that this material is correctly attributed to Ibn Ishaq as part of his book? Or are they more correctly attributable to Wahb as part of his book? To complicate matters further, Newby points out that this tale (where three stones speak to David and declare themselves to be the stones of Abraham, Isaac, and Jacob; they promise to kill Goliath) is also found in *Midrash Shmuel*, a Jewish commentary on Samuel.[96] One possibility of course is that Wahb translated *Midrash Shmuel* into Arabic and that Ibn Ishaq incorporated excerpts of Wahb's translation into his text. But then who shall we say is the author, especially given the fact that tales like these probably had a long oral tradition before being written down? A more reasonable possibility in my view is that these are texts with both oral and written components passed down during the eighth century in a world where the boundaries of authorship – and of religious communities – were porous. When incorporated into al-Tabari's monumental works, these texts, and the names of their supposed authors, lend a sense of age and authority to al-Tabari's compilation. But taking quotations out of this context and reformatting them in a manner that accords with modern sensibilities of single-authored books gives us a misleading picture of early eighth-century scholarship.

Gordon Newby's study emphasizes the pious boundaries of religious communities that, I believe, formed an important characteristic of Umayyad proto-scholars. In Newby's words,

> the biographies of Muhammad and his prophetic predecessors were a result of a hagiographic and hermeneutic process in Islam that continued the living traditions of Midrashic and Haggadic studies found in the Jewish communities encountered by Muslim scholars. The stories, anecdotes, tales, and legends in the *Sirah* are the crystallized remains of an intellectual process among early Muslim scholars who

[94] Newby, *Making*, 157. Wahb is often cited in this book. Interestingly, Ibn Ḥabīb's *Taʾrīkh* includes some of the same stories as found in Newby's reconstructed text, but attributes them to Ibn Abbas.

[95] Ibid., 158.

[96] Ibid. The date of *Midrash Shmuel* is disputed, but it is thought to have been composed about this same time.

were continuing the traditions of their Jewish counterparts. When early Muslims incorporated salient aspects of the Jewish and Christian methods of treating holy persons and texts, the details, the anecdotes, and the themes naturally followed.[97]

There is good evidence to believe that Newby is right to argue for a shared intellectual project, though I would interpret the evidence slightly differently. Ibn Ishaq's *Kitāb al-Mubtada'* was thought to have been composed as a preface to his *Sīra* (biography of Muhammad) which has come down to us in an excerpted form from the Egyptian scholar Ibn Hisham (d. 219/834). Similarly, the papyrus fragments of Wahb b. Munabbih's *History of King David* were discovered with an undated *Life of Muhammad*, and Ibn Habib's *Ta'rīkh* contains short biographies of pre-Islamic prophets, followed by a biography of Muhammad and continuing with biographies of the *'ulamā'*. Newby suggests that "in the generation after Ibn Ishaq the use of extra-Islamic sources fell into disrepute."[98] It seems plausible to me, however, that in the seventh century (and perhaps continuing on in smaller circles as late as the ninth century), Muhammad's life was only comprehensible to these early Muslims within the context of the lives of earlier prophets, and that these collectors of stories were very much the face of Islam during this early period. With time, figures like Ibn Abbas and Wahb b. Munabbih were discounted by later scholars as interested in *Isrā'īlīyāt*, a passing scholarly fad; stories of King David and Moses receded and stories of Muhammad increased in number and significance. Ibn Ishaq's *Kitāb al-Mubtada'* is forgotten and only his life of Muhammad is remembered. A gradual increase in Muhammad's centrality over time also helps to explain the fact that ninth-century legal scholars seemed as interested in the words and deeds of Muhammad's companions as they were in the *sunna* of God's last prophet.

CONCLUSIONS

The historical period under consideration here, 680–750, was one of great diversity: multiple stories about self-identity, some of which continued into the next period and some of which died away. Our survey of the physical evidence demonstrates the following (1) Arabic had undergone a significant period of development, from a rudimentary script that served more as a mnemonic device to a full-fledged writing style with

[97] Ibid., ix.
[98] Ibid., 4.

several variations. (2) Arabic was only one of several languages in use during this period, with significant remains in Greek, Coptic, Syriac, and Pahlavi. (3) In only one area did Arabic have exclusive presence: the writing of Qurʾans. In all other areas (diplomacy, taxation, numismatics), Arabic gradually took over from other preexisting traditions. (4) Major works in these other languages continued to be produced during this period, perhaps even the Talmuds. (5) These other works employed scholars, whether priests or rabbis, who underwent a specific program of training to be able to compose these works. (6) The sophisticated correspondence of the early chancery, and the painstaking production of Qurʾans, required experts of a sort as well, but they are distinguished from the true scholars of the Christian and Jewish traditions by methods of training and the utilitarian focus of their work.

While it may be that God considered Islam to be complete before Muhammad's death in 632, the meaning of that Qurʾanic statement changed dramatically over the next century as the realities of new leaders and the religious and social ocean of the Near East nearly drowned this new religion. But this is not a new story. Unity in the face of diversity is always a struggle, from the diverse audiences mentioned in the Qurʾan (Muslims, "believers," Christians, Jews, polytheists, "hypocrites," and believers only in fate [*dahr*]) to the diversity of the Umayyad period to that after 750. Any narrative (pre-modern or modern) that presents a unified notion of "Islam" with clear boundaries, and a singular perception of history must therefore be considered an artificial construction. This is especially the case when one considers that the categories of Muslim, Jew, Christian, Arab, or Persian are themselves diffuse, subject to change over time. That said, such constructions are informative, since even they tell us a great deal about their audiences; further, they must often deal with certain events and facts that are true but inconvenient to their narratives.

As I have pointed out in this chapter, our physical evidence for this period, rich as it is, tells us almost nothing directly about the proto-scholars. Indirectly, we can see their influence through analysis of Abbasa's tombstone, Qurʾan manuscripts, and theological statements minted on coins, but the attempt to reconstruct written texts from this period is, I believe, fatally flawed. Nonetheless, while we cannot know the thoughts of individual proto-scholars, we can make reasonable speculations about the general outlines of their activity. In terms of theology, it is reasonable to date the first great disputes to this period: whether human beings have a role in determining the moral value of their acts, whether people are bound to obey rulers that God puts in their place, whether heaven and hell are eternal. In terms of legal development, both the categories and the content of law appear to be established at this time as well, long before the debates on the theory, or the systematic incorporation of the Qur'an into a notion of Islamic law. And as for the Qur'an, interpretation appears to be tied up with historical concerns, as people seek to tie verses of the Qur'an together with events in the Prophet's life, and with grammatical issues as the use of Arabic spreads.

History, of course, was important to all these disciplines, and here the evidence of early manuscript fragments forms an important corrective to any characterization of these fields of theology, law, or hermeneutics as uniquely Islamic. While we cannot know precisely who circulated stories of King David's exploits, for example, it is evident that these tales were part of an interconnected oral environment in which material of value was shared among Jew, Christian, and Muslim alike. We should not, therefore, draw boundaries between Muslim and Christian theological speculation, or Muslim and Jewish legal thinking, which may not have existed in this period. As I will discuss in Chapter 3, it is only in the subsequent period that questions are raised about how the Qur'an and the Prophet's example are relevant to law and theology. In fact, our earliest written texts demonstrate both an interest in incorporating these "Islamic" sources into an already-existing body of law and also some serious confusion as to how these sources are to be squared with what these earliest experts already know to be true. Disagreements on these matters would eventually result in the establishment of several valid schools of law and theology, as well as others considered heretical by some.

3

Rise of the Muslim Scholar, 750–820

The first seventy years of the Abbasid period reveal clear evidence of scholarly activity: five undated papyrus fragments that probably derive from the late eighth century, others that likely date from the early ninth century, and many manuscripts from the late ninth and tenth centuries that preserve texts initially composed before 820. In contrast with the reconstruction of putative early eighth-century texts discussed in Chapter 2, the process of reconstructing texts during this period can be based on a much more rigorous methodology. Nonetheless, most texts from the early Abbasid period were still fluid, with generations of students adding and modifying material that was initially put together by an earlier scholar; therefore, most of these must be classified as texts or writings, not books. This fluidity of boundaries between oral and written texts, between one text and another, and between authors[1] is indicative of the fact that there is no specific moment when scholarly communities burst onto the scene. The rise of Muslim scholars to positions of importance, and their increasing sense of themselves as a class, is a process stretched out over centuries. What we can discern in the period covered in this chapter are the beginnings of a clearer organization and a new culture surrounding the study and transmission of texts.

[1] Just as I argue here for a restriction of the word "book", so also Motzki has questioned whether we should properly speak of authors in this period (Motzki, "The Author and His Work"). Ultimately, however, he rejects alternatives, such as "editor," "compiler," etc. as unsatisfactory, as do I.

Also new is the fact that we can observe these scholarly processes directly through examination of the material evidence. Interestingly, the texts produced by scholars in the early Abbasid period are both highly sophisticated and also original in form and content, not directly dependent on the advanced literary cultures of surrounding civilizations. This is in contrast with the seventh century, when the Prophet's own Companions were said to study Jewish texts, and papyrus evidence, including evidence of bilingual scribes, described a multilingual, multi-religious world. Even in the Umayyad period, there is still some evidence of dependence on Jewish and Christian scholarly texts. In the Abbasid period, however, those direct influences wane, even though indirect dependence remains.

As we have seen previously, material evidence alone can lead us astray; if we pay attention only to dated Arabic manuscripts, we would see a gradual emergence of Arabic literary activity beginning in the early ninth century, not the late eighth century as I suggest here. No literary manuscripts can be securely dated previous to 229/824; thereafter, progress is slow: only six fragments are known to have been written previous to 250/864, and one of these is a Gospel of John (three are Qur'ans). As I will discuss in Chapters 4 and 5, the one hundred years after 250/864 see a great flourishing of manuscript witnesses, though the lion's share comes from Egypt and North Africa. Again, if we were dependent on material evidence alone, we might reasonably conclude that North Africa was the heart of early Islamic scholarly activity. But such a conclusion is untenable. First, many of the texts preserved in these earliest manuscripts are already quite sophisticated, with an impressive organizational structure and complex reasoning; second, all our *literary* sources point to Syria, Iraq, and Khurasan as important sites of scholarly activity, and many later manuscripts purport to preserve texts from authors writing there in the ninth and even eighth century. Physical evidence is also misleading in that it does not support a significant role for the practices of the chancery; therefore, it may over-emphasize the independence of scholarly activity from state power and authority. Finally, as detailed in the Appendix, the earliest dated manuscripts that have survived cover a limited range of scholarly subjects.

One solution is to contextualize material evidence with literary sources, but how one goes about that task is debatable. On one side, Fuat Sezgin simply accepts the accounts of Muslim historians and reckons their descriptions of literary production as factual. On the other side, Norman Calder treats the biographical literature as imagined reconstructions, rejects the claims of early scholarly writings, and redates those putative texts to later periods.[2] This debate replicates the broader gulf between the descriptive approach and the skeptical view that I described in the Introduction. The majority of scholars today reject Calder's radical redating of early legal literature without fully acknowledging the force of his arguments. For example, Ahmed El Shamsy recognizes the biographical dictionaries as performative texts that express "cultural memory,"[3] yet he continues to mine these texts for factual information. Likewise, Gregor Schoeler uses sophisticated reasoning and a broad reading of the literary sources to back his reconstruction of early scholar development.[4] I argue here that we can set this whole discussion on a far firmer foundation. The Kairouan cache of manuscripts not only provides a remarkably thorough picture of Muslim scholarly texts from the Hijaz, Egypt, and North Africa, it also gives us direct information on the literary centers of Cordoba, Syria, and Iraq and points farther east, evidence that a nascent scholarly tradition active in the late eighth century is making use of texts as enhancements in a highly oral environment.

There is more. Manuscript evidence survives to allow the reconstruction of two early texts, the *Muwaṭṭa*ʾ of Malik b. Anas (d. 179/795) and much of *al-Mukhtaṣar al-kabīr* by Ibn Abd al-Hakam (d. 214/829). The first of these survives in several recensions, demonstrating a certain unified mode of construction, but without the necessary social structures (or perhaps the personal will) to control the process of transmission. The *Mukhtaṣar*, on the other hand, is a kind of missing link. Due to a unique collection of surviving manuscripts, it is the first text that we can prove was written in a single redactionary effort, probably before 200/815, and then subjected to a controlled transmission. In other words, Ibn Abd

[2] Calder, *Studies in Early Muslim Jurisprudence*. See the important review article by Miklos Muranyi, "Die frühe Rechstslitertur zwischen Quellenanalyse und Fiktion," *Islamic Law and Society* 4 (1997), 224–241.

[3] El Shamsy, *Canonization*, 9 (discussion of cultural memory [with a nod toward Jan Assmann]) and 12 (El Shamsy's own methodology). To my knowledge, all historians of Muslim scholarly communities (Hallaq, Melchert, Motzki, etc.) base their analyses almost entirely on a critical reading of the literary sources. Schacht, in contrast, undertook ground-breaking research in manuscript libraries (in, for example, his article "On Some Manuscripts in the Libraries of Kairouan and Tunis," *Arabica* 14 (1967), 225–258), but his work is now outdated.

[4] I discuss Schoeler's ideas below. My own inclinations follow the methods of Michael Cooperson, who is more interested in the motivations of those who preserved specific tales about, for example, Ibn Hanbal, than he is in what actually may have occurred in history (Cooperson, *Classical Arabic Biography*, esp. 129–153).

al-Hakam's *Mukhtaṣar* is our first book, clear evidence of a scholarly community that had developed the tools and self-awareness to perpetuate itself through the propagation of fixed texts that accurately represented the thought of specific scholars. While this finding seems to vindicate Schoeler's claim that "actual books" (*syngrammata* as he calls them) were produced in the late eighth century,[5] it also highlights the significant limitations of that claim, based as it is on literary sources.

In contrast, my argument that Ibn Abd al-Hakam's *Mukhtaṣar* is a book arises from the congruity of literary accounts with a broad collection of ancient manuscripts. That manuscript record, in turn, provides us with a foundation for analysis and critique of other manuscripts that claim to preserve texts from this period, allowing us to reconstruct the rise of scholarly communities, especially in Egypt and the Hijaz, in the late second/eighth century. While I believe it is useful and important to trace out the precise emergence of book culture in Islamic history, it is the transition from individual scholars to scholarly communities that is the more significant cultural development. As I will discuss below, books are both cause and effect of these communities. On the one hand, without scholarly communities, there could be no books as I have narrowly defined them, because verbatim transmission (what Schoeler calls publication)[6] requires a disciplined collective with a shared purpose. On the other hand, books allow for the establishment of new scholarly commentaries and the linking of distant communities with one another. We have some sense of this development in the literary sources, but the Kairouan manuscripts allow for an unparalleled reconstruction of some early communities on the basis of actual artifacts from the period.

Again, however, the material evidence taken alone can be misleading. As impressive as they are, the Kairouan manuscripts bear witness only to a small slice of scholarly activity in the early Abbasid period. Literary sources suggest that we have here only the fruits of a few of the era's great minds, further limited by what later generations of students saw fit to preserve. Here, therefore, I focus less on the content of these texts than on the techniques of textual transmission as witnessed by the manuscripts. I suggest that just as we can see these techniques clearly spread from

[5] Schoeler, *Genesis*, 63 defines a *syngramma* as "an actual book, composed and redacted according to the canon of stylistic rules, and intended for literary publication."

[6] I find Schoeler's definition of publication (he calls it *ekdosis*) to be inadequate, since it includes transmission of a text to a single individual (*Genesis*, 87–89) as well as "oral publication" (ibid., 69).

Egypt to North Africa, so also it is safe to speculate that similar communities of scholars existed in the eastern half of the Islamic world and that secretarial practices in the chancery may have been a source for some of these techniques. While it is right to be skeptical of literary descriptions from later generations, the riches of this one provincial library lend credence to accounts that regard the early Abbasid period as a transition from an oral to a literate scholarly culture.

This transition is of key importance in the history of all areas of Muslim scholarship: law, theology, history, exegesis, etc. First, a formal community gives a clear direction and purpose to scholarly thought by building consensus and establishing the inertia of precedent. Whereas Umayyad proto-scholars looked to Jewish, Christian, and Arabian examples to give their opinions weight, Abbasid scholars could begin to draw on a history of Muslim precedent.[7] Second, Arabic itself was gaining in prestige; not only did caliphs support the translating of Greek and Persian texts into Arabic, Christians themselves began to use Arabic as a scholarly language. The scholarly public became a reading public. Finally, formal scholarly communities are the essential prerequisite for the "schools" of law and theology that would dominate the scholarly landscape in the ninth century and beyond.[8] The discipline of verbatim written transmission would be a useful tool for students who sought to determine clear lines between Muʿtazili and Ashʿari, or between Hanafi and Shafiʿi. In the mid-eighth century, however, these lines still did not exist, and it is well known that both al-Shafiʿi (d. 204/820) and al-Shaybani (d. 189/805) studied with Malik b. Anas.[9]

The tales that historians record from this era imagine a scholarly world quite different from the one ascribed to the earlier periods discussed in Chapters 1 and 2. As we have seen, Umar b. al-Khattab was thought to have consulted certain knowledgeable individuals (and then ignored their advice), and Umar b. Abd al-Aziz was portrayed as having exchanged edifying letters with famous savants. In these cases, proto-scholars appear

[7] Behnam Sadeghi, *The Logic of Lawmaking*, 26

[8] Christopher Melchert, *The Formation of the Sunni Schools of Law, 9th–10th Centuries. CE*, Studies in Islamic Law and Society (Leiden: E. J. Brill, 1997), 32–47.

[9] According to most historians, the eighth century is the time when regional schools transformed into personal schools, reflecting conventions in the literary sources. I suggest, however, that these conventions are misleading insofar as they overplay the development and societal impact of Islamic law and theology in the eighth century, while also implying that the lines between Muslim, Jewish, and Christian communities were clearer than was apparently the case.

as isolated individuals who have attained knowledge through personal experience. In contrast, the early Abbasid period sees an increasing number of tales describing scholars and their students in communities devoted to the pursuit of knowledge, apart from any political interests. Of course, these tales are recorded centuries later and are often highly artificial in construction, but it is worth noting that it is the literary sources themselves that suggest the early Abbasid period as the first time when scholarly communities seem to have formed. For example, Qadi Iyad b. Musa (d. 544/1149) collected immense detail on the activities of Malik b. Anas, including this excerpt from a chapter on Malik's character:

> Abdallah b. Abd al-Hakam [d. 214/829] said: Malik invited [his] students [to dinner] while I was among them, so we went with him to his dwelling (*dārihi*). When we had entered the courtyard (*dār*), he said: this is the restroom (*al-mustarāḥ*) and here is water. Then we entered the sitting room (*al-bayt*), though he did not enter with us but afterwards. Then he brought us something to eat, though he did not bring water beforehand for the washing of our hands but afterwards.
>
> So when the people had left, I asked him about what I had seen. He said: As for my showing you the restroom and water, I mentioned [it to] you to be of benefit to you; perhaps one of you needed to urinate or something and would not know where to go to relieve himself. As for my leaving you to enter the sitting room yourselves, perhaps if I had said: "Over here Abu So-and-So: sit down, and over here Abu So-and-So: sit down" I might have forgotten one of you, and he would take this as a slight. So I left you to take your own places and entered afterwards. And as for my omitting to bring water before the meal, ablutions before [a meal] is a foreign custom (*sunnat al-aʿājim*), while there is a *ḥadīth* about [bringing it] afterwards.[10]

Malik, as mentioned above, was the teacher of many famous scholars and is the author of the *Muwaṭṭaʾ*, one of the earliest texts in the Islamic legal tradition. This story is one of many in Iyad's collection that records the intimate relationships between Malik and his students. Malik's paternal concern for his students – from their bodily needs to their sensitivities regarding issues of status – suggests a sense of community that reached beyond the mere transmission of knowledge. Further, the content of that "knowledge" is apparently not limited to matters of law or theology but also extends to questions of etiquette. Perhaps already for his students,

[10] ʿIyāḍ, *Tartīb*, 1:129. For more entertaining tales of Malik's teaching, see El Shamsy, *Canonization*, 18–20. Unlike El Shamsy, though, I see no reason to regard these tales as representing "al-Shāfiʿī's own account of his study with Mālik" (p. 12). I do, however, regard these stories as generally indicative of a change from individual savants to scholarly communities.

and certainly by the time of Iyad, Malik had become the paragon of what it meant to be a scholar, and so every detail of his daily life was worth recording and imitating.

To be sure, certain individuals earlier in Islamic history are also said to have had students – Ibn Abbas and A'isha, for examples, are remembered as having been pressed for their memories of the Prophet, reflected in the many *ḥadīth* that include them in the chains of transmission. But the tales related about scholars from the early Abbasid period are different, since these later stories are focused on the social activities of teaching, not merely on the transmission of wisdom from the Prophet. Other stories from a little later in the Abbasid period concern themselves with the shift from oral knowledge to written materials. The following tale of scholarly rivalry captures the interplay of oral and written authority; it was so popular that it appeared in one collection after another over the centuries, here in the famous *Muqaddima* of Ibn Khaldun (d. 1406):

> Asad b. al-Furat [d. 213/828] traveled from Ifriqiya (to the East) and studied first with the followers of Abu Hanifa, but then changed over to the school of Malik. He studied with Ibn al-Qasim all the chapters of jurisprudence and wrote down what he learned. He brought his book back to Kairouan. It was called *al-Asadiya*, after Asad b. al-Furat. Sahnun studied it with Asad (himself). He, then, traveled to the East and met Ibn al-Qasim. He studied with him and confronted him with the problems of the *Asadiya*. [Ibn al-Qasim] reconsidered many of them, and Sahnun wrote down his own problems in a systematic work, and stated which of the problems of the *Asadiya* he had reconsidered. Ibn al-Qasim and he together wrote to Asad and asked him to delete from the *Asadiya* the problems that had been reconsidered (by Ibn al-Qasim and Sahnun) and to accept the book of Sahnun. Asad, however, refused to do that. As a result, people disregarded Asad's book and followed the *Mudawwana* of Sahnun, despite the fact that (in the *Mudawwana)* different problems were (confusingly) lumped together in the various chapters. Therefore, the *Mudawwana* was called *Mudawwana-and-Mukhtalita* (the "mixed up, confused one"). The inhabitants of Kairouan concentrated upon the *Mudawwana*, whereas the Andalusis focused on the *Wadiha* and the *Utbiya*.[11]

As Miklos Muranyi has pointed out, this story does not match our manuscript evidence and must be rejected as apocryphal.[12] However,

[11] Ibn Khaldūn, *The Muqaddimah: An Introduction to History*, trans. Franz Rosenthal, 3 vols. (Princeton: Princeton University Press, 1958), 1:14–15; slightly modified. I discuss a different version of this tale, its history and meaning in "Contradictory Evidence and the Exemplary Scholar: The Lives of Sahnun b. Sa'id (d. 854)," *International Journal of Middle East Studies* 43, no. 1 (2011), 115–132, at 121–122.

[12] Miklos Muranyi, *Beiträge zur Geschichte der Ḥadīṯ und Rechtsgelehrsamkeit der Mālikiyya in Nordafrika bis zum 5. Jh. d.H.* (Wiesbaden: Harrassowitz, 1997), 42–43.

I am not interested in it for its specific information on the texts but for the way that it captures the interplay between oral and written sources, something that still made sense to Ibn Khaldun many centuries later. First, we have an original text from Asad, based on his studies with both Hanafi and Maliki authorities. Then we have Sahnun as a student, first studying this text with Asad and then travelling himself to Egypt to discuss it with Ibn al-Qasim. Through the process, Ibn al-Qasim is not perceived as the author of a text. Rather, his responses to questions form the stuff of two written texts, one by Asad and another by Sahnun. Further, Ibn al-Qasim seems well aware of the unique power of the written word, expressing anxiety that Asad continues to teach his original responses, which he has now revised.[13] Finally, Ibn al-Qasim's personal authority is the reason that the *Asadiyya* was forgotten and that the *Mudawwana* is still taught, despite (we are told) its imperfections. The ultimate lesson, therefore, is that books were not authoritative in themselves, but only when connected with the imprimatur of the great scholars whose knowledge they purported to pass on.

The other important aspect of this story is the way it connects Kairouan to major centers of learning in Egypt, Iraq, and Arabia. Manuscript evidence suggests that Asad did indeed serve as a conduit for Hanafi learning in Kairouan,[14] and the institution of *al-riḥla fī ṭalab al-ʿilm* (travelling in search of knowledge) was already well-established. As I will discuss below, this institution resulted in the extraordinary library of Kairouan, a library that preserves many of our oldest witnesses to texts produced in Egypt and other centers. In other stories, Asad is portrayed as a judge in the province of *Ifrīqiya* and as the leader of troops into battle. Iyad b. Musa records Asad's speech upon his departure for Sicily in 210/825 when he proclaimed: "I have only reached what you see by scholarship. So strive yourselves and persevere in the laying down of knowledge; by it you will gain both this world and the next."[15] Knowledge, in this tale, is far more than a matter of personal piety or individual salvation. It is what propels simple scholars to positions of worldly importance, granting them the authority to judge and to lead troops in battle.

[13] The fact of ongoing revision itself is not regarded by any of these characters, including Iyad, as problematic.

[14] Jonathan Brockopp, "Asad b. al-Furāt" in Kate Fleet, Gudrun Krämer, Denis Matringe, John Nawas, and Everett Rowson (eds.), *Encyclopaedia of Islam – Three* (Brill Online, 2015).

[15] ʿIyāḍ, *Tartīb*, 3:305–306.

There are many other stories that connect scholars in this period to political power,[16] but after the 820s we see a significant change. In addition to those scholars who were said to serve the bureaucracy of great leaders (Asad leading troops, Abu Yusuf administering the tax collection and appointing of judges for Harun al-Rashid, Ibn Abd al-Hakam serving the Egyptian governor Ibn Tahir, etc.), we also have new stories about scholars resisting political power, thereby setting themselves up as a societal force to be reckoned with.[17] As I will discuss in Chapter 4, there are many examples of this resistance, including Ahmad b. Hanbal surviving the inquisition (*miḥna*) in Baghdad. In later years, resistance to political authority becomes an expected part of any respectable scholar's biography, a sign of the independent power of the scholarly community.

My point in retelling these stories is simply to underline the fact that scholars in the early Abbasid period are portrayed as students, teachers, and community leaders. The early Abbasid period, therefore, is depicted as the essential moment when scholarly communities form and begin to achieve their full sociological function within Islamic society. While the institutionalization of these functions is only partially visible during this period, between 750 and 820, this is when we see scholars explicitly training one another to pass down specific knowledge. As such, they affect not only isolated individuals, but the whole fabric of society, determining and enforcing Islamic norms. It should not surprise us that this rise to power leads to clashes with other groups, especially the holders of political power. To see this progression, however, we must again build a framework of inquiry, based on the material evidence.

PAPYRI AND THE ROLE OF WRITING IN EIGHTH-CENTURY SCHOLARSHIP

In this period we have no more need of such blunt instruments as coins and architecture to infer scholarly activities. Now, finally, we have scholars' own writings, and the beginning of this period offers us our first tantalizing glimpses of scholarly activity. Many years ago, Nabia Abbott published a three-volume study of important papyrus fragments, five of

16 Muhammad Qasim Zaman, *Religion and Politics under the Early ʿAbbāsids: The Emergence of the Proto-Sunnī Elite*, Islamic History and Civilization, Studies and Texts, vol. 16 (Leiden: E. J. Brill, 1997), 12, calls this a "pattern of collaboration."

17 I agree with Zaman (ibid., 11–12) that collaboration continues after the *miḥna*, but I believe that his view of the development of the ʿ*ulamā*ʾ over time needs to be nuanced and geographically differentiated.

which she dated to the second/eighth century: one of a *maghāzī* text that she attributed to Maʿmar b. Rashid (d. 154/771),[18] a second of a text on the caliphs by Ibn Ishaq (d. 150/767),[19] a fragment of *al-Wujūḥ wa l-naẓāʾir* by Muqatil b. Sulayman (d. 150/767),[20] a fragment of Malik's *Muwaṭṭaʾ*, and a short text attributed to Amr b. al-As (d. 42/663).[21] In addition to these fragments, Abbott dated several others to the early ninth century, a clear testament to the increasing literacy of the period. While the dating of these papyrus fragments is impressionistic at best, in aggregate they demonstrate that writing is an increasingly important aspect of scholarship. The specific areas of scholarship represented here (history, Qurʾan commentary, Islamic law) fit into both the broader pattern I have been describing and also the evidence of the ninth-century manuscripts. Nonetheless, these extremely short fragments leave many questions unanswered. Because they contain no titles, the only way to identify them is to compare them with manuscripts of texts from much later periods. This is more problematic than Abbott allows, as I will demonstrate by looking at the *Muwaṭṭaʾ* fragment in more detail.

Malik's *Muwaṭṭaʾ*: An Early School Text

Few other scholarly texts have as many manuscript witnesses as does the *Muwaṭṭaʾ*, attributed to Malik b. Anas though actually compiled by his students. According to our literary sources, Malik was born between 708 and 716 CE and was the most famous jurist from Medina by the time of his death in 179/795.[22] He studied with several experts on *ḥadīth*, some of whose parents knew the Prophet. Malik attracted students from all over the Islamic world, and the *Muwaṭṭaʾ* was taught in all medieval centers of learning, especially Egypt, Baghdad, North Africa, and Spain. This information is verified by a large number of early manuscript copies, including a beautifully rendered copy, now preserved in the Chester

[18] Abbott, *Studies*, 1:65–79.
[19] Ibid., 1:80–99.
[20] Ibid., 2:92–113.
[21] Ibid., 2:114–128.
[22] Umar F. Abd-Allah, *Mālik and Medina: Islamic Legal Reasoning in the Formative Period*, Islamic History and Civilization, vol. 101 (Leiden: E. J. Brill, 2013); Yossef Rapoport, "Malik ibn Anas (d. 179/795)" in David Powers, Susan Spectorsky, and Oussama Arabi (eds.), *Islamic Legal Thought: A Compendium of Muslim Jurists* (Leiden: E. J. Brill, 2013), 27–41; Yasin Dutton, *The Origins of Islamic Law: The Qurʾan, the Muwaṭṭaʾ and Madinan ʿAmal*, Culture and Civilization in the Middle East (Richmond, Surrey: Curzon, 1999).

Figure 3.1a: Recto of undated fragment of the *Muwaṭṭa'* on papyrus (A. P. 00263 Pap; PERF 731. Each page approx. 18 × 18.5 cm), © Austrian National Library, Vienna.

Beatty library in Dublin (see Figure 5.4); I will discuss that important manuscript in Chapter 5. Here, however, I begin by outlining the limitations of any speculation based on the papyrus fragment that Abbott analyzes.

Paleographic dating is more art than science, and so Nabia Abbott's suggested date (before 179/795) for this fragment (Figure 3.1) must be taken with a grain of salt. We simply have no basis for scientific comparison, since our earliest dated manuscript of any text from the Maliki school was written more than fifty years later, and our earliest dated copy of the *Muwaṭṭa'* was written down more than a hundred years after the supposed date of this manuscript. Abbott suggests that the key piece of

Figure 3.1b: Verso of undated fragment of the *Muwaṭṭa'* on papyrus (A. P. 00263 Pap; PERF 731. Each page approx. 18 × 18.5 cm), © Austrian National Library, Vienna.

information that puts this papyrus into the period before Malik's death is the lack of specific formulae (e.g., *ḥaddathanī* or *akhbaranī*) within the chain of authorities or at the beginning of these chains.[23] While it is true that appearance of the phrase *ḥaddathanī Yaḥyā* (Yahya told me [that Malik said]) would argue for the manuscript postdating Malik's life, the lack of this phrase does not prove it was written before Malik's death. In fact, a distinctive marker of the Chester Beatty manuscript 3001, which was certainly written centuries after Malik's death, is the removal of the phrase *ḥaddathanī Yaḥyā* from the text. In other words, Abbott's

[23] Abbott, *Studies*, 2:121.

arguments are based on information in literary texts (the date of Malik's death, the timing of Yahya b. Yahya's trip to Medina), not on paleographic evidence. This is, in part, due to the paucity of dated texts from this period. Abbott is forced to compare this fragment with a small number of manuscripts of other texts, but these were written by scribes from different backgrounds and disparate training. Paleographic dating is based on a linear evolution of letter shapes, but with so many centers of literacy in this period, the differences between geographical locations may be greater than differences across time.[24] Nonetheless, even if we accept her dating for the purpose of argument, this fragment still does not prove that Malik wrote a book; all our other evidence strongly suggests that he did not.

First, like most of the fragments that Abbott analyzes, this one is quite short (less than a page), and so it is impossible to determine whether it derives from a longer "book" or simply represents notes taken by students. Abbott remarks on the congruency of the *Muwaṭṭa'* fragment with the printed version of the text, but as discussed in Chapter 2, this does not prove that the *Muwaṭṭa'* is an authored text, produced in a single redactional effort and passed on, intact, to future generations. Not only could the correspondence between the fragment and the printed version be a coincidence, the printed version itself is no critical edition, without indication of its manuscript basis.[25]

Second, literary evidence tells us that Malik was constantly revising his text (theoretically as a way of preventing the caliph from using it as the basis for a legal code),[26] and so he never finished a complete version. This story may be apocryphal, but it dovetails nicely with the fact that many versions of the *Muwaṭṭa'* exist, several of which have been published. Yasin Dutton argues, however, that "The basic text was in place by the year 150 AH, but underwent various editorial changes over the next thirty years which are reflected in the different transmissions that have survived to this day."[27] It is true that comparison of the extant

[24] Also, if I am right that scholarly writing developed from the school of Qur'an scribes and not the chancery, then dated bureaucratic correspondence may be of no help at all in dating these earliest literary texts.

[25] Miklos Muranyi, *Die Rechtsbücher des qairawāners Saḥnūn b. Sa'īd: Entstehungsgeschichte und Werküberlieferung*, (Stuttgart: Franz Steiner, 1999), ix.

[26] Abbott, *Studies*, 2:123. See also Ignacz Goldziher, *The Ẓāhirīs. Their Doctrine and Their History, a Contribution to the History of Islamic Theology*, trans. Wolfgang Behn (Leiden: E. J. Brill, 1971), 89.

[27] Dutton, *Origins*, 22. Abbott agrees with this assessment (2:123), but Dutton argues (p. 24) that the papyrus fragment is of a different recension of the *Muwaṭṭa'* than that of Yahya b. Yahya.

transmissions reveals a common core of both juristic dicta and also *ḥadīth*, but these variants are far more significant than Dutton's phrase "editorial changes" would seem to suggest.[28] The key point here is that Abbott's fragment is witness to a text that was subject to an ongoing process of revision; it is not a book, and there is no way to confidently isolate the "basic text" that Dutton claims was established by Malik.[29] Simply excerpting the material common to a few of the recensions runs the risk of producing a text quite different from any that Malik himself might have put together.

This distinction between text and book might seem picayune, but it has clear implications for the role of writing in scholarship and for the nature of scholars and the scholarly community during this period. First, when dealing with the *Muwaṭṭa'*, we are in a different league than we were with Wahb b. Munabbih's *History of King David*. In the case of that text, we had no way to discern material that may have stemmed from Wahb from that which was ascribed to him by his students or later generations. In contrast, comparison of Abbott's fragments with other early manuscripts of the *Muwaṭṭa'* reveals a core of material spread by a variety of different students; the common denominator of this material is Malik.[30] Second, while we cannot reconstruct a book written by Malik, this common core of material provides evidence of a process of teaching and learning underway in the late eighth century, and Abbott's papyrus is witness to the fact

[28] I remain firm in my judgment, fifteen years ago, that that Malik "exercised no authorial control over his text and also that no scholastic structure was in place to maintain the integrity of the text" (Brockopp, *Early Mālikī Law*, 77). Even Schoeler agrees with me on this point, saying that the *Muwaṭṭa'* is "not an actual book ... its author did not give it a definitive shape" (Schoeler, *Genesis*, 63).

[29] The same reservations apply to Abbott's other fragments. For example, we have no manuscript copies of any of Ibn Ishaq's texts, only quotations preserved in later texts. Therefore, even if we accept Abbott's judgement that the Ibn Ishaq fragment dates to the 770s, we still cannot prove it is from Ibn Ishaq himself, and there seems to be no reason to suggest that it stems from a book, despite Schoeler's claims to the contrary (Schoeler, *Genesis*, 61–63). Schoeler's language is a bit slippery here. While he calls Ibn Ishaq's text a *syngramma*, and says it was published for the caliph and his court (p. 63), he later admits that the version that has come down to us reflects redactions made by subsequent generations (p. 72). Likewise, he claims that Malik "had in mind" to write an actual book (p. 73).

[30] This reasoning is similar to, though not the same as, the "common-link" reasoning used by Schacht, Motzki, and others. The important difference is that dated manuscripts of the *Muwaṭṭa'* and other Maliki texts bring us within one hundred years of Malik's life. In contrast, the manuscripts of hadith collections can often be dated no earlier than several centuries after the death of the putative sources, leaving much more room for interpolation, contamination, and outright forgery.

that this process had both oral and written components. Therefore, we are now reaching the stage where material evidence is strong enough to safely remove the third possibility: that Malik never wrote a text and that what we have is a pious forgery.

This more limited finding partially vindicates Schoeler's speculative reconstruction of this period, based on his review of literary sources and reconstructed texts. According to Schoeler, this period was dominated by *hypomnēnata*, texts that served as aides to support the largely oral teaching methods. He writes:

> Three characteristics suggest that the systematically organised works we have been discussing qualify as notes or notebooks rather than as actual books. First, none of these works has survived in its original form; second, the texts we do have are dependent on later transmissions, dating from the ninth century at the earliest; and third, whenever several recensions of one of these works exist, these recensions often show considerable textual divergence.[31]

This finding also fits with Norman Calder's description of early texts as "school texts" in the sense that they had no single author but were compiled over generations by groups of students.[32] We saw this process quite clearly in my discussion of the *History of King David*, attributed to Wahb b. Munabbih, where very similar stories were attributed to Wahb, Ibn Ishaq, and *Midrash Shmuel*. So long as we only have unique manuscripts (whether of the *History of King David* or of Muhammad's life), we cannot say for certain that this manuscript is the end of the process – it may in fact preserve only one version of a text that was then subject to a continuing cycle of revision and emendation by later students.

Defining the Book

Calder and Schoeler's insights are important; not only do they highlight the problems of working with manuscript fragments in isolation, they also expose our notions of authorship, authenticity, and intellectual property as modern artifacts. In my view, however, Schoeler goes too far when he presses on to speculate that in addition to these *hypomnēnata* there were also "actual books" in the early Abbasid period, naming Ibn Ishaq,

[31] Schoeler, *Genesis*, 76.

[32] Calder, *Studies*, 11; he writes that school texts "grew organically in response to ongoing problems and perceptions that emerged and disturbed the scholars who preserved this material."

Abu Yusuf (d. 182/798),[33] and Sibawayh (d. 180/796?) as authors. To date, no material evidence can support this conjecture, and here is where I find the primary weakness of Schoeler's model: his definition of a book depends more on an author's intent than on the social context of that authorial effort.[34] Unless we have direct evidence from the author, it is impossible to know their intent apart from what later generations choose to tell us. Further, it is unclear what, if any, social meaning can be derived from a "book" produced by an isolated genius and never discussed with students. This is precisely the case with Sibawayh who, according to Schoeler, authored "the very first book properly speaking in all of Islamic scholarship."[35] Yet, as Schoeler himself admits, the literary sources claim that Sibawayh himself never taught his book, and offer us only a cryptic story of him passing the book on to a colleague who then himself taught it to his students.[36] This history is reflected in the transmission records of the manuscripts, all of which "ultimately lead through al-Mubarrad, al-Māzinī and al-Akhfash to Sībawayhi."[37] Schoeler's claim that Sibawayh is the true author, and that al-Akhfash and the others passed down his book verbatim, is only one way to make sense of this evidence, since it is equally as possible that al-Akhfash (or one of his students) compiled notes from Sibawayh and ultimately composed the book. The impressive findings of internal consistency forwarded by Geneviève Humbert only suggest that what has come down to us is a fixed text, not when that text was fixed or by whom.[38]

These fine distinctions matter because they reveal Schoeler's claim to be quite limited. Because he argues that "actual books" grew out of court culture, with "men of letters" producing them "for the exclusive use of

[33] He calls Abu Yusuf's text "one of the very first actual books in the field of law to have survived" (Schoeler, *Genesis*, 63).

[34] I find the same problem with El Shamsy's reconstruction of al-Shafiʿi's various uses of writing (*Canonization*, 149–154) in which he claims to be able to recognize "his powerful authorial voice" (166). Yet, as El Shamsy points out, the "community of interpretation" that would value a verbatim transmission of al-Shafiʿi's works did not arrive until a generation later.

[35] Schoeler, *Genesis*, 87.

[36] Ibid., 89; Geneviève Humbert, "Le Kitāb de Sībawayhi et L'autonomie de L'écrit," *Arabica* 44, no. 4 (Oct. 1997), 553–567, at 555; Sezgin, *Geschichte*, 9:53–54. Sezgin (9:52) also points out that we know very little about Sibawayh's life, and that dates for his death vary widely.

[37] Schoeler, *Genesis*, 89.

[38] Humbert, "Le Kitāb de Sībawayhi."

the caliph and his court,"[39] their broader social impact was negligible. At the same time, Schoeler misses the real revolution happening among what he terms the "traditional scholars" whom he claims continued to depend on *hypomnēnata* in the ninth century "when, everywhere else in the Muslim world, literary works, i.e. actual books, had begun to circulate."[40] While Abbott's edited papyri demonstrate the importance of *hypomnēnata* in the eighth century, the Kairouan collection of manuscripts helps to show that at least in some cases "traditional scholars" developed a highly sophisticated book culture, including both *hypomnēnata* and *syngrammata*. Moreover, as I will discuss in Chapter 4, the relationship between oral and written texts rapidly changed in the early ninth century.

To summarize, I agree with Schoeler and Calder that scholars produced written materials in the late eighth century, and so the literary accounts that point to the existence of private libraries and the use of writing in the course of study are believable. We ought, however, to translate *kutub* not as "books" but simply as writings. Ibn Lahiʿa (d. 174/790), for example, was said to have had a library that burned in 170/786.[41] He was also famous for wandering around Fustat with writing material in a sort of leather wallet that he hung around his neck for the purpose of collecting *ḥadīth* from visitors to Egypt.[42] Al-Shafiʿi (d. 204/820) is remembered to have consulted Ibn Abd al-Hakam's library of Malik's teachings when he lived in Egypt toward the end of his life.[43] Ibn al-Qasim (d. 191/806) also had such a library. These accounts are consistent with the notion that the writing of notes in *kurrāsa*s (quires of papyri or parchment leaves, sewn together[44]) was part of the normal course of study. The fragment from Malik's writings that

[39] Schoeler, *Genesis*, 63. On page 59, Schoeler writes "traditional scholars can consequently best be characterised as *transmitters*, whereas the state secretaries and authors of Persian origin are *men of letters* or *writers*" (emphasis in original).

[40] Ibid., 24. Arguably, actual books had long circulated in the Muslim world, just not books in Arabic.

[41] Raif Georges Khoury, *ʿAbd-Allāh Ibn-Lahīʿa, [97–174/715–790]: juge et grand maître de l'école égyptienne* (Wiesbaden: Harrassowitz, 1986); Franz Rosenthal, "Ibn Lahīʿa, ʿAbd Allāh" in *Encyclopaedia of Islam*, 2nd ed., 3:853.

[42] Rhuvon Guest, introduction to al-Kindī, *Kitâb el umarâ (el wulâh) wa Kitâb el qudâh*, Rhuvon Guest (ed.) (Leiden: E. J. Brill, 1912), 35. See also my "Formation of Islamic Law."

[43] Brockopp, *Early Mālikī Law*, 29.

[44] François Déroche, *Islamic Codicology: An Introduction to the Study of Manuscripts in Arabic Script* (London: Al-Furqān Islamic Heritage Foundation, 2006), 71–80.

Abbott analyzes might well be part of one of these student notebooks, originally preserved in one of these private, scholarly libraries. The informal nature of production, however, does not mean that these writings had only personal value. When Ibn Wahb died, in 197/812, the sources record that he left behind a substantial library of *kutub* that was sold off for hundreds of dinars.[45]

I further agree with Schoeler and Calder that while writing formed an increasingly important part of education, it remained an adjunct to oral modes of learning for centuries. Where we disagree is with the date of the appearance of the first scholarly books and the role that these "actual books" played within the overall scholarly endeavor. Schoeler argues that books existed already by the early Abbasid period, albeit in a very limited circulation, and were produced by "men of letters" in the court; he further argues that the first books of law were not produced by "traditional scholars" but by bureaucrats, such as Abu Yusuf, already associated with the court. Calder does not include this nuanced discussion of court culture but agrees that we must wait for the late ninth century before any actual books appear. While accepting that Schoeler's reconstruction of court culture is possible, I argue that until we have clear evidence, it must remain conjecture. Moreover, I suggest that by 200/815, we do have evidence of both books being used by "traditional scholars" as well as the scholarly communities to pass them on to others. Abbott's papyri cannot resolve this argument, but I believe that analysis of later manuscripts can.

USING NINTH- AND TENTH-CENTURY MANUSCRIPTS AS A SOURCE FOR EIGHTH-CENTURY SCHOLARSHIP

I hold that the preponderance of the evidence is best explained by regarding the end of the second Islamic century as a crucial moment in the development of Muslim scholarly communities. Yet, it must be admitted that we have no direct evidence of the activity of these scholars. This poses a particular problem for historians because the material evidence is weakest for those areas of the world (Iraq, Persia, Khurasan) that the literary sources tell us were the most active. Just as almost nothing remains of the famous round city of Baghdad, very few of our oldest manuscripts appear to have been produced in the eastern part of the

45 Brockopp, *Early Mālikī Law*, 27n. and the discussion there.

Islamic world, and no dated literary manuscripts have survived from before 820, the period addressed in this chapter. Therefore, we are left trying to reconstruct history not on the basis of actual artifacts from the eighth century, but on the basis of ninth- and tenth-century manuscripts that purport to preserve eighth-century texts. It would seem that we are left in the same conundrum we faced when analyzing Sibawayh's *Kitāb*, with sanguine and skeptical historians reading the same evidence in different ways. Yet, when we follow our earliest manuscripts, a very different picture appears. In fact, it is Egypt, not Iraq, that emerges as a literary powerhouse.

A Brief Overview of Ninth-Century Manuscripts

In 1989, François Déroche published a list of the forty Arabic manuscripts that he felt could be securely dated to the year AH 300 (about 912 CE) or earlier. This is a surprisingly small number that is further reduced when one realizes that of the forty manuscripts in Déroche's list, fourteen are fragments of the Qur'an while twelve preserve texts deriving from the Christian tradition. The remaining fourteen manuscripts cover a narrow scope of fields, including several aspects of law, and *ḥadīth* (Déroche rejects, for various reasons, the age of certain philosophical, medical, and literary manuscripts that had been dated to the ninth century).[46]

I will analyze this group more fully in Chapter 5, but it would be folly to suggest that these fourteen manuscripts are representative of Muslim scholarly writing from the third/ninth century. Only the Maliki school is represented here in any detail, with the other schools of law contributing merely one book each; nothing is present from other areas of knowledge: theology, Sufism, grammar, poetics, astronomy, etc. This skewed representation is related to the fact that nearly half of Déroche's manuscripts derive from three collections: the Egyptian national library, the ancient mosque-library of Kairouan, Tunisia, and the monastery of St. Catherine in the Sinai. Missing, of course, are remains of libraries from northern and eastern portions of the Islamic world, where climatic conditions were less conducive to the survival of manuscripts. Further, as Déroche points out, the current location of these manuscripts (e.g., Ireland, Germany, Egypt, Syria) cannot tell us much about where they were produced and studied. Déroche does note the preponderance of Tunisian manuscripts, however

[46] Déroche, "Les manuscrits arabes," 350–351.

(seven of the forty), he warns us against drawing overly hasty conclusions from this fact, writing: "il est fallacieux de tenir pour identique le lieu de conservation d'un manuscript et l'endroit où il a été copié."[47] In other words, even with seven third-century manuscripts from the same library, careful analysis is required to determine the provenance of these precious fragments and their relationship to one another. Thankfully, this task is made easier by the work of Miklos Muranyi and others during the twenty-five years since Déroche published his essay. As I outline in the Appendix, we can now add sixteen more manuscripts written before AH 300, more than doubling the number of Islamic literary manuscripts known to have been written in the third/ninth century. Altogether then, we have twenty-three third/ninth-century manuscripts from a single location, Kairouan, allowing for a sea change in what we can know about scholarly communities based on a completely new methodology.

The Kairouan manuscripts share many physical features (similar size, parchment, binding, ink, etc.),[48] and many can be matched with a list (*sijill*) made a few centuries later; therefore, we have high confidence that most were produced in Kairouan. This common provenance allows for an unparalleled comparison of scripts and even, in some cases, identification of individual scribes, allowing dozens of undated manuscripts to be securely placed well before the year 1000.[49] These manuscripts, combined with a few finds from Egypt, such as an undated fragment from the *ḥadīth* collection of Ibn Lahiʿa (d. 174/790) on papyrus, offer a remarkably rich picture of the intellectual life of Fustat and Kairouan from about 780 through the eleventh century; this collection also has important implications for our understanding of the rise of the scholarly class in Spain. These dated manuscripts from Kairouan provide us with a rich context similar to dated strata in an extensive archeological site.[50] Together with undated manuscripts, they are like artifacts discovered *in situ*, providing us much more information about the texts they preserve, and the community that produced them, than any individual manuscript on its own. I will focus on the scholars of Kairouan in Chapter 5, but here

[47] "To regard the place where a manuscript is preserved as identical with the area where it was copied is fallacious." Déroche, "Les manuscrits arabes," 351 and notes.

[48] A rough paper appears occasionally as well, but it is rare.

[49] Muranyi, *Beiträge*.

[50] An analogy first put forward by Miklos Muranyi, "Neue Materialien zur *tafsīr*-Forschung in der Moscheebibliothek von Qairawān," in Stefan Wild (ed.), *The Qurʾan as Text* (Leiden: E. J. Brill, 1996), 228–234.

I am interested in using these manuscripts as a conduit to an earlier community, that of Fustat, Egypt, in the second/eighth century.

Early Scholarly Activity in Egypt

The importance of Egypt as the site for early Muslim scholarly activity has been downplayed,[51] perhaps because its most important city, Alexandria, was not fully incorporated into the new Muslim polity. Since ancient times, Alexandria was the site of major philosophical, astronomical, and medical advances, and papyri from Alexandria and other scholarly centers in Egypt detail the continued influence of scholarship and writing well into the Islamic period.[52] Classified as an outpost (*thaghr*) due to its position on the sea, Alexandria does not play a significant role in Arab historical imagination.[53] For the first few decades of the Islamic era, as the Arab conquests continued westward, administrative and commercial life continued in Alexandria, while Fustat served as the base for raids and eventual expansion to North Africa and Europe. Early coins demonstrate that when the mint was finally brought to Fustat from Alexandria, coins were still marked with Greek letters, demonstrating the same slow process of Islamicization detailed in Chapter 1.[54] Early papyri were composed in Greek, Arabic, and Coptic as Copts quickly filled positions left open by fleeing Byzantine functionaries.[55] Only in 87/706 was the *dīwān* changed from Coptic to Arabic.[56]

[51] Brockopp, "Formation of Islamic Law."

[52] For an overview of recent finds, which include an estimate that there are more than 150,000 Arabic papyrus fragments awaiting analysis, see Lennart Sundelin, "Introduction: Papyrology and the Study of Early Islamic Egypt," in Petra Sijpesteijn and Lennart Sundelin (eds.), *Papyrology and the History of Early Islamic Egypt* (Leiden: E. J. Brill, 2004), 1–19. For analysis, see Mikhail, *Byzantine and Islamic.*

[53] The pharaohs preferred capitals in Upper Egypt (Thebes) or at the point where upper and Lower Egypt met (Memphis). Alexandria's position and prestige was dictated by its accessibility first to the Greco-Roman empire and then to the Byzantine. This same position caused it to be vulnerable to attack from the sea until such time as the Muslims built a navy.

[54] At first, only copper coins were minted in Egypt, with the name changing from ALEX to MASR (but still in Greek letters) sometime in the late seventh century (Warren Schultz, "The Monetary History of Egypt, 642–1517," in Carl F. Petry [ed.], *The Cambridge History of Egypt*, 2 vols. [Cambridge: Cambridge University Press, 1998], 1:318–338, at 325).

[55] The papyri found in Aphrodito are in all three of these languages. See Abbott, *Kurrah Papyri*, and Rāġib, "Lettres nouvelles de Qurra b. Šarīk."

[56] Hugh Kennedy, "Egypt as a Province in the Islamic Caliphate, 641–868," in Petry (ed.), *Cambridge History of Egypt*, 1:62–85, at 69.

Umar b. Abd al-Aziz, the future Umayyad caliph, may have been born in Egypt and probably spent time there during the twenty years when his father served as Egypt's governor.[57] Umar is credited with supporting the study of Islamic law in both Egypt and North Africa,[58] and as caliph he was also famously lenient toward new converts.[59] Whether Umar played a pivotal role or not, our earliest proto-scholars in Egypt appear to date from the late Umayyad period, including a Nubian convert to Islam, Yazid b. Abi Habib (d. 128/745),[60] a well-regarded transmitter of many *ḥadīth*s. Local Umayyad governors also had an active and well-trained chancery, as demonstrated clearly by the Qurra papyri.

The change in ruling dynasty from Umayyad to Abbasid led to an Egypt of increasing independence. By the 780s, Egypt was striking its own gold and silver coins,[61] a prerogative normally reserved to the capital. From this period we also have our first scholars of note: Abd Allah b. Lahiʿa (d. 174/790) and al-Layth b. Saʿd (d. 175/791), two men who loom large in the literary sources. Many years ago, Khoury edited a papyrus fragment from a *ṣaḥīfa* of Ibn Lahiʿa; even though it is not dated, I believe it should be considered among our oldest manuscripts. First, internal evidence suggests a date before 219/834, the death of Uthman b. Salih, a well-known student of Ibn Lahiʿa whose name appears in the manuscript.[62] Second, the disorganized nature of this collection of *ḥadīth*, only some of which are of legal significance, justifies an early date. This is especially the case when we compare it with a manuscript attributed to Abdallah b. Wahb and produced in North Africa at about the same time the papyrus roll was written; it also preserves many *ḥadīth* of Ibn Lahiʿa, but these are organized into the familiar chapters of Islamic law.[63] This evidence makes clear that, like Malik b. Anas, Ibn Lahiʿa did not compose

57 Paul Cobb, "ʿUmar b. ʿAbd al-ʿAzīz," in *Encyclopaedia of Islam*, 2nd ed., 10:821.

58 Al-Suyūṭī, *Ḥusn al-Muḥāḍara*, 1:258.

59 The reversal of this policy under Umar's successors may have led to a long period of Coptic revolt. See Mikhail, *Byzantine to Islamic*, 118–127.

60 Sezgin, *Geschichte*, 1:341–342; Yazid is also mentioned by Harald Motzki, "The Role of Non-Arab Converts," 303); on p. 311, Motzki notes his Nubian descent, but not his residence in Alexandria; he also dismisses any connection to Coptic Christianity. See also Khoury, *ʿAbd-Allāh Ibn-Lahīʿa*, 114–115.

61 Schultz, "Monetary History", 327.

62 Khoury, *ʿAbd-Allāh Ibn-Lahīʿa*, 118 and 232.

63 Miklos Muranyi, *ʿAbd Allāh b. Wahb: Leben und Werk. Al-Muwaṭṭaʾ, kitāb al-muḥāraba* (Wiesbaden: Harrassowitz, 1992), 320–321. It must be admitted, however, that the attribution of these remarks in the text is ambiguous and that they may actually stem from Ibn Wahb's student, Yunus b. Abd al-Aʿla (d. 264/877); see ibid., 83.

actual books. But it also strongly argues for an early date for this papyrus fragment. This manuscript marks, I believe, our earliest demonstrable community of scholars, scholars whose work would be largely unknown to us were it not for the unique collection of manuscripts in Kairouan.

The Manuscripts of Kairouan

When Joseph Schacht examined the collection of the mosque library of Kairouan fifty years ago, he wrote, "In verifying the authors of these manuscripts and their works, I almost felt as if I had been admitted to a family party of the Malikis of the first two or three generations."[64] The sense of "a family party" that Schacht refers to is precisely the qualitative difference between the material basis for reconstructing the history of scholarship in Egypt and North Africa compared with that for the rest of the Islamic world. Some of my fondest memories of working on manuscripts come from the times I was sitting with the late Shaykh al-Sadiq Malik al-Gharyani in a room of the old Sidi Abid Zaouia in Kairouan. The manuscripts – thousand-year-old pieces of parchment – were in cardboard file boxes, stacked on the stone floor of the eighteenth-century building. We worked by the natural light of the room, with the Shaykh at a small desk near the window and me at another desk nearby; he served hot, sweet tea in small, Turkish-style glasses, which he set right next to the precious documents. Whereas I was in fear of spilling the tea, using a tissue to turn the pages, the Shaykh had a different attitude. At one point, I discovered that a fragment I was reading looked very much like the one I had been reading a few days earlier, and I was able to conclude that the fragments derived from the same manuscript. The Shaykh, excited by my discovery, took the parchment and proceeded to write the correct title on the manuscript itself in pencil – a violation of everything I had learned about manuscript conservation. To me, these documents had value because of what they could tell us about centuries past, but to the Shaykh they were part of his living heritage, and he was simply continuing the tradition of scholars writing notes in the margins of the manuscript.[65]

64 Schacht, "On Some Manuscripts," 226.

65 This recollection stems from my visit in spring of 2000. During my most recent trip to Kairouan, in December of 2015, I was given latex gloves before being allowed to touch the manuscripts. Still today, though, the Shaykh's marks on the manuscripts are visible as he underlined names and other key details in his attempt to identify loose parchment pages. I should also add that even for the Shaykh, writing on a manuscript was an

I recount this tale to emphasize the ways that the Kairouan manuscripts are different, especially from those scattered in European libraries. Because we have so many manuscripts from roughly the same period, we can compare handwriting of fragments, reconstruct texts, and discern copied colophons from originals. Further, the Shaykh's interaction with the manuscripts is a faint trace of the community of scholars that once surrounded this collection. While the Shaykh's methods are different from those of past scholars, the habit of making notations on manuscripts was widespread in Kairouan, with use of a specific terminology. We can note definite trends in marginalia and even trace the influence of certain teachers and students throughout the collection. The handwriting of some individuals can also be discerned.[66] The result is that while we are forced to reconstruct texts from Syria, Iraq, and Khurasan from manuscripts dating centuries after the fact,[67] in North Africa we have manuscripts that are sometimes as old as the texts they preserve.

The Kairouan collection is particularly rich with the writings of four Egyptian scholars from the generation after Ibn Lahiʿa: Abd al-Rahman b. al-Qasim (d. 191/806), Abd Allah b. Wahb (d. 197/812), Ashhab b. Abd al-Aziz (d. 204/819), and Abdallah b. Abd al-Hakam (d. 214/829). According to literary evidence, they were key players in the Egyptian intellectual community, and many of their writings are now known to be extant. Muranyi has recently published a fragment of Ibn al-Qasim's recension of Malik's *Muwaṭṭa*ʾ as well as an important fragment of Ibn al-Qasim's *Samā*ʿ.[68] Because of the oversized role Ibn al-Qasim plays in

extraordinary occasion. Most of his notes were placed on separate sheets of paper with which he wrapped the fragments. On a few occasions, he invited me to write notes on these sheets as well, and so my rectilinear schoolboyish Arabic handwriting has now become part of the collection.

[66] In personal communications, Miklos Muranyi has told me that he can easily distinguish the handwriting of Abu l-Arab al-Tamimi (d. 333/944), for example.

[67] For example, it seems reasonable to suggest that Muhammad al-Shaybani (d. 189/805), the famous Iraqi jurist, actually wrote *al-Jāmiʿ al-ṣaghīr* and that it was a book; much like early Maliki texts, it demonstrates an interest in first- and second-order questions and formed the basis of early commentaries. However, any such judgment must remain provisional, since the earliest manuscript for this text dates to AH 759 (although there is a commentary dated to AH 521; Sezgin, *Geschichte*, 1:428). Likewise, our oldest witnesses to other texts attributed to al-Shaybani were first written down many centuries after his death: *Kitāb al-aṣl* (oldest manuscript dated to AH 639; Ibid., 1:422, though there is a partial commentary dated 590; ibid., 1:423); *al-Jāmiʿ al-kabīr* (sixth Islamic century; ibid., 1:423; commentaries dated as early as 559; ibid., 1:424); and many more texts that Sezgin attributes to al-Shaybani (ibid., 1:421–433).

[68] Miklos Muranyi, "A Unique Manuscript from Kairouan in the British Library: The Samāʿ-Work of Ibn al-Qāsim al-ʿUtaqī and Issues of Methodology," in Berg (ed.), *Method and*

Sahnun's *Mudawwana*, these textual transmissions are of particular importance. They represent the ways that writing was used as a supplement to a fundamentally oral teaching method.

As for Ibn Wahb, Muranyi completed a three-volume study of Ibn Wahb's life and work twenty years ago in which he presented editions of the Kairouan manuscripts of Ibn Wahb's *Jāmiʿ* and *Muwaṭṭaʾ*.[69] Both texts are only partially dependent on the work of Malik b. Anas, despite the common title (*muwaṭṭaʾ* like *mudawwana*, can mean work that is set down in writing or a "well-worn path"). Both in these works as well as in quotations from Ibn Wahb in the *Mudawwana*, he comes across as far more interested in *ḥadīth* than were his colleagues, reflecting an eighth-century Egyptian debate on the validity of this literature as a basis for Islamic law.[70] The works of Ashhab are still in manuscript, and to Sezgin's brief mention of his *Kitāb al-Ḥajj* may be added the extensive notes and description by Schacht.[71] More recent finds by Muranyi include a *Kitāb al-daʿwa*, a *Kitāb al-ʿitq*, and the *Majālis*.[72] As for Ibn Abd al-Hakam, I have published studies of both his *Major* and *Minor Compendium*,[73] and the complete text of the latter has now been edited.[74]

This list of recently discovered early texts is quite impressive, and I believe it is clear evidence of a community of scholars, of true *ʿulamāʾ* in Medina and Fustat at the end of the second/eighth century. Because of the broad implications of this claim, let me be clear as to why these mostly fourth/tenth-century manuscripts should be taken as trustworthy witnesses to late second/eighth-century texts, even while I continue to be

Theory, 325–368; ʿAbd al-Raḥmān b. al-Qāsim, *al-Muwaṭṭaʾ*, Miklos Muranyi (ed.) (Beirut: Dār al-Bashāʾir al-Islāmī, 2012. See further discussion in Chapter 4.

69 Muranyi, *ʿAbd Allāh b. Wahb*; Abdallah b. Wahb, *al-Ǧāmiʿ: tafsīr al-Qurʾān (die Koranexegese)*, Miklos Muranyi (ed.) (Wiesbaden: Harrassowitz, 1993); and ʿAbd Allāh b. Wahb, *al-Ǧāmiʿ: tafsīr al-Qurʾān, Koranexegese*, 2. Teil, Miklos Muranyi (ed.) (Wiesbaden: Harrassowitz, 1995). More recently, Muranyi added to the published chapters of Ibn Wahb's *Muwaṭṭaʾ* with ʿAbd Allāh b. Wahb, *al-Muwaṭṭaʾ*, *kitāb al-qaḍāʾ fī al-buyūʿ*, Miklos Muranyi (ed.) (Beirut: Dār al-gharb al-islāmī, 2004).

70 Brockopp, "Competing Theories."

71 Sezgin, *Geschichte*, 1:466–467; Schacht, "On Some Manuscripts," 233–235.

72 Miklos Muranyi, "Fiqh," in Helmut Gätje (ed.), *Grundriss der arabischen Philologie*. 2 vols. (Wiesbaden: Reichert, 1987), 2: 229–325, at 314; see also Muranyi, *Materialien zur mālikitischen Rechtsliteratur* (Wiesbaden: Harrassowitz, 1984), 23 for commentary on the *Kitāb al-Daʿwa*. See the Appendix to this book for some early manuscripts of Ashhab's work.

73 Brockopp, *Early Mālikī Law*; idem, "The *Minor Compendium* of Ibn ʿAbd al-Ḥakam."

74 Unfortunately, the edition by ʿUmar ʿAlī Abū Bakr Zāryā (al-Riyāḍ: Dār Ibn al-Qayyim lil-Nashr wa l-Tawzīʿ, 2013) does not include the Kairouan manuscripts, but is extracted from a late commentary.

skeptical about other early manuscript witnesses. First, the external evidence for these manuscripts is unparalleled. No other collection of early Muslim literary manuscripts has this many examples from such a narrow window of time. Therefore, we can compare quality of parchment and ink, methods of binding, and also habits of commentary across a large number of witnesses. As I will discuss in more detail in Chapter 5, this allows us to identify individual scribes, sometimes by name, and to reconstruct who studied and who taught specific texts, all without recourse to literary sources. Second, the internal evidence is also unique. Not only does the Kairouan collection preserve copies of well-attested books, like the *Muwaṭṭa'*, we also have books that are barely mentioned in the historical record, such as those of Ashhab and Ibn Abd al-Hakam.[75] Further, we have multiple texts from these Egyptian authors and can trace precisely how their students used these texts in producing their own works. However, only in the case of Ibn Abd al-Hakam do we have multiple manuscripts of a single text that appear to be verbatim copies, a distinction that allows definite identification of his texts as actual books.

The Missing Link: Ibn Abd al-Hakam's *Major Compendium*

The information that can be gleaned from manuscripts of Ibn Abd al-Hakam's *Minor Compendium* and *Major Compendium* may be used to analyze the writings of his contemporaries in Egypt and elsewhere. Personally, I find the writings of Ibn Abd al-Hakam to be especially useful because they form a sort of intellectual dead end. Unlike Ibn al-Qasim and Ibn Wahb (but very much like their colleague Ashhab b. Abd al-Aziz), Ibn Abd al-Hakam's name has been all but forgotten in the living traditions of the great Maliki madrasas of North and West Africa, as well as in the historical study of Islamic law. Yet the evidence from Kairouan and elsewhere demonstrates that his texts were widely read for more than two hundred years after his death, and that sporadic study continued for hundreds of years after that. These facts provide certain advantages for the historian: first, the relative unimportance of Ibn Abd al-Hakam as an authority in the later school means that it is unlikely that texts would be falsely ascribed to him – in fact (as I will discuss below regarding the

[75] This interaction of literary and manuscript material allows us also to assess the reliability of North Africa literary sources. I summarize some of the main findings in my "Saḥnūn's *Mudawwanah*."

Gotha manuscript), it is more likely that his writings would be ascribed to yet more famous individuals. Second, because Ibn Abd al-Hakam's texts had fallen out of fashion, almost all our manuscripts were written as part of the course of study when they formed an active part of the teaching curriculum. His texts, therefore, give us evidence about the nature of scholarly communities in this period – not only the texts they treasured, but also what they rejected or forgot. Third, the representation of manuscript fragments only partially accords with the literary histories of this period, written centuries later, and this gives us a good basis for understanding the ways that specific facts are represented in those histories. In general, material evidence vindicates the broad outlines of biographies: names, death dates, and much specific information about scholarly communities.

The literary texts tell us that Ibn Abd al-Hakam died in 214/829 and that he wrote three compendia of jurisprudence in varying lengths. So far, we have evidence of only two of these: the *Major* and *Minor Compendia.* If a "middle" compendium existed, it appears to be lost to history. Examination of these texts demonstrates that Ibn Abd al-Hakam was, in fact, a student of Malik b. Anas; however, Malik is not the sole source of information. Not only does Ibn Abd al-Hakam cite numerous authorities besides Malik, the very nature of his texts interrupts the scholarly focus on transmitting information from recognized authorities.[76]

As Norman Calder pointed out, compendia are a particularly sophisticated accomplishment, since they move beyond the simple gathering and organizing of the raw materials of legal thinking toward the systematization and application of law. He wrote: "[Compendia] are authored texts. They represent the effort by particular named individuals to bring the inherited tradition, with all its diversity of oral and written sources, to order."[77] Calder also rightly regarded compendia as a marker of a change in the way that legal scholars were being trained: "Their purpose is clearly educational. They were the earliest constituents of a formal curriculum, and they mark, accordingly, the transition from the world of the jurist who gained his knowledge through experience of life and participation in the process of juristic discussion, to the world of the academic trainee. [Institutionalization of that training] signals the end of the formative and the beginning of the classical period."[78] But Calder also held that jurists

76 *Pace* Schoeler, *Genesis*, 63.
77 Calder, *Studies*, 245.
78 Ibid., 246.

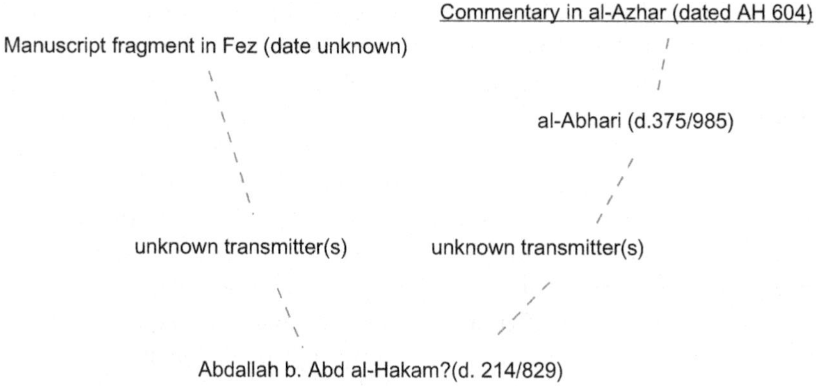

Figure 3.2: Known manuscripts of the *Major Compendium* in 1980

of the second/eighth century were not such a sophisticated lot, and that legal compendia could not have arisen before the beginning of the fourth/tenth century.

Consulting the most authoritative reference of its time, Sezgin's *Geschichte des arabischen Schrifttums*, Calder would have found nothing in the manuscript record to disabuse him of this notion. According to Sezgin, only Ibn Abd al-Hakam's *Major Compendium* had been preserved, and that in a single fragment of thirty folios found in Fez; also, several parts of a commentary by Abu Bakr al-Abhari (d. 375/985) were located in the library of al-Azhar and dated to AH 604.[79] I illustrate this state of knowedge in Figure 3.2, and based on this information, Calder could argue in a similar vein to what I wrote about Wahb b. Munabbih in Chapter 2. While Ibn Abd al-Hakam was said to be the author, our only witnesses appeared to have been written four hundred years after his death, so we could not know this work was really his.

More recent research has turned up new evidence that completely changes that assessment. Manuscripts have several ways of giving us information. They often start chapters (the *incipit)* with a chain of authorities (*riwāya*) through which the text was transmitted; this information is also often found in the colophon, a similar statement at the end of chapters or sections that sometimes includes a date of completion.[80] The information in these statements must be used with caution, however,

[79] Sezgin, *Geschichte*,1:467–468. The Fez manuscript is actually thirty-two folios.
[80] Déroche, *Islamic Codicology*, 318–330.

since incipit and colophon can be simply copied from older manuscripts, making it seem that the manuscript is older than it is. Also, there is always the possibility of pseudepigrapha, as scholars cite famous authorities to give more credence to their work. The veracity of these statements is difficult to check, but comparison with marginalia, notes written in the blank space surrounding the text, offers fuller information. These notes include corrections from the original scribe, collations with other manuscripts (often including a note with the name of the collator and the date of the collation), and "auditions" of the text. These latter are from students who, upon completion of a book chapter or a section, would record their accomplishment on the manuscript itself. Finally, there are library remarks and notes from donors who gave manuscripts to libraries as an endowment (*waqf* or *ḥubus*). When found on manuscripts from the rich collection of Kairouan, this information is far better than that found in a chain of *ḥadīth* transmitters, since claims can be dated and cross-checked.

For example, the Fez manuscript of the *Major Compendium* can be dated by a reader's remark to be earlier than AH 391 (1001 CE).[81] Also, comparison of that text with portions of the commentary in Egypt shows that the commentary faithfully records the entire text verbatim before adding comments in an interlinear fashion. Furthermore, on the basis of closer analysis, I discovered that the Egyptian manuscript is at least two hundred years older than initially thought, having been written before AH 405, making it the oldest legal manuscript in al-Azhar's collection.[82] As impressive as these new dates are, they barely challenge Calder's basic thesis, since only the earliest manuscript witness can date the existence of a text – and even then, it may only preserve one version of a text, which was then changed by later students. These isolated manuscripts, from the beginning of the eleventh century, still fit his scheme.

This problem is perfectly exemplified by the Gotha manuscript, which we now know to be a copy of al-Abhari's commentary on Ibn Abd al-Hakam's *Major Compendium*. Sitting in an important European library for many years, the manuscript was thoroughly described in an 1880 catalogue.[83] That catalogue dutifully recorded the title found on the

[81] Brockopp, *Early Mālikī Law*, 215.

[82] Ibid., 212–213. Also, Sezgin's reference to a "*Masā'il wa-ağwibatuhū*" (Sezgin, *Geschichte*, 1:468) may be removed according to Muranyi (*Materialien*, 12).

[83] W. Pertsch, *Die arabischen Handschriften der herzoglichen Bibliothek zu Gotha*, 5 vols. (Gotha: Perthes, 1877–1892), 2:352–354.

Figure 3.3: Final pages of Gotha manuscript, including colophon (Ms. Orient. A 1143, fol. 224b–225a), Universität Erfurt, Forschungsbibliothek Gotha.

manuscript itself: *Kitāb masāʾil li-imām Mālik li-ahl al-Andalus* (Book of Legal Issues Put to the Imam Malik by the People of al-Andalus); it also transcribed the colophon (Figure 3.3), which dates the manuscript to the seventh Islamic century.

The title should have raised suspicions. Malik is certainly not the author of this text, though his is the most famous name mentioned therein; also, none of the scholars mentioned in the text come from al-Andalus, though that may have been the origin of the manuscript before it came into German hands. Schacht recognized the title to be a later addition, prompting his remark that Gotha 1143 "is certainly apocryphal,"[84] but in his monumental history of Islamic literature, Sezgin nonetheless places this text among writings attributed to Malik b. Anas.[85] Only when Miklos Muranyi was able to compare the Gotha manuscript with the Fez manuscript did it become clear that the text was that of

[84] J. Schacht, "Mālikism," in *Encyclopaedia of Islam*, 2nd ed., 6:264.
[85] Sezgin, *Geschichte*, 1:464.

al-Abhari's commentary on *al-Mukhtaṣar al-kabīr fi l-fiqh*.[86] Even though al-Abhari's name appeared clearly in the colophon, no one had made this connection, perhaps because the colophon itself is problematic. It states that the scribe, Marwan b. Hassan al-Qushayri (death date unknown), based his copy of the text on an exemplar written in Egypt and completed in AH 435. This exemplar was itself based on the original text (*al-umm al-masmūʿa*) which was taken directly from al-Abhari, who died in 375/985. However, the date given for completion of the manuscript is Thursday, the ninth of Ramadan "*sana // wa sittu-miʾa* (the year six hundred and //)." The meaning of these slashes is unknown; they could be an idiosyncratic way of writing 11, except that Ramadan 9 was a Monday in 611.[87] The most reasonable explanation appears to me that this colophon was itself copied and that these slashes mark a lacuna in the copied manuscript. In other words, the Gotha manuscript must be from some date later than the seventh century, but it preserves a transmission record that is much older. No other names or readers' remarks appear on the manuscript to offer further information, nor do we know how the manuscript itself was acquired. It is a perfect example of the intriguing, but ultimately useless, nature of artifacts taken out of their cultural contexts.

Thankfully, the Kairouan collection allows for a sea change in our understanding of Ibn Abd al-Hakam's writings. First, the collection contains five more fragments of the *Major Compendium*: numbers 85 (twenty-three folios), 1646 (fifteen folios), 1662 (one folio), 3/498 (two folios), and 5/342 (eight folios, heavily damaged).[88] It also has evidence that al-Abhari's commentary to the *Major Compendium* was studied in Kairouan.[89] Manuscripts of Ibn Abd al-Hakam's *Minor Compendium* have now also come to light: a fragment of the text in Kairouan and a complete manuscript of a commentary by al-Barqi (d. 291/904) in Istanbul.[90] With the addition of these witnesses to Ibn Abd al-Hakam's work, we can now say a great deal about his texts and the subsequent study of

[86] Muranyi, *Materialien*, 11–13.

[87] It cannot be any other number, because Ramadan 9 fell on a Thursday only in 655 (not 600, 611, 622, 633, 644, 666, 677, 688, or 699).

[88] Kairouan 85 was described by Joseph Schacht ("On Some Manuscripts," 239–340); I identified the other manuscripts with the assistance of al-Sadiq Malik al-Gharyani during a research trip to Tunisia in 1996.

[89] I identified the Kairouan fragment with the assistance of Dr. Mourad Rammah during a research trip in the spring of 2000, supported by the Fulbright Foundation. A full description is found in Chapter 5.

[90] For the history of these discoveries, see Brockopp, "*Minor Compendium*."

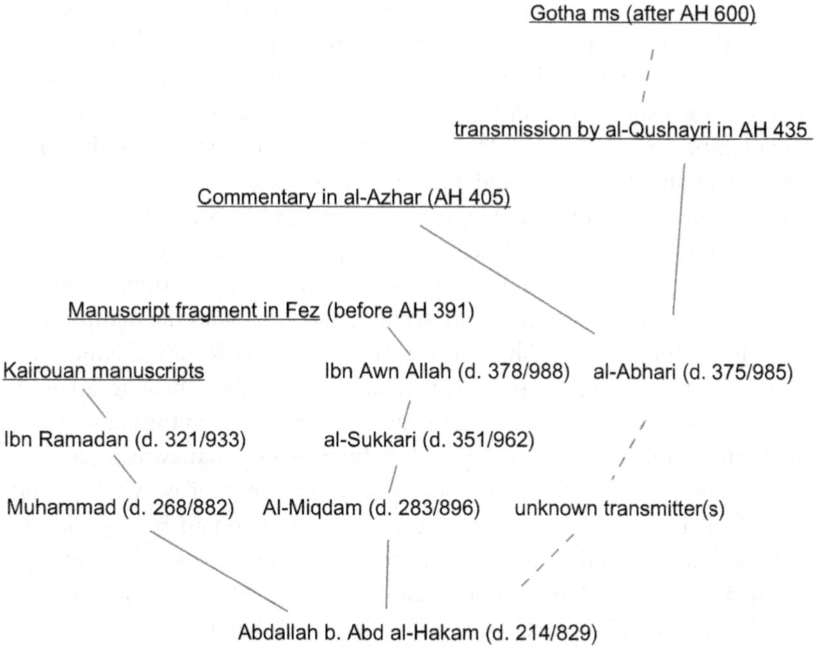

Figure 3.4: Revised transmission of the *Major Compendium*

his work by scholars in Egypt, North Africa, and Andalusia, all based on documentary evidence (illustrated in Figure 3.4).

For example, marginal notes on these manuscripts provide us with a few firm dates to begin our inquiry: according to an incipit, a Kairouan manuscript (number 1646) of the *Major Compendium* was taught by Ali b. Muhammad b. Masrur (d. 359/970) to an anonymous student in AH 355; the Fez manuscript (number 810) contains a margin note that collation and recitation (*al-muqābala wa-l-qirāʾa*) of the manuscript was completed under the tutelage of al-Faqih Abu Umar Ahmad b. Ibrahim b. Abd al-Rahman (d. 391/1000);[91] and, as stated above, the commentary on al-Abhari (Azhar 1655) was completed before 405. There is every reason to believe that all the manuscripts from Kairouan are from the fourth/tenth century, but it is possible to do much more with this rich material.

[91] This Cordoban scholar was known as Ibn al-Ḍaḥā and died in *Jumādā al-ūlā* according to ʿIyāḍ, *Tartīb*, 2:678.

The Kairouan manuscripts of Ibn Abd al-Hakam's *Major Compendium* contain the same basic transmission record: from Muhammad b. Ramadan b. Shakir (d. 321/933), who received his copy from Muhammad b. Abdallah b. Abd al-Hakam (d. 268/882), who in turn took his text from his father Abdallah b. Abd al-Hakam. This information accords well with the basic skeleton of information found in the biographical dictionaries.[92] I will return to these individuals in Chapter 5, where I address the impact of this text in Kairouan in the fourth/tenth century. My interest here, however, is, first, in proving that these manuscripts are faithful representations of a book written by Ibn Abd al-Hakam and, second, in seeing what the manuscripts can tell us about scholarship during Ibn Abd al-Hakam's lifetime and before. Given the significance of this undertaking, we must tread with caution. For example, despite the seeming accord between the claim in the literary texts and these manuscripts (that Ibn Abd al-Hakam was the author of the *Major Compendium*), we should consider another possibility: that either Muhammad b. Ramadan b. Shakir or Muhammad b. Abdallah b. Abd al-Hakam could have been the actual authors of the text, perhaps collating notes from Ibn Abd al-Hakam's lectures. Moreover, placing the composition of the *Major Compendium* before Muhammad b. Ramadan's death date (321/933) instead of a century earlier fits better with Norman Calder's linear scheme of the development of Islamic legal thought.[93] Luckily, we have three witnesses to the text that do not come from Kairouan, manuscripts now found in libraries in Fez, Cairo, and Gotha.

Already in my dissertation I laid out the stemmatic analysis that proves this early transmission,[94] though I did not then understand the full implications of my finding; I will only summarize the results here. The key piece of evidence is the fact that the Fez manuscript (written before AH 391) contains a transmission record that differs from the path found in the Kairouan manuscripts, from Ibn Awn Allah (d. 378/998) to Ahmad al-Sukkari (d. 351/962) to al-Miqdam b. Dawud (d. 283/896) to Ibn Abd al-Hakam.[95] On the one hand, comparison of the manuscripts

92 I have argued elsewhere that biographical dictionaries are trustworthy regarding names of students and relationships, but less so regarding their history of textual production. Further, that while biographies of famous individuals, such as Malik and Sahnun, lend themselves to an accretion of contradictory detail, those of lesser-known figures, such as the jurists mentioned here, were not subject to this activity.

93 Calder, *Studies*, 246.

94 Brockopp, *Early Mālikī Law*, 81–90.

95 The transmission record appears at the beginning of the several chapters. One of these records (fol. 27a) is extended to include Ibn Awn Allah at the beginning of the chain of

demonstrates important "separative errors," small scribal mistakes that demonstrate the independence of the two main branches of transmission.[96] On the other hand, comparative analysis also demonstrates that the bulk of the text matches nearly perfectly; therefore, we can say that it was transmitted faithfully along both paths, pointing to a common antecedent, a book written by Abdallah b. Abd al-Hakam in a single redaction and passed on verbatim to a community of scholars who preserved the original text.

Reevaluating Egyptian Scholarship

Miklos Muranyi called 200/815 the "magical boundary," the point at which a real change took place in Egyptian scholarship.[97] The secure dating of Ibn Abd al-Hakam's *Major Compendium* to this same period vindicates Muranyi's assessment and opens up a wealth of information about Muslim scholars in Egypt and Medina during this period. While the particular configuration of manuscript witnesses to Ibn Abd al-Hakam's *Major Compendium* is unique, it seems very unlikely that this text is a complete outlier, that it is the only true book from this period, and that no other books were written until many decades later. The very fact that Ibn Abd al-Hakam's *Compendium* fits my strict definition of a book mitigates against this possibility, since a book depends on a *community* of scholars to enforce its verbatim transmission. The systems of transmission, class sessions, and personal loyalties that effected this transmission could not have existed just for this one book. It is immediately obvious to me, for example, that the *Minor Compendium* is also a book, even though its manuscript basis is much more narrow,[98] and we might well share this designation with other texts from Egypt that have a strong internal structure.

transmission. Further, in another manuscript in Kairouan, the *Kitāb al-nawādir wa l-ziyādāt* by Ibn Abī Zayd al-Qayrawānī (d. 386/996), Ibn Abī Zayd mentions a copy of Ibn Abd al-Hakam's *Mukhtaṣar* that he used this text with a recension which went back through Muhammad b. Masrur to al-Miqdam b. Dawud (Muranyi, *Materialien*, 47). Muhammad b. Masrur is the father of Ali b. Muhammad b. Masrur who appears in the Kairaoun manuscripts as having transmitted the text from Ibn Shakir from Muhammad b. Abd al-Hakam; evidently, he brought both transmissions with him to Kairouan, and only one is preserved in manuscripts available to us today.

[96] Brockopp, *Early Mālikī Law*, 77–81, 84.

[97] Muranyi, *Rechtsbücher*, 78.

[98] Brockopp, "*Minor Compendium*," 157–161.

Even so, it is also evident that Ibn Abd al-Hakam's book is unusual in at least two ways. First, many writings from this period continue to show signs of interpolation from later scholars. That is, they continue to serve as *hypomnēnata*, not *syngrammata.* While we can prove that the apparatus existed to make books possible, only a few early texts appear to have been passed on verbatim. Ibn Abd al-Hakam's texts may have been subjected to this treatment because they served a different purpose, signaling a shift in the study of Islamic law (as Calder suggested above). Like the *Muwaṭṭa'*, and al-Majishun's book, the compendia are organized into chapters, signaling a division of law into commonly accepted categories. While it is clear that some smaller categories are still developing, such as separate chapters on different sorts of slaves,[99] there is remarkable agreement on the categories, and even the content, of Islamic law in these very earliest texts.[100]

The second way in which Ibn Abd al-Hakam's book is unusual is that it utilizes a compact, referential style; it is a second-order text, one that summarizes debating points without rehashing the debates themselves.[101] Rarely does it provide proof texts for its pronouncements. I believe that this difference in style denotes a difference in attitude toward the law. Texts such as Sahnun's *Mudawwana* reflect a pious devotion to the study of law itself, while Ibn Abd al-Hakam's *Compendia* provide a pragmatic shortcut that must have been useful to students and bureaucrats alike. Whereas the *Mudawwana* requires a living guide to help the student comprehend the text, the *Compendia* are immediately accessible as texts alone.

Finally, the very size of Ibn Abd al-Hakam's two compendia is worth mentioning. As for the *Major Compendium*, it is a significant book and probably larger than the *Muwaṭṭa'*, though it is impossible to determine precisely how large it was since we have no complete copy. It is a

[99] Brockopp, *Early Mālikī Law*, 148–150.

[100] Schoeler, *Genesis*, 4–6. Categorization is important because it is an artifice that organizes materials. As such, it signals a common language shared by scholars in various parts of the empire and suggests basic agreement on many major aspects of law. However, we have no reasonable explanation for the provenance of this scheme of categorization – there is no basis for it in the Qur'an; no precedent claimed for Muhammad and no clear evidence of borrowing from surrounding cultures. It is true that books of law broken down into categories were well attested in the region, but none of their categorization schemes can be mapped directly onto the scheme we find in Islamic legal texts. Further, while the very fact of categorization was a widespread notion, this still does not explain how one particular scheme of categorization became so commonly accepted.

[101] Brockopp, "Saḥnūn's Mudawwanah," 137–138.

significant achievement to maintain authorial control over such a long text, and this fact underscores both the sophistication of the Egyptian scholarly community and also the fact that there must have been other books that preceded it.[102] The *Minor Compendium*, however, is definitely the shortest comprehensive law book known, less than one-fifth the size of the *Muwaṭṭa*ʾ, on which it seems to be dependent.[103] The ability to reduce God's law to such a minimal text reveals an extraordinary confidence in the ability to comprehend the law long before the development of the discipline of legal theory.

SCHOLARLY COMMUNITIES AND POLITICAL POWER

In Chapter 1, I laid out two possible roles for proto-scholars based on stories about Umar and Uthman. The Umaric path exemplified by his *dīwān* successfully established a bureaucratic system for training men to serve the state as secretaries, governors, and emissaries. Its relationship to religion was entirely pragmatic, invoking its power only in the most general terms. In contrast, the Uthmanic path, represented by the compilation of the Qurʾan, would have yoked religious power to buttress political power. Its failure led to a development of private expertise in the arts of Qurʾanic commentary and of gathering the stories of the Prophet and his early Companions. We can make too much of this separation, however. Rulers also like to hear stories of past heroes and they need legal advice, so it is not surprising that one of the persistent themes of Islamic history is the proper relationship between scholarly expert and political power. Malik b. Anas is an exemplary figure in these histories, in part because of the way he is said to have resisted Abbasid attempts to use his text, the *Muwaṭṭa*ʾ, as the basis of a legal code. Malik's ruse was to prevaricate by telling the caliph that his text was not quite finished, and the evidence of this fact is plain in the many extant versions of the *Muwaṭṭa*ʾ, some of which deviate substantially from others. This

[102] I am thinking here both of the works of Ashhab b. Abd al-Aziz, who was reported to be fifteen years older than Ibn Abd al-Hakam, and also of the influence of other scholarly communities, particularly those of Iraq. In other words, I believe that the *Major Compendium* is an indirect witness to significant Iraqi books, such as the works of Muhammad al-Shaybani (who was reported to be twenty-three years older than Ibn Abd al-Hakam). For an extensive comparison of the *Major Compendium* with other early legal texts, including three texts attributed to al-Shaybani, see appendix B in Brockopp, *Early Mālikī Law*, 285–292.

[103] Brockopp, "*Minor Compendium*," 172.

story may not be entirely a fiction – it is quite reasonable for any ruler to desire a code of law, one backed not only by the coercive power of the state but also by the religious authority of the scholars – but the way Malik's solution is represented appears also to be a convenient way to explain the lack of authorial control over texts in this period.

It is no accident that this altercation between Malik and the caliph is played out through texts. As both Umar and Uthman knew, writing is power, a power that can serve the state or stand in opposition to it. It is perfectly reasonable, therefore, as Schoeler suggests, that the state would produce bureaucratic texts – grammar, history, law – for its own purposes. The fact that Ibn Abd al-Hakam produced two books in Egypt by 215/800 is further circumstantial evidence that a similar book culture existed in Iraq at that time. But Ibn Abd al-Hakam's text was not produced by the state or for it, and in that sense it is evidence of an independent basis for power. A community of scholars that can maintain the training and discipline to pass on books verbatim is a social force to be reckoned with. These forces will in fact clash head-on during the *miḥna* (inquisition) of 833–848, as I will discuss in Chapter 4.

Despite the apparent power of the Egyptian scholarly community, and the wealth of texts they left behind, most histories of pre-modern Islam continue to focus primarily on the central lands of Syria, Iraq, and Iran. This focus is reasonable, due to the political importance of these areas, yet it is also deeply problematic. First, it is far too dependent on literary texts, which have their own agendas for the selecting of information. Pre-modern authors of biographical dictionaries, for example, make clear distinctions between the "people of Kufa" and the "people of Medina," but they fold Egyptians and North Africans into the latter category, thereby effacing the independence of thought we find in the manuscripts.[104] Nor do literary histories accept any notion of development – if anything, schools are represented as a decline from the Golden Age of Jaʿfar al-Sadiq, Abu Hanifa, Malik, al-Shafiʿi, and Ibn Hanbal when our manuscripts suggest that the schools significantly expanded, developing books and sophisticated methods of transmission. Second, by mirroring this Golden Age narrative, modern surveys preserve an illusion of a far more coherent Islamic world during this period than the evidence supports. Not only were these paragons not the "founders" of legal schools,

[104] Even El Shamsy (*Canonization*, 96) falls into this trap when, after a reasonable account of Egyptian history, he represents Egypt as merely the recipient of scholarship from Medina.

they weren't necessarily its most illustrious members. The fragments of Ashhab's text reveal a keen legal mind, perhaps more sophisticated than that of either Malik or al-Shafiʿi. The variety of opinions and genres of writing preserved only in the surviving manuscripts from Egypt and North Africa is astonishing, though it is not reflected in the literary texts. Third, accounts of scholarly texts from the central lands can work only with those texts that later scholars saw fit to preserve. Without the Kairouan manuscripts, we would know almost nothing of al-Majishun or the independent works of Ibn Wahb, Ashhab, Ibn al-Qasim, and Ibn Abd al-Hakam, while Sahnun and Malik would still be well-represented.[105] We can well assume that the other legal and theological schools would look very different if we had more texts from more scholars of the early period. Finally, without these manuscripts, it would be impossible to note the interplay between oral and written texts that must have obtained throughout the Arabic-speaking world, leaving modern scholars either to become skeptics and reject all early texts as imaginative reconstructions, or to be sanguine about the ability of manuscripts written in the twelfth or thirteenth century to faithfully reproduce texts supposedly written in the eighth or ninth centuries.

[105] Note the many manuscripts of the *Mudawwana* in Damascus, for example. See Janine Sourdel-Thoumine and Dominique Sourdel, "Nouveaux documents sur l'histoire religieuse et sociale de Damas au moyen age," *Revue des Etudes Islamiques* 32 (1964), 1–25.

4

Scholarship and the Literary Turn, 820–880

In the first three chapters of this book, I have taken pains to stay very close to the material evidence as a way of correcting our reading of the much more ample literary sources. In this chapter, which covers a period two hundred years removed from the Prophet's life, material sources remain central, especially since we have five important manuscripts dated to this period. Analysis of these manuscripts gives us important insights into the communities that produced them. Yet the very fact that we have only five such manuscripts reveals, more than ever, the inadequacy of the material evidence as a direct source for the history of Muslim scholars. Archeology, numismatics, and literary evidence all point to the ninth century as a period of remarkable wealth and power; visitors to the Abbasid capital of Baghdad were awestruck by its beauty and sophistication. The lists of scholars who flourished during this period, the literary culture that they produced, and vast number of fields of academic inquiry are all justly celebrated in numerous historical texts. The fact that only five manuscripts can be confidently dated before the year 880 is evidence of the ephemeral materials on which they were written, not of a lack of activity.

The paucity of material evidence causes problems when we try to understand the precise development of scholarly communities during this period. This is particularly frustrating because the sixty-year period covered in this chapter is one that Christopher Melchert and others have highlighted as a key transitional moment for legal and theological schools.[1]

[1] Melchert uses Makdisi's three stages of regional, personal, and guild (or classical) schools (*Formation*, xxv). The period covered here, according to Melchert, sees the transition from regional to personal schools (ibid., 32 ff.).

As I demonstrated in Chapter 3, Muslim scholarly communities emerged by the year 800 and were growing in sophistication and influence. One would have hoped that material evidence would enable a fine-grained analysis of their activities that would complement analysis of the copious literary sources. Unfortunately, the five manuscripts that can be dated to this period are now located in four different libraries, two of these in Europe. Because these artifacts have been removed from their places of origin, they lack the contextual evidence that can truly inform us about the broader social impact of scholarly communities. As I will discuss below, our ability to understand who wrote these texts and why – and whether these texts were actual books or merely student notations – is extremely limited. Yet even this limited information gives us some guidance for understanding this formative period.

First, two of these earliest dated manuscripts come from Kairouan, and remarks on those manuscripts can be interpreted within the context of a much larger collection. Again, of our thirty Arabic literary manuscripts dated before AH 300 (excluding Qurʾans and Christian texts), twenty-three come from Kairouan. This extraordinary concentration of manuscripts from a single location allows us to see in detail precisely how a scholarly community was built and how it functioned. I will devote Chapter 5 to a close examination of this community, but the Kairouan manuscripts provide us with a clear indication of how a "writerly culture"[2] helped to establish scholarly communities as nodes of independent power. If such a community of scholars existed in the small provincial outpost of Kairouan by the year 850, we should feel confident about literary accounts of more sophisticated communities established earlier in Cordoba, Fustat, Medina, Damascus, Kufa, Baghdad, and other major centers.

A second guidepost is provided by the new ways that writing is being used in these emerging scholarly communities. In Chapter 3, I argued that a unique array of manuscripts allowed us to identify Ibn Abd al-Hakam's *Major Compendim* as a book written before 800 CE Every indication is that the *Minor Compendium* is also a book, perhaps composed even earlier. These books demonstrate that the late eighth century in Egypt was a time of intellectual ferment, and they lend credence to claims that other innovative texts from Egypt, including the *Risāla* by

[2] I borrow this terms from Shawkat M. Toorawa, *Ibn Abī Ṭāhir Ṭayfūr and Arabic Writerly Culture: A Ninth-Century Bookman in Baghdad*, RoutledgeCurzon Studies in Arabic and Middle-Eastern Literatures 7 (London: RoutledgeCurzon, 2005).

al-Shafiʿi (d. 204/820) and the writings of Ashhab b. Abd al-Aziz (d. 204/820), were actually composed by their putative authors, though we cannot rule out later emendations by students. From a broader perspective, the existence of these books demonstrates both an increasing devotion to the authority of exemplary scholars from the past, whose words must be transmitted verbatim, and also new, highly disciplined methods of training students to reproduce these books.[3] While not supported by the same manuscript evidence, it is reasonable to speculate that Iraq was ahead of this Egyptian-Medinan developmental curve, and that texts attributed to Abu Yusuf (d. 182/798), al-Shaybani (d. 189/805), and others could also have been books. In fact, the innovative use of books in Iraq may have influenced developments in Egypt, because this new technology allowed authority to be transportable. The five manuscripts dated to this period contain clear evidence that, already in the early Abbasid period, scholars from across the region are becoming organized into interlinked communities, centers of authority, independent from government structures.

The material evidence that is the focus of this chapter must therefore be seen within a writerly culture. While oral instruction remains at the heart of scholarly formation, texts allowed the paragons of the past, such as Abu Yusuf, Malik, and al-Shafiʿi, to be transported from their limited time and space to inhabit new places and times. The development of a writerly culture effected a transition between an oral culture dependent on personal relationships to a written one where books, with their carefully controlled transmission of information, allowed for direct access to the *imāms*, the exemplars of the scholarly ideal. Already, in Chapter 3, we saw a story in which the authority of Malik b. Anas extended to areas of etiquette, but the farther these exemplars retreated to the distant past, the greater their accomplishments seemed to become with Malik appearing in dreams, al-Shafiʿi foretelling the future from his deathbed, and Ibn Hanbal performing miracles.[4]

The authority of the scholarly expert, I would argue, rises alongside the proliferation of books, whether in the fields of law, grammar, or medicine. One of the motivations for a book, as opposed to simple class notes,

[3] What cannot be determined, however, is that these communities have yet developed a definite program of study such as the one that Melchert associates with Ibn Surayj (d. 306/918) in his discussion of the earliest "classical" school, that of the Shafiʿis (*Formation*, 87–115).

[4] Brockopp, "Theorizing Charismatic Authority," 144–145; Cooperson, *Classical Arabic Biography*, 145.

is to preserve the author's words verbatim, presumably because the author of those words has greater authority than any subsequent teacher.[5] With classroom notes, it is the present, living teacher who has the greatest authority, but with books, the teacher's authority pales in comparison with that of the author. This phenomenon is most clearly seen with the intact transmission of the Qur'an; regarded as God's own speech, it was carefully preserved. All may recite it and comment on it, but no one may reach God's authority. The shift to book culture, then, has many implications,[6] but one is a hierarchy of elite knowledge. At first, the expert who teaches the Qur'an to others is merely a conduit to divine works. As knowledge accumulates, however, greater expertise is required to unlock the full meaning of the sacred text. Eventually, Muhammad b. Idris al-Shafi'i would describe knowledge in three categories: that required of the general public, that found among specialists, and that which only a chosen few can attain:

> Al-Shāfiʿī said: Someone asked me: "What is knowledge? What knowledge is incumbent on people?" Knowledge is of two kinds, I replied: knowledge of the general public, which any person who has reached his majority and who is of sound mind may not ignore. "Like what?" he asked. Like the five prayers, I replied … That category of knowledge in its entirety is found in explicit texts in the Book of God and is widely extant among the adherents of Islam …
>
> "What," he asked, "is the second kind?" It is the subsidiary obligations that apply to God's servants, I replied, and the particular rulings among them, and other things for which there is no explicit scriptural prooftext …
>
> There is indeed a third aspect, I replied. "Describe it for me, then," he said, "and cite the authority for it, what is binding, who is bound, and who is not bound thereby." This is a level of knowledge to which the general public does not have access, I said, nor have all of those specially concerned with it been charged with it. As for those specially concerned with it who are able to have access to it, it is not possible for all of them, as a whole, to let it lapse.[7]

[5] My interest here is on the social meaning of books. But there are other ways to look at the effect of this technology on the teaching of Islamic law. For example, Ahmed El Shamsy argues that al-Shafi'i uses writing to convey the notion of a scholar as "autonomous interpreter of canonized scripture" who "could only speak for himself" (El Shamsy, *Canonization*, 147). I remain skeptical of arguments from the intention of authors, but I do agree that al-Shafi'i's way of looking at law was defined by a writerly culture.

[6] As Asma Afsaruddin pointed out to me in a private communication (December 2015), this shift may have also resulted in the near erasure of female scholars from the historical record. See now Asma Sayeed, *Women and the Transmission of Religious Knowledge in Islam*, Cambridge Studies in Islamic Civilization (Cambridge: Cambridge University Press, 2015).

[7] Muḥammad ibn Idrīs al-Shāfiʿī, *The Epistle on Legal Theory*, Joseph E. Lowry (ed. and trans.) (New York: New York University Press, 2013), 259–261. See also al-Shāfiʿī,

Here al-Shafi'i provides a framework that explains why the judgments of scholars should carry weight, and there is every reason to believe that al-Shafi'i's words reflect scholarly views during this period.[8] To be sure, he argues that all Muslims must have some basic knowledge, including the times of prayers and those things that are forbidden or required of all Muslims. But knowledge of "subsidiary obligations" and "particular rulings" requires a specialist to explain, someone who has devoted time to studying the sacred texts and their interpretation. Still, this form of authority is derivative of the sources; anyone who could read should be able to obtain this level. That is why al-Shafi'i's third level is so interesting; he tells us that "the general public does not have access ... nor have all of those specially concerned with it been charged with it."[9] This rank of scholars, beyond that of common religious specialists, has the "prophetic inheritance" mentioned in *ḥadīth*, and al-Shafi'i compares them to warriors in the jihad who gain heavenly rewards for their efforts.[10]

MUHAMMAD'S HEIRS – ON THE MEANING OF KNOWLEDGE

In the introduction to this book, I offered a definition of religious knowledge as an intrinsic personal quality, a social phenomenon with tangible effects, and also a divine gift. With al-Shafi'i's definition, we can finally see this third aspect coming in to play. Up to now, we have noted the rise of individual specialists, experts on religious knowledge, and especially

al-Risāla, Aḥmad Shākir (ed.), second printing (Cairo: [n.p.], 1979, 357–360; Majid Khadduri, *Islamic Jurisprudence: Shafi'i's Risala* (Baltimore: Johns Hopkins University Press, 1961), 82–83. Khadduri's translation is still worth consulting, but is superseded in every way by Lowry's work.

8 In dating the *Risāla*, I follow Joseph Lowry ("The Legal Hermeneutics of al-Shāfi'ī and Ibn Qutayba: A Reconsideration," *Islamic Law and Society* 11, no. 1 [2004], 1–41, at 2–3) against Melchert (*Formation*, 68) who largely follows Calder's reasoning, though he has more recently moderated his position. Part of the problem, I believe, is that Melchert reads the *Risāla* as a founding document of the classical (guild) school of law, while I see there strong arguments for the personal schools. As Lowry points out, al-Shafi'i organizes the *Risāla* around the notion of *bayān*, not around a four-source theory of Islamic law (Lowry, *Early Islamic Legal Theory*, 23).

9 Al-Shāfi'ī, *al-Risāla* (ed. Shākir), 360 (trans. Lowry, 261).

10 On p. 361 of the *Risāla* (ed. Shākir), al-Shafi'i describes the support of scholars as a collective duty, incumbent on all the community, just as supporting warfare is a collective, not an individual duty. For an analysis of the connection in the literary sources between the *'ālim* and the *mujāhid*, see Houari Touati, *Islam and Travel in the Middle Ages*, trans. Lydia Cochrane (Chicago: University of Chicago Press), 201–220. My thanks to Elizabeth Lambourn for this reference.

pious individuals. We have also noted that the line between those individuals and the authority of other major religious traditions (especially Judaism and Christianity) was fuzzy at best. By the end of the second Islamic century, however, scholars are no longer isolated individuals but joined together in interconnected communities that coalesce around texts; the first books appear. Al-Shafiʿi's discussion above perfectly captures this changing culture, where scholars begin to see themselves as an elite class, akin to soldiers; they form a vital part of the emerging Islamic polity.

The notion that these scholars are recipients of a divine gift is an essential source of their social authority; however, this idea emerges slowly and unevenly during the period covered in this chapter. It occurs as the lines between religious traditions are becoming clearer and as Islam itself gains a history. As I will discuss below, the five surviving manuscripts from this period help to track this shift. The *History of King David* by Wahb b. Munabbih is attached to a story from Muhammad's life, and so we see the emergence of Muhammad in the mold of a biblical prophet/king, still dependent on the history of Judaism. At the same time, scholars such as Sahnun and Abu Dawud are writing texts that focus on the authority of single scholars (Malik and Ibn Hanbal, respectively) whose interpretation of law and theology is held to be exemplary. This, I argue, is the beginning of a turn toward divinely ordained charismatic authority. In the mind of later generations, Malik and Ibn Hanbal were not merely devoted scholars, they were the heirs of the prophets. With this inheritance, Islam supplants and supersedes the traditions from which it emerged.

Only when this connection is well-established does the Prophetic *ḥadīth* that forms the central organizing theme of this book seem to apply to Muslim scholars exclusively, even though this longer version, found in the collection of Ibn Maja, could easily refer to scholars of other religions:

Nasr b. Ali al-Jahdhami related to us that Abdallah b. Dawud related to him on the authority of Asim b. Raja b. Haywa on the authority of Dawud b. Jamil on the authority of Kathir b. Qais, who said:

I was studying with Abu l-Darda in the mosque of Damascus when a man came up to him and said: "O Abu l-Darda, I have come to you from Medina, the city of God's messenger (God's blessing and peace be upon him), about a *ḥadīth* which, I understand, you narrated from the Prophet (God's blessing and peace be upon him)." [Abu l-Darda] responded: "Did you not come [to Damascus] for commerce?" He said: "No." [Abu l-Darda] said: "Did you not come for anything else?" He said: "No." [Abu l-Darda] replied: "I certainly heard God's messenger (God's blessing and peace be upon him) say: "Whoever follows a path in the pursuit of knowledge, God will smooth his path to Paradise. The angels lower their wings in approval of the seeker of knowledge (*ṭālib al-ʿilm*), and all who are in the heavens and on earth pray for forgiveness for the seeker of knowledge, even the fish in the sea. The superiority of the scholar over the [average] worshipper is like the superiority of the moon above the planets. The scholars are the heirs of the prophets, for the prophets passed on neither dinars nor dirhams, rather they passed on knowledge, so whoever takes it has inherited a bountiful share."[11]

Whereas al-Shafiʿi clearly understands religious knowledge to arise from the Qurʾan and the *Sunna* of Muhammad, this *ḥadīth* is not so obvious, yet both texts understand knowledge to be a divine gift with tangible consequences. What may seem like a simple differentiation of tasks in al-Shafiʿi's discussion of knowledge, then, is revealed to be much more, due in part to the use of coded language. In the quotation above, Lowry translates al-Shafiʿi's use of the word *khāṣṣ* as "those specially concerned with [law]" and the *ʿāmm* as the "general public." But these terms can also be read as referring to the elect and the masses, a sense far more congruent with Abu l-Darda's *ḥadīth* and with the growing influence of the *ʿulamāʾ*.

Aligning the scholars with the prophets is a claim to authority. While others control riches and armies, the scholars alone control God-given knowledge. This ethereal power has implications far beyond the simple teaching of law and theology. As noted above, writing is a form of power; it gives scholars a source of authority independent from that of court and caliphate. A clash of these two forms of authority occurred during the early ninth century in the famous "inquisition" (*miḥna*) in which scholars were marched before the political authorities and questioned about their beliefs. Much has been written about the inquisition, which was carried out to varying degrees throughout the Islamic world of the time.[12] What interests me here, however, are two aspects. First, the very fact that the inquisition occurred, and that the scholars won, suggests to me that the scholarly community had grown powerful enough to be a threat to the administration.[13] Also, surviving the *miḥna* would have created a kind of

[11] Muḥammad b. Yazīd Ibn Māja, *Sunan Ibn Māja*, 5 vols. (Lahore: Kazi Publications, 1993–1996), *kitāb al-muqaddama*, *ḥadīth*, 228; Gilliot, "ʿUlamāʾ," 10:801; Wensinck; *Concordance*, 4:321.

[12] Our understanding of this event is colored by highly polemical sources that exaggerate the role of some individuals, such as Ibn Hanbal; see Christopher Melchert, "The Adversaries of Aḥmad Ibn Ḥanbal" *Arabica* 44 (1997), 234–253; Nimrod Hurvitz, "Miḥna as Self-Defense" *Studia Islamica* 92 (2001), 93–111; idem, *Formation of Hanbalism: Piety into Power* (London: RoutledgeCurzon, 2002), 115–157. Here, I am less interested in the actual history of these trials than I am in their reception by later historians.

[13] Zaman, *Religion and Politics*, 108.

group solidarity, such that resistance to political authority would become a trope within scholarly biographies. This leads to the second aspect: the process by which heroes of the inquisition, such as Ahmad b. Hanbal (d. 241/855), are seen as being the recipients of divine favor.[14] This process was integrally connected to the stories that disciples collected and passed on about these heroes, stories that became embellished over time. There is no better example of this process than in the story of Ibn Hanbal's flogging.

The full story is long and complicated; Ibn Hanbal comes across as a stubborn man, unwilling to argue except on his own terms. Finally, the caliph delivers on his threat to flog him; al-Maqrizi (d. 845/1442) records the scene in the words of one of Ibn Hanbal's devotees:

> At the twenty-ninth stroke, the waistband of his trousers at the edge of the cloth was cut, and the trousers fell to his privates. I said: Now he is disgraced! But Abu Abdallah [Ahmad b. Hanbal] fixed his gaze on heaven and moved his lips, and I cannot say how, but his trousers remained [up] and did not fall.
>
> Maymun [continued]: I visited Abu Abdallah seven days after [his flogging] and asked him: Oh, Abu Abdallah, I saw on the day that they beat you that your trousers had loosened, and that you raised your eyes to heaven; I saw you move your lips: what did you say? He replied: I said: Oh God! Surely I ask you for the sake of your name with which the Throne is filled, if You know that I am in the right, do not disgrace me by [letting my] cover [fall].[15]

This story of Ahmad b. Hanbal has been retold throughout the centuries; by the time of this version by al-Maqrizi we have definitely reached the point when scholars are raised above the level of ordinary human beings and regarded as heroic figures,[16] exemplary individuals who make the boundaries between good and evil clear to others. This remarkable tale is the culmination of Ibn Hanbal's trial; earlier in al-Maqrizi's

[14] Hurvitz, *Formation*, 159–163, argues that it was simply the strength of Ibn Hanbal's ideas and personality that caused him to be so influential. However that may be, one should not ignore the role of the biographers in selecting and enhancing these qualities. See Cooperson, *Classical Arabic Biography*, 107–153.

[15] Walter Melville Patton, *Aḥmed ibn Ḥanbal and the Miḥna* (Leiden: E. J. Brill, 1897), 109–110. This is my translation from one of Patton's extensive quotations from the Arabic sources. It reflects the consensus of the later sources that Ibn Hanbal was a saint and that he founded the Hanbali school; in Patton's words (p. 4) due to his "intense devotion to the things most venerated and cherished by the people: God, the Prophet, the Ḳorân, the Tradition, the Sunna of the Prophet, and the Communion of the Faithful, endeared him to the mass of the common folk." Another version of the story has a golden hand appear to repair the trouserband.

[16] Cooperson, *Classical Arabic Biography*, 133–134, draws similar conclusions from an earlier (and less elaborate) version of the story by Abu Nuʿaym al-Isfahani (d. 430/1038).

version, Ibn Hanbal makes the Muslim confession of faith and points the caliph to a *ḥadīth* of the Prophet that the life and property of a Muslim are inviolable. With this action and throughout the trial, Ibn Hanbal clarifies the ideal role for the scholar as a counterweight to political authority. Moreover, like Muhammad, legal scholars gather a community of followers who remember their actions and recount exemplary tales. While the story here was recalled centuries later, it fits in well with the prophetic *ḥadīth* and al-Shafiʿi's division of knowledge. A hallmark of this new writerly culture, then, is an increase in myth-making. While books provide the technology for passing words on verbatim, myths provide the justification for the preservation of the words of particular scholars. Moreover, as early scholars are noted for their quasi-miraculous achievements, even appearing in the dreams of pious scholars from later generations, their personal authority rested uneasily alongside that of Qurʾanic norms, Muhammad's practices, and local custom.[17] Again, our five earliest manuscripts demonstrate this variety, as each seems to depend on a very different notion of religious authority.

THE EARLIEST DATED SCHOLARLY PRODUCTIONS, 844–880

Ibn Abd al-Hakam's *Major* and *Minor Compendia* give us a unique insight into the scholarly world of Egypt before the year 800. However, the manuscripts that preserve those texts, that is, the actual material artifacts, date from a century afterward and even later. In contrast, the manuscripts under consideration here are the only ones we currently know to have been produced in the mid-ninth century.[18] The five texts preserved in these earliest manuscripts provide us with a remarkable, if accidental, overview of Muslim scholarship in this century, and most of these texts have received sustained, if not exhaustive, attention in the

[17] Abū Muṣʿab, *Mukhtaṣar*, Fās, Qarawiyyīn 874, fol. 2b. See also Malik's letter to al-Layth b. Saʿd (Robert Brunschvig, "Polémiques médiéval autour du rite de Malik," *al-Andalus* 15 [1950], 377–435).

[18] Again, I am excluding Qurʾans (several fragments are dated from before 880) and also Christian texts, of which there are four: a fragment of the *Gospel of John*, a collection of letters and acts of the apostles, a *Life of the Martyrs*, and a theological treatise. See Déroche, "Manuscrits," 343–379. Also, the high bar that I am using for dating manuscripts eliminates the undated papyrus fragments that Abbott believes belong to the ninth century (Abbott, *Studies*); the existence of these other manuscripts, however, only reinforces my point about the extensive writerly culture of this period.

secondary literature. So far as I know, however, these five texts have never been analyzed together as the material remains of a scholarly process, and I believe that this evidence provides us with three important implications for the rise of the Muslim scholar. First, none of these texts is clearly a book, and some have been proven to have undergone significant changes after the death of their putative authors. Just because books existed does not mean that they were widespread, or that they supplanted the most common use of writing as an adjunct to oral teaching methods. Second, these texts all show evidence of being in conversation with other forms of writing; they are in a sense commentaries on earlier texts and perhaps the earliest stages in canonizing texts and their authors. Together they can provide important insights on the stages of scholarly development. Third, these texts demonstrate the ways that writing causes knowledge to be transportable, offering us an insight into the linking of travel with scholarship.[19]

The five earliest manuscripts are Wahb b. Munabbih's *History of King David* (dated *Dhū al-Qaʿda* 229/July–August 844); Sahnun's *Mudawwana* (several third/ninth century manuscripts [see the Appendix], the earliest is 235/849–850); *Gharīb al-Ḥadīth* by al-Baghdadi (d. 223/838) (dated 252/886); Yahya b. Sallam al-Basri's (d. 200/815) *Tafsīr al-Qurʾān* (before 260/873–874); and the *Masāʾil ibn Ḥanbal*, collected by Abu Dawud (d. 275/889) (manuscript dated 266/880). Together, these manuscripts represent disciplines of history, jurisprudence, *ḥadīth*, and Qurʾan scholarship. They also represent a wide variety of manuscript production, in terms of both materials (three on parchment, one on papyrus, and one on paper) and quality. Before discussing these manuscripts in detail, it is worth noting that I am excluding two others that may also date from this period. The first of these is a fascinating scrap of paper that contains the oldest fragment of the *Thousand Nights* (later called the *Thousand and One Nights*) that we possess; it is also the oldest example of *belles lettres* in Arabic, but its dating is controversial.[20] Apparently, it was used as scrap by a notary, who practiced writing the date "Ṣafar 266" (October 879) on it several times. Nabia Abbott argued that by the time that the notary wrote these lines, the manuscript must have already been old; François Déroche, in contrast, does not accept this as a definitive dating,

[19] See discussion in the last section of this chapter and in Chapter 5.

[20] Nabia Abbott, "A Ninth-Century Fragment of the 'Thousand Nights.' New Light on the Early History of the Arabian Nights," *Journal of Near Eastern Studies* 8, no. 3 (1949), 129–164.

but does not exclude a third century origin.[21] I agree with Déroche that without context, we do not know what to make of the scribe's actions. But I also remain uncertain as to whether this literary work can give us much insight into Muslim scholarly communities during this period; therefore, I exclude it from consideration.

The second questionable manuscript is of a different order altogether; it is a substantial fragment of al-Shafiʿi's *Risāla* that has been thought to date to AH 265.[22] In fact, Déroche writes "avant 265."[23] I am at a loss, however, in attempting to understand his reasoning. Déroche cites only Bernhard Moritz, who himself actually argued for a fourth-century date.[24] Though Déroche does not cite the editor of this fragment, Ahmad Shakir, Shakir responded to Moritz, claiming that this manuscript was a copy belonging to al-Rabi, one of al-Shafiʿi's most illustrious students, and so dated it before his death in 270/844.[25] The secondary literature I know of does not provide any new information on this dating controversy,[26] so it seems that Déroche has uncharacteristically repeated Shakir's date, even though he is normally skeptical of this type of reasoning.

This famous treatise on jurisprudential theory presents a mélange of styles and content; it has been widely discussed and analyzed.[27] In his recent translation, Joseph Lowry gives preference to Shakir's edition in his own reading of the text, arguing quite reasonably that this is one of the earliest and most important manuscripts of Muslim jurisprudence. More interesting for our purposes, Lowry addresses the question as to whether the *Risāla* (or, as he calls it, the *Epistle*) is a book, arguing that

[21] Déroche, "Manuscrits," 351.

[22] Cairo, Dār al-Kutub, *uṣūl al-fiqh* 41 (paper, 62 fol.).

[23] Déroche, "Manuscrits," 346.

[24] Bernhard Moritz, *Arabic Paleography* (Cairo: Khedivial Library, 1905), plates 117–118.

[25] Al-Shāfiʿī, *al-Risāla*, Shākir (ed.), 22–23.

[26] See Khadduri (trans.), *Al-Shāfiʿī's Risāla*, 48–51; Ahmed El Shamsy, review of *Early Islamic Legal Theory: The Risāla of Muḥammad ibn Idrīs al-Shāfiʿī* by Joseph E. Lowry in *Journal of the American Oriental Society* 128, no. 1 (Jan.–Mar. 2008), 185–186, at 186. Lowry addresses some of these issues in the introduction to his 2013 translation of the *Risāla* (*Epistle on Legal Theory*), xxxi.

[27] See, for examples, Joseph Schacht, *The Origins of Muhammadan Jurisprudence* (Oxford: Clarendon, 1950); Norman Calder, "Ikhtilāf and Ijmāʿ in Shāfiʿī's Risāla," *Studia Islamica* 58 (1983), 55–81; Nasr Hamid Abu Zayd, *al-Imām al-Shāfiʿī wa-taʾsīs al-aydiyūlūjiyya al-wasaṭiyya* (Cairo: Sīnā li-l-Nashr, 1992); Wael Hallaq, "Was al-Shafii the Master Architect of Islamic Jurisprudence?" *International Journal of Middle East Studies* 25 (1993), 587–605; idem, *Origins*, 114–119.

> although the *Epistle* may not exhibit all the features of the kinds of integral texts that were produced by those authors who wrote later in the third/ninth centuries, its content exhibits a high degree of coherence and its form a discernible deliberateness and clear relationship to that content . . . the *Epistle* comes close to being a *syngramma* . . . but because the *Epistle* was likely intended for a restricted audience of students, it remains 'literature of the school.'[28]

Lowry therefore follows Schoeler in speculating on intent as a hallmark of the *syngramma.* I agree that the *Risāla* is not a book (though it is very close), but I disagree as to why. Rather than look at intent, I argue that the *Risāla* has significant structural inconsistencies that demonstrate that it was not constructed in a single redactional effort. It certainly is possible that al-Shafiʿi himself combined disparate pieces into a whole, or this compilation could be the work of a student.[29] The ascription of these ground-breaking ideas to al-Shafiʿi, however, seems reasonable to me, despite remaining questions about the date when this manuscript was produced. I have greater confidence, however, in the dating of the other five manuscripts.

The Manuscript Basis of Wahb's *History of King David*

As discussed in previous chapters, Wahb b. Munabbih's *History of King David* is a unique papyrus manuscript, currently located in Heidelberg (see Figure 2.5). This heavily damaged document is made up of fifty folios, approximately 20 cm high by 25 cm wide.[30] The manuscript came to Heidelberg along a path that is all too familiar in the history of Muslim artifacts. The collection is known as the Schott-Reinhardt collection after a Swabian industrialist Friedrich Schott (who made his money in cement) and a Bavarian orientalist-adventurer, Carl Reinhardt, who worked at one time as a "dragoman" for the German embassy in Cairo.[31] Reinhardt arranged for Schott to purchase more than a thousand papyrus pieces in the early twentieth century, forming the foundation of Heidelberg University's collection. The origin of many of these fragments is unknown.

[28] Lowry, *Epistle on Legal Theory*, xxix. He makes here a note to Schoeler, *Genesis*, 21, 76.

[29] El Shamsy gives a fine overview of al-Shafiʿi's writing styles (*Canonization*, 149–154), though he is rather sanguine in ascribing authorship to al-Shafiʿi for all these texts.

[30] Khoury, *Wahb b. Munabbih*. The catalog has been digitized; see http://zaw-papy.zaw.uni-heidelberg.de/fmi/xsl/Arabisch/home.xsl. I was able to examine this manuscript personally in June 2015. This is number 2 in Déroche, "Manuscrits," 345.

[31] Khoury, "Les papyrus arabes de Heidelberg disparus. Essai de reconstruction et d'analyse," in Alexander T. Schubert and Petra Sijpesteijn (eds.), *Documents and the History of the Early Islamic World* (Boston: Brill Academic Publishers, 2014), 249.

This manuscript (PSR Heid. Inv. Arab. 23) actually contains two texts, a fragment from the Life of Muhammad (twenty-one folios) and the History of King David (twenty-nine folios), though a date only appears on the latter and reasonably the editor (Raif Georges Khoury) conservatively limits the date to the one fragment. Khoury is also at a loss to explain the provenance of the date, which appears in a different hand and is not a typical reader's remark (*samāʿ*), nor an explanatory note from the scribe. The fact that the fragment has neither incipit nor colophon, however, suggests to me that the date may have been copied there from one of these pages by a librarian when the colophon or incipit was disintegrating.[32] In my earlier discussion of this text in Chapter 2, I referred to the difficulty of determining just who the author is, when it was composed, and whether the text was subjected to a disciplined transmission process. Likewise, with this manuscript, we cannot be certain that what we have here is an actual book, composed and passed on intact. However, we can treat this manuscript as an artifact from the year 229/844 and make several observations about scholarship in that period.

First, the scholar who wrote out *History of King David* is clearly in conversation with other texts. The Qurʾan is quoted at several occasions, and the author appears to be familiar with texts from the Hebrew Scriptures.[33] Certain stories found in the *History* also have parallels in the *Midrash Shmuel* as well as writings attributed to Ibn Ishaq.[34] While we may rightfully speculate about the status of these texts as actual books or simply notes from lectures, the *History* is participating in a writerly culture, where texts from a wide variety of sources are being woven together into new forms. The *History* is also a manifestly religious text, citing the hand of God in working through history to effect his will. That said, the text also demonstrates the fuzzy boundaries among the various religious traditions of the period; still in the early third/mid-ninth century, texts from other traditions may be drawn upon to elucidate the Qurʾan's messages. We may surmise, therefore, that Jewish and Christian scholarly

[32] With the help of Fr. Fuchs, a technician at the Heidelberg Papyrus Institute, I was able to determine that the *History of King David* was bound *behind* the *Life of Muhammad.* Therefore, this date actually appears in the middle of the manuscript. This may not, of course, reflect the original order of the texts, only the one that obtained when the worms did their damage.

[33] Nabia Abbott in her review, *Journal of Near Eastern Studies* 36, no. 2 (Apr. 1977), 103–112, at 105.

[34] Newby, *Making of the Last Prophet*, 157–158.

communities continued to have an impact on emerging scholars from the Islamic world at this time.

The most important lesson to be gleaned from this text, however, is the role of history as a key scholarly discipline. We have some sense of the size of this field from Ibn al-Nadim's catalogue (*fihrist*) of books from the year 377/987, in which he recorded hundreds of history texts that he had seen or heard of.[35] Fuat Sezgin, in his monumental *Geschichte des arabischen Schrifttums*, builds on this and other lists, adding information on extant manuscripts, where available. He separates history writing into several subcategories, recording nineteen texts on Muhammad's life and early battles in the Umayyad period, and dozens more in the early Abbasid period.[36] While these lists cannot be taken as accurate representations of actual scholarly production in this period, they underline the fact that, along with Jewish and Christian scriptures, the Qur'an shares the conviction that God works within history; therefore, the study of history, like the study of nature, can provide insights into the lessons that God has for humankind. The Qur'an makes this assertion many times.[37] It is worth emphasizing, however, that Wahb's text, like the Qur'an, suggests a shared monotheistic history, rather than a uniquely Islamic history, and this may be reason to place its composition earlier than 229/844. However, the copying of this text in the third/ninth century suggests that its perception of history was still in vogue. In our next manuscript, we can start to see the creation of a uniquely Islamic history, a necessary part of establishing Islam as an independent religious tradition.

Sahnun's *Mudawwana*, a Well-Attested Text

The next oldest manuscript is an ancient fragment of Sahnun's *Mudawwana*, the oldest dated manuscript in the Kairouan collection.[38] Like most

[35] Ibn al-Nadīm, *Kitāb al-Fihrist*, Gustav Flügel (ed.), 2 vols. (Leipzig: Vogel, 1872). He makes no mention of this or any other book by Wahb, however. I quote from the standard edition, though mention should be made of a new edition by Ayman Fu'ad Sayyid, 4 vols. (London: Al-Furqan Islamic Heritage Foundation, 2009).

[36] Sezgin, *Geschichte*, 1:275–302. Other categories include the history of pre-Islamic Arabs, world history, local history, and cultural history (ibid., 1:235–370).

[37] Franz Rosenthal, "History and the Qur'ān," in *Encyclopaedia of the Qur'ān*.

[38] As mentioned in Chapter 3, I have seen this fragment and provide an analysis in "Saḥnūn's *Mudawwana*." Like all Kairouan manuscripts, it has no proper catalog number; but this fragment does not even have a serial (*rutbī*) number; rather, it is located with dozens of other loose parchment pages in folder (*milaff*) number 69. This manuscript was unknown to Déroche, "Manuscrits."

of the recent finds from Kairouan, this manuscript is not mentioned in Sezgin's chapter on jurisprudence, which must be completely rewritten regarding the Maliki school.[39] Sezgin does list numerous manuscripts of the *Mudawwana*, however, in contrast to Ibn al-Nadim, who makes no mention of Sahnun's text, even though his chapter on Maliki jurisprudence is quite extensive. This tells us both of the limitations of Ibn al-Nadim's catalogue (which contains no mention of many texts from North Africa and Andalusia, though Ibn al-Nadim was aware of his own contemporary Ibn Abi Zayd al-Qayrawani[40]) and also of the limited reach of the *Mudawwana* in the tenth century; today it is regarded as the most important Maliki text to arise from North Africa, and it was subject to centuries of continuous study.[41]

In many ways, this fragment could not be more different from the manuscript of Wahb's *History*, and it thereby offers an important marker of both specialization and differentiation in the scholarly world of the mid-third/ninth century. To begin, the *Mudawwana* fragment is on parchment, not papyrus. Also, in contrast to Wahb's *History*, we have numerous ancient manuscripts of this text. While this oldest dated fragment comprises only one folio, many more dated manuscripts of Sahnun's *Mudawwana* are found in Kairouan (the oldest fragments have readers' remarks from AH 256, 258, 279, and 294; see the Appendix), and there are many undated fragments as well.[42] The large number of manuscripts bear witness to an intense study, as well as to sophisticated attempts to

[39] Brockopp, "Re-reading the History of Early Mālikī Jurisprudence," *Journal of the American Oriental Society* 118 (1998), 233–238.

[40] Ibn al-Nadim, *Fihrist*, 201.

[41] Wesley Thiessen, *The Formation of the Mudawwana*. Ph.D. dissertation, University of Victoria (2014).

[42] There is no catalogue of the Kairouan manuscripts; the most important overview of the manuscripts pertaining to Sahnun is Miklos Muranyi, *Rechtsbücher*; on p. 18, he states that the oldest dated colophon is from 256/869 with a secondary remark from 292/904, but now, of course, this is superseded by the remark from 235. Muranyi does not include catalogue numbers because of his distrust of the organizational system in Raqqada, but I have seen the AH 256 manuscript (listed as number 38; see Sezgin, *Geschichte*, 1:469) and also number 1/1786, dated AH 258 (see the Appendix). For Muranyi's other comments on Kairouan manuscripts of Sahnun's *Mudawwana*, see also idem, "„man ḥalafa 'alā minbarī āṯiman ...": Bemerkungen zu einem frühen Traditionsgut," *Die Welt des Orients* 18 (1987), 92–131, at 94–95; idem, *Materialien*, 3–4; and idem, *Beiträge*, 33–39; on p. 79, Muranyi describes a small fragment that he argues must be dated before 276.

Before Muranyi, two undated *kurrāsas* (twelve and eighteen folios) of the *Mudawwana* were identified by Schacht in "On Some Manuscripts," 242. See also Sezgin, *Geschichte*, 1:469. To this work we may now add the analysis of Thiessen (*Formation of the*

collate what can only be called a critical edition in the early eleventh century by Ali b. Muhammad al-Qabisi (d. 403/1012).[43]

The *Mudawwana* distinguishes itself further from Wahb's *History* in its literary qualities. While both the *History of King David* and the *Life of the Prophet* are narratives, the *Mudawwana* is focused on Islamic law. Even so, it is an odd text, one that represents law more as the site of devotional meditation than as a practical tool for meting out justice.[44] As such, it has far more in common with Jewish texts such as the Talmud than it does with Ibn Abd al-Hakam's *Compendia*. The text is organized according to familiar chapters of jurisprudence, however, incorporating several genres of legal drafting, including the question and answer form (*masāʾil*), listings of relevant *ḥadīth*, and paragraphs without any attribution to authority.

Short as this fragment is, it has much to teach us. First, two student notations are still legible at the bottom of the page (the end of the chapter on pilgrimage): "I heard this from Sahnun ... the original and Saʿid b. Muhammad b. Rashid heard it," and then on the next line: "I heard this from Sahnun, reciting it back to him, in the year 235." This second remark was written five years before Sahnun's death, making this unique among these earliest literary manuscripts as it was written within the lifetime of the author. Earlier speculation by Norman Calder suggested that the *Mudawwana* was actually compiled in AH 250, a date that I have called both too early and too late.[45] It is too early because Miklos Muranyi and Wesley Thiessen have demonstrated that the process of compilation continued well into the eleventh century, with some additional work thereafter. But it is too late because this manuscript is very closely, although not perfectly, aligned with those later versions.

The student remarks on the bottom of the page also highlight another difference between this manuscript and that of Wahb's *History*. In the case of the Heidelberg papyrus, we have little guidance for understanding the specific notation that we now use to date the manuscript. In contrast, we can compare the Kairouan fragment with numerous others from a similar place and time, noting that students often wrote remarks just like the one on this manuscript. It is also interesting to note that the individual

Mudawwana), who unfortunately was not able to access the Kairouan manuscripts for his study.

43 Muranyi, *Rechtsbücher*, 49–53.

44 Brockopp, "Saḥnūn's *Mudawwana*."

45 Ibid., 131–132.

mentioned here, Saʿid b. Muhammad b. Rashid, is not otherwise known to us. In other words, biographical dictionaries and other literary sources capture only a portion of the individuals directly participating in the writerly culture of the time. We might well presume this to be the case, but manuscripts prove it to be so.

Turning to the contents of the *Mudawwana*, this short excerpt differs from the printed version (itself based on just one manuscript from Fez) in that it elides the contribution from Abd al-Rahman Ibn al-Qasim (one of the great Egyptian authorities profiled in Chapter 3), leaving Malik b. Anas as the only identified authority in this text.[46] We can only speculate on the meaning of this elision, but in most other aspects it reflects the printed version precisely. The concerns in this fragment are typical of the *Mudawwana* as a whole in that they reflect more of a fascination with interstitial categories than they do practical matters of law. As Calder correctly observed, the *Mudawwana*'s jurisprudence "is not a logical presentation of known rules but a reflection of developing thought about rules."[47] It is, as I have discussed elsewhere, a disquisition on second-order questions, concerned with small details, interstitial categories, and controversies that arise in discussions about law. In fact, I believe it is our first example of a pure "second-order" text in the Medinan tradition, just as Ibn Abd al-Hakam's *Minor Compendium* is our earliest example of a pure first-order text.

Finally, like all early *fiqh* texts, the *Mudawwana* makes no effort to defend or adhere to a four-source theory of Islamic law, being far more interested in Malik's ideas. Yet while the *Mudawwana* does not often mention the Qurʾan, it is evidently connected to a writerly culture, though not necessarily in the way we would imagine. Due to the wealth of Kairouan manuscripts, we actually have some sense of the texts that Sahnun himself passed on to others, including works by Ibn Wahb and Ibn al-Qasim, both of whom appear in the *Mudawwana*. Yet we do not find direct quotations of these texts in the *Mudawwana*, just as Calder found that Sahnun did not follow the *Muwaṭṭaʾ* in reasoning through certain arguments. Like a modern scholar who does not always cite every book in his own library, Sahnun's omissions are hard to explain, yet the manuscript evidence on this count is incontrovertible: he certainly knew these other sources because ancient remarks on manuscripts show that he

[46] A subtitle is also missing in this fragment, suggesting that the full organizational scheme of the *Mudawwana* was still under development.

[47] Calder, *Studies*, 7.

himself transmitted them to others (suggesting that he taught them), yet he does not cite them in his own work. Therefore, the *argumentum e silentio* is disproven: just because a scholar does not cite a source does not mean that he does not know it.

The Earliest Work of Iraqi Scholarship

The next manuscript (Figure 4.1), written seventeen years later, offers yet another striking contrast. In comparison with short, fragmentary scraps written on papyrus or parchment, *Gharīb al-Ḥadīth* by Abu Ubayd al-Qasim b. Sallam al-Baghdadi (d. 223/837),[48] dated Dhū al-Qaʿda 252 (866),[49] demonstrates sophistication in every way.

First, the manuscript is written on very fine paper. Second, it is a work of remarkable erudition, fully supporting the literary accounts that see its author as a polymath grammarian of Byzantine heritage. According to the *Fihrist* of Ibn al-Nadim, Abu Ubayd was author of twenty books,[50] and several of these have survived in manuscript. *Gharīb al-Ḥadīth*, as its name implies, focuses on difficult problems, especially issues of grammar, that arise in the study of *ḥadīth*.

As with the Heidelberg manuscript of Wahb b. Munabbih's *History*, this manuscript was brought to Europe by an antiquarian, in this case Levinus Warner, a Dutch diplomat of German descent who died in Istanbul in 1665.[51] During his twenty years in the Ottoman Empire, he collected hundreds of Arabic manuscripts, all of which are now preserved in the University library of Leiden. The manuscript is in excellent condition, but it presents a number of puzzles. First, it is bound in a fine leather cover that is evidently much later than the manuscript proper. Despite the binding, the pages are out of order, and only after painstaking research was DeGoeje able to determine that the manuscript contains most of twelve of an original twenty quires.[52] Second, scholars have been at a loss to explain the combination of excellent paper and the script. The

[48] H. L. Gottschalk, "Abū ʿUbayd al-Ḳāsim b. Sallām," in *Encyclopaedia of Islam*, 2nd ed.

[49] Leiden Or. 298. Number 6 in Déroche, "Manuscrits," 346. M. J. de Goeje, "Beschreibung einer alten Handschrift von Abû ʿObaid's Ġarîb-al-ḥadîṯ," *Zeitschrift der Deutschen morgenländischen Gesellschaft* 18, no. 4 (1864), 781–807. The text was edited by Muhammad Azim al-Din, 3 vols. (Hyderabad: Osmania Oriental Publications Bureau, 1964).

[50] Ibn al-Nadīm, *Fihrist*, 71.

[51] See the forward to P. S. van Koningsveld, *Levinus Warner and his legacy. Three Centuries Legatum Warnerianum in the Leiden University Library* (Leiden: E. J. Brill, 1970).

[52] DeGoeje, "Beschreibung," 785.

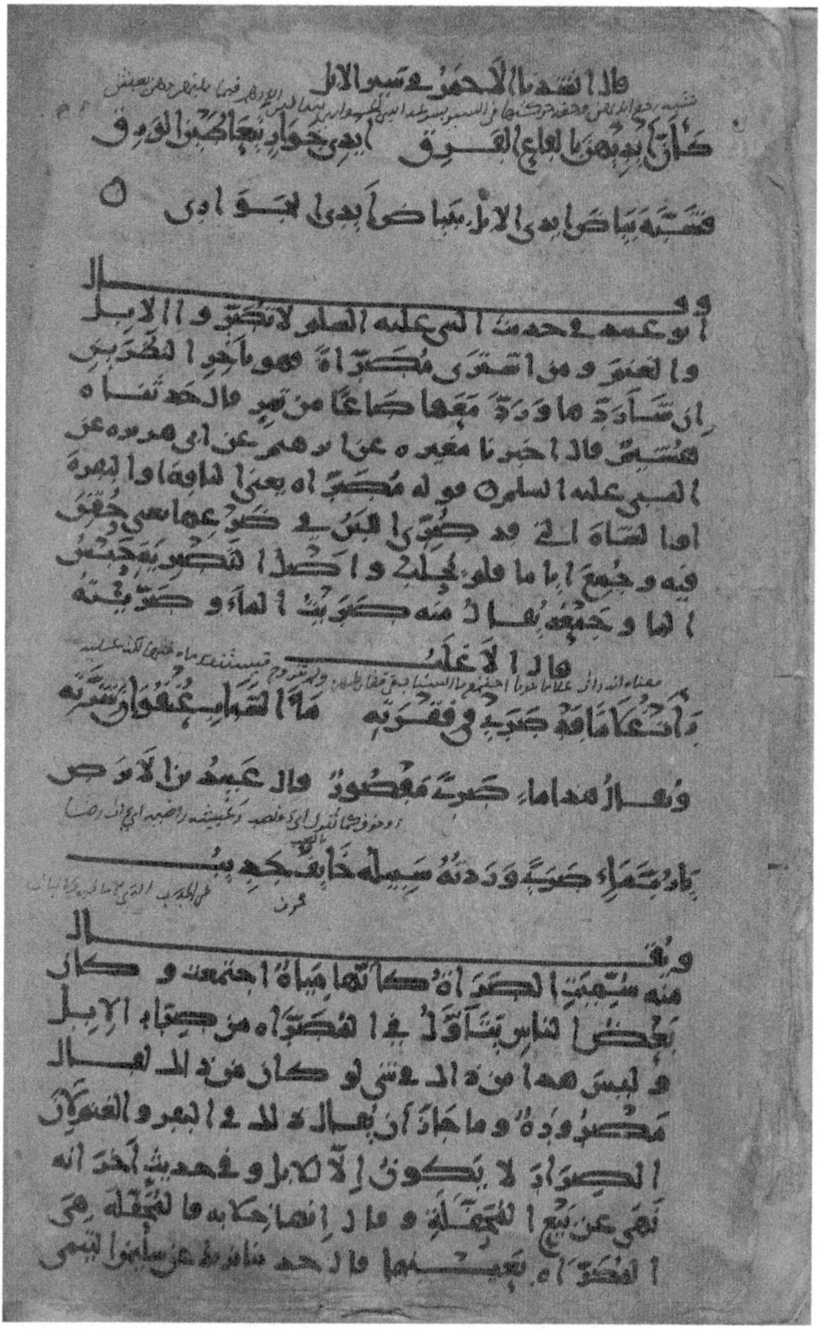

Figure 4.1: *Gharīb al-Ḥadīth* (Ms. Or. 298, fol. 2b), University Library Leiden.

presumption is that paper of this fine of quality would only have been produced in the east, perhaps "in one of the paper-mills of Samarkand or Bagdad."[53] Given the fact that two of our earliest manuscripts from Kairouan are also on paper, however, this presumption may not be accurate.[54] The script, in contrast, was described by DeGoeje as similar to old western (*maghribī*) script.[55] I confirm that it is similar to script forms found in Kairouan manuscripts, yet with some idiosyncrasies. Without further information, we can only speculate on the history of this interesting manuscript.[56]

Sezgin records nearly one hundred compilers of *ḥadīth* collections who died before 880 CE, many of whom composed more than one text; all of these, of course, are based on much later manuscripts.[57] Abu Ubayd's *Gharīb al-Ḥadīth* is very much a secondary text, which seems to confirm the existence of a long history of discussion as well as the oral and written texts of previous scholars. The published edition is based on more recent manuscripts, since even at 241 folios the Leiden manuscript only covers the final third of the text.[58] Examination of the contents confirms that Abu Ubayd's interest in prophetic *ḥadīth* is largely limited to questions of the study of language. After quoting a *ḥadīth*, he often focuses on a specific definition of a word, quoting al-Asmaʿi, the famous lexicographer who died in 213/828, or other authorities. All this suggests that *ḥadīth* had been the subject of study and analysis for quite some time when this work was written down. Furthermore, time and distance seem to have rendered the meaning of words obscure, requiring the explanations that

[53] Jan Just Witkam, "The Oldest Known Dated Arabic Manuscript on Paper (Dated Dhu al-Qaʿda 252 (866 AD)," www.islamicmanuscripts.info/e-publications/witkam_oldest_dated/index.html, accessed November 10, 2015.

[54] See numbers 11 and 17 in the Appendix, dated AH 273 and 282. Granted, this is more than twenty years after the *Gharīb al-Ḥadīth* manuscript, and the quality of the Kairouan paper is not as fine, but it does suggest that paper-making spread quickly throughout the southern Mediterranean basin.

[55] De Goeje, "Beschreibung," 781; see also Muhammad Azim al-Din's Introduction to the edition, p. xvi.

[56] There are many possibilities; for example, the paper could have been brought to Cordoba, the text written there and preserved by some scholar who brought it to Istanbul after the fall of Grenada, but we cannot know for certain.

[57] Sezgin, *Geschichte*, 1:84–153.

[58] The close correspondence among the manuscripts lends confidence to the reconstruction. A study of these other manuscripts is found in G. Lecomte, "A propos de la résurgence des ouvrages d'Ibn Qutayba sur le hadît aux VIe/XIIe et VIIe/XIIIe siècles. Les certificats de lecture du *K. Garīb al-Ḥadīt et du K. Iṣlāḥ al-ġalat fī ġarīb al-hadīt* li-Abī ʿUbayd al-Qāsim b. Sallām," *Bulletin d'Études Orientales* 21 (1968), 347–409.

Abu Ubayd provides. Finally, this work is direct evidence of a highly advanced writerly culture, and whatever the origins of script and paper, it certainly suggests a broad geographical range to these sophisticated discussions.

Qur'an Exegesis

As discussed in Chapter 2, Fuat Sezgin claims that the scholarly study of the Qur'an goes back to Ibn Abbas himself, and he finds more than a dozen authors who died before 880.[59] It certainly seems reasonable that the Qur'an formed the initial focus of Muslim scholarly study, but the development of an organized interpretive analysis *(tafsīr)* covering the entire text of the Qur'an may not have come about until the early Abbasid period.[60] Our earliest manuscript witness to this activity comes from Kairouan,[61] a *tafsīr* written by Yahya b. Sallam al-Basri (d. 200/815), who, as his name indicates, was born in Iraq; he lived in Kairouan, however, and died in Egypt. As with many texts from Kairouan, there are numerous old copies of the *tafsīr* in the collection, including several complete parts *(ajzā')* and other loose fragments, the oldest of which has a reader's remark from 260/873–874.[62] A portion of the *tafsīr* has been published, and the editor makes use of several distinct

[59] Sezgin, *Geschichte*, 1:25–55. Ibn al-Nadim also includes an extensive list of Qur'an commentators; Yahya b. Sallam al-Basri does not appear in his list, however.

[60] I am aware that this is a controversial claim, as a good deal of scholarship is based on the notion of an incremental development of exegesis, based on reconstructed early texts. But my concerns raised in Chapter 2 still apply: (1) the notion that early figures wrote books is a misreading of *kitāb*, which can simply mean a text; (2) we cannot distinguish between texts written by early authorities and lectures that were compiled by students; and (3) pious forgeries are possible. Further analysis of Yahya b. Sallam's writings, in my view, could provide firmer ground for arguing the authenticity (or inauthenticity) of Umayyad-era scholarly projects.

[61] If Muranyi's claim regarding an undated twenty-four-folio manuscript under serial numbers 1779 and 1781 is ever proven correct, there may be a yet older *tafsīr* in Kairouan; the *tafsīr* in this manuscript is attributed to Ibn Wahb from the *Jāmi';* see Muranyi, *'Abd Allāh b. Wahb*, 53–54.

[62] First described by Schacht, "On Some Manuscripts," 233, though he noticed only later marginalia, evidence that this manuscript was still in use at the end of the fourth/tenth century. Muranyi, *Beiträge*, 16–20, describes the earlier *samā'* remark and includes an excerpt on pp. 390–396. This manuscript was unknown to Déroche, "Manuscrits." There are several studies of this text: Al-Fadil Ben Ashur, *al-Tafsīr wa-rijāluh* (Tunis, 1966 [reprint Cairo, 1970]); Hamadi Sammoud, "Un exégète oriental en Ifriqiya: Yahyâ Ibn Sallâm (742–815)," *Revue de l'Institut des Belles Lettres Arabes* 33 (1970), 227–242; Ismail Cerrahoğlu, "Yaḥyā b. Sallām ve tafsirdeki metodu." *Ankara üniversitesi Ilāhiyat*

manuscripts with dates ranging from AH 307 to the eighth century of the *hijra*, demonstrating a pattern of continuous study through the centuries.[63]

Yahya b. Sallam's *tafsīr* has been the subject of a good deal of research, but much more remains to be done. For example, few scholars have tried to sort through the large number of remaining manuscript fragments,[64] and almost no one has attempted to analyze Yahya b. Sallam's work as a whole.[65] This is unfortunate, because we know of several texts by him, all based on ancient Kairouan manuscripts. A stemmatic analysis of these manuscripts might give us increased confidence that the texts we see in these manuscripts were actually composed by Yahya b. Sallam; it might also be possible to prove that the *Tafsīr* is a book, according to my narrow definition. Even more important, the opportunity to compare several works from the same author, including two different analyses of the Qur'an, can shed light into the development of a scholarly profile over a person's lifetime. In other words, if these texts can all be shown to derive from Yahya b. Sallam, and not his students, then we would have a window into second-/eighth-century scholarship that would complement and perhaps surpass what we can learn from the *Compendia* of Ibn Abd al-Hakam.

Yahya b. Sallam's *Tafsīr* was reworked by other early scholars, and some of these texts have also received attention.[66] Miklos Muranyi has undertaken an analytical comparison of the *Tafsīr*, an early commentary/summation by the Ibadite Hud b. Muhakkam (died end of the third/ninth century), and a summation (*mukhtaṣar*) by Ibn Abi Zamanin (d. 399/1008).[67] I will

Fakultesi Yayınları 89 (1970), 3–211; Walid Saleh, "Marginalia and Peripheries: A Tunisian Historian and the History of Quránic Exegesis," *Numen* 58 (2011), 284–313.

63 Edited by Hind Shalabi, 2 vols. (Beirut: Dar al-kotob al-ilmiyah, 2004), 1:17–25. Interestingly, Shalabi does not seem to know of Muranyi's work, nor does she mention the existence of this most ancient fragment. In a private communication in 2013, Muranyi told me that some of the other sections of this text had been published in Tunisia as a dissertation under the direction of Mohamed Talbi.

64 Shalabi and Muranyi are exceptions.

65 Both Muranyi and Shalabi offer some preliminary analysis, but nothing in detail. The inaccessibility of the Kairouan manuscripts and the sheer number of known fragments, and the very real possibility of additional, as yet unidentified fragments, makes the job extraordinarily difficult.

66 Claude Gilliot, "Le Commentaire Coranique de Hud b. Muhakkam/Muhkim," *Arabica* 44 (1997), 179–233; Ibn Abī Zamanīn, *Mukhtaṣar tafsīr Yaḥyá ibn Sallām li-Abī 'Abd Allāh Muḥammad ibn Abī Zamanayn*, 'Abd al-Salām b. Aḥmad al-Kanūnī (Tetouan?, 2001); M. J. Hermosilla, "Corán 22,52 en el tafsīr de Yaḥyà b. Salām," *Al-Qanṭara: Revista De Estudios Árabes* 12 , no. 1 (1991), 271–272.

67 Muranyi, *Beiträge*, 390–396.

not focus too much on the contents of the *Tafsīr*, however, since the manuscript basis has not been sufficiently analyzed – specifically, the text of the most ancient dated fragment has not been published. From what has been published, however, it appears that the *Tafsīr* is also highly engaged with an interregional writerly culture, including *asbāb al-nuzūl* literature (which uses history to explain why verses of the Qurʾan were revealed), along with Iraqi and Hijazi ideas; variant readings are also addressed. So not only is this the oldest manuscript of a text devoted to Qurʾan interpretation, it also provides direct evidence of an individual transmitting Iraqi ideas to North Africa.

An Important Text from the Hanbali School

The final manuscript from the period covered in this chapter is *Masāʾil ibn Ḥanbal*, collected by an unnamed student of Abu Dawud al-Sijistani in AH 266, well before Abu Dawud's death in 275/889. The earliest discussion of law from the Hanbali school, this manuscript was written only twenty-five years after Ibn Hanbal's death. The manuscript currently resides in Damascus,[68] though its provenance is unknown. The text has been edited and published, though the earlier edition (Cairo, 1934) is based primarily on the much later, and faulty, Medinan manuscript. A more recent edition (1999) is based primarily on the Damascus manuscript, with reference to the Medinan manuscript and an additional witness from the Escorial library.[69] As Susan Spectorsky points out in her study and partial translation, Abu Dawud's is one of three extant transmissions of Ibn Hanbal's *responsa*, all of which differ substantially one from another, though they share an interest in exploring the fine nuances of Islamic law.[70]

Given the stark differences in content among these transmission lines, it is unclear what we are looking at with this manuscript. Spectorsky argues that certain characteristics of Ibn Hanbal's thought do come through, such as "his refusal to let the exposition of the jurist take

[68] Ẓāhiriyya, *ḥadīth* 334 (eighty-six folios). Number 12 in Déroche, "Manuscrits," 346. First (briefly) described by Helmut Ritter, "Philologika II," *Der Islam* 17 (1928), 249–257, at 250.

[69] Abū Dāwūd al-Sījistānī, *Masāʾil al-Imām Aḥmad*, Abu Muʿādh Ṭāriq b. Awād Allāh b. Muḥammad (ed.) ([Cairo]: Maktabat Ibn Taymiyya, 1999), pages و- ز followed by sample facsimiles of the Damascus and Escorial manuscripts.

[70] Susan Spectorsky in *Chapters on Marriage and Divorce: Responses of Ibn Ḥanbal and Ibn Rāhwayh* (Austin: University of Texas Press, 1993). Spectorsky used the then-available published version, supplemented by her own reading of the Damascus manuscript. See her translation of Abu Dawud's transmission on pp. 60–90; her description of the manuscripts is on pp. 255–290.

precedence over the study of *ḥadīth*," or a certain "moral dimension to Ibn Ḥanbal's responses."[71] Yet these impressions could be explained in other ways, such as a set of practices and attitudes common within a certain circle of scholars. It is possible, in fact, that the *masāʾil* format, both here and in the *Mudawwana*, does not reflect actual conversations but serves rather as a literary device, a way of exploring legal minutiae while also honoring the memory of exemplary scholars from the past.[72] By the time that Abu Dawud composed these lines, Ibn Hanbal's exploits during the inquisition had perhaps already become the stuff of legend, placing him on par with the paragons of a previous generation, Malik b. Anas and Abu Hanifa. What we can be sure of is that Abu Dawud is helping to cement Ibn Hanbal's reputation through this text.

Masāʾil ibn Ḥanbal is therefore a fitting bookend to this group of manuscripts, since it bears witness both to the narrative power of Wahb's *History*, written down thirty-seven years earlier, and the drafting conventions of Sahnun's *Mudawwana*, written down thirty-one years earlier. As Spectorsky has already undertaken a thorough analysis of its content, I will not delve into that here, but it is worth repeating her reflections of the meaning of this text within the writerly culture of the third/ninth century. She writes:

> By the third century of Islam, virtually all questions of *fiqh* had already been asked and various answers already given. These different answers were incorporated into all *fiqh* works, whether implied in the way questions were posed or explicitly, in special chapters devoted to disagreement (*ikhtilāf*). The different answers were also reflected in the thousands of traditions in circulation, many of them contradictory, through which the growth of legal doctrines can be charted. Some of the questions asked and answers given were practical; others, theoretical or casuistic ... But not all jurists discussed all questions, and they certainly did not use all available traditions. Rather, they made use of the *ḥadīth* and *fiqh* material available to them for their own purposes.[73]

In other words, as we press forward in time, the work of the modern researcher becomes infinitely more complicated, since the scholarly context of the period is essential to understanding the content of these texts. We must now pay attention to the motivations of audience, student, and teacher, and we need to understand that arguments are sometimes made through leaving specific references unsaid. This need for context is one

[71] Ibid., 7.
[72] Calder, *Studies*, 10.
[73] Spectorsky, *Chapters on Marriage*, 4.

reason that so many modern scholars ignore the actual history of early manuscripts. If we restrict ourselves to proven, dated materials from the ninth century, as I have done in this chapter, then we are forced into a state of ignorance. It is obvious that these texts are all engaging with a highly literate society, but we do not have contemporary witnesses to those conversation partners; we have only five manuscripts, after all, and these five are from substantially different contexts. Yet acknowledging the limited nature of our material evidence not only allows us to build stronger arguments for accepting the historicity of other early texts, it also gives us guidelines for doing so. Moreover, as I will discuss in Chapter 5, the Kairouan manuscripts allow us to document what is merely implied in texts such as Ibn Hanbal's *Masāʾil*, since we see the interactions of a mature scholarly community at work.

SCHOLARLY POWER AND "CONNECTIVITY"

Limited as it is, the material evidence from this period gives us an extraordinary opportunity to comment on the rise of Muslim scholarly communities to a position of authority and influence in Muslim societies. Until now, most researchers have used these manuscripts as windows into a yet deeper past, rather than as evidence from the period in which they were produced. To a certain extent, of course, the manuscripts themselves dictate this. The fragment of Wahb's *History of King David*, for example, contains almost no marginalia at all, and without student remarks we cannot say how it was used. Further, because we have so little literary papyrus, the dating of this manuscript seems to be an anomaly (and reasonably raises questions). If this manuscript were part of a collection, we might well be able to find similar dating marks and be able to say with more certainty why the date was written in this way, but isolated from its original context, it is rendered mute.

This lack of external context is mirrored by the contents of these five texts, which also seem strangely disconnected from political, economic, and social worlds of the time. Very occasionally, specific places (Egypt, the Nile, Medina) are mentioned, but the overall impression is one of timeless truths. The *History of King David*, for example, is full of legendary and miraculous acts. Sahnun's *Mudawwana*, like the *Masāʾil Ibn Ḥanbal*, is devoted to arcane discussions of little applicability to the real world. The *Gharīb al-Ḥadīth* and the *Tafsīr* also involve an internal, scholarly discussion of grammar and lexicography. We are hard pressed to make any judgments about the personalities – or personal lives – of the authors, and this fact makes the historical accounts of the biographical dictionaries that much more important. But it also emphasizes the fact that this early community of scholars was a world unto itself. Ahmad b. Hanbal may have suffered under the *miḥna*, but whatever real world troubles these men had, they did not bring them into their texts, which were purely devoted to the service of knowledge. The insularity of this community, I would argue, is the very source of their power. While torture is painful, it cannot last; and it is therefore unimportant in comparison with the timeless work of scholarship.

The Scholars Are the Heirs of the Prophet

According to one strand of Muslim tradition, Muhammad's sole miracle was that he received divine revelation, a holy book. That sign of divine favor gave him and his followers the ability to succeed against overwhelming odds. Yet the Qur'an does not detail Muhammad's suffering and setbacks – it rarely mentions him at all. Likewise, we see almost nothing of Ibn Hanbal's torture, described at the beginning of this chapter, in his *responsa* passed on to Abu Dawud. In a similar fashion, Sahnun b. Saʿid's *Mudawwana* is known for carefully ascribing most every legal injunction to Malik b. Anas or some other exemplary scholar of the past; he himself is almost absent, rarely expounding his own views.

In contrast, literary sources tell us that Sahnun suffered significantly under the Muʿtazili judge Ibn Abi al-Jawad.[74] Toward the end of his life the local Amir, Muhammad b. al-Aghlab, tried to name Sahnun to the position of judge, but Sahnun refused the nomination. When pressed by the Amir, he delayed, forcing the Amir to accept a number of conditions, one of which was that he was to have leave to prosecute injustice, even into the Aghlabid family itself. When these conditions were finally met and sworn upon, Sahnun reluctantly accepted the position on Monday, the third of Ramadan in 234 (March 30, 849).[75]

Sahnun's assertion of independent judicial authority was, of course, very important to the later historians who recorded this story, and it recalls similar altercations that Malik, al-Shafiʿi and Ibn Hanbal all had

[74] We have a unique account of the events in Kairouan from Abu l-Arab al-Tamimi, a local historian who lived two generations after Sahnun and who wrote our earliest surviving biography; see his *Kitāb al-Miḥan*, Yaḥyā Wahīb al-Jabbūrī (ed.) (Beirut: Dār al-Gharb al-Islāmī, 1983); the entry on Sahnun is found on pp. 449–452. For analysis, see Brockopp, "Contradictory Evidence," 124–126.

[75] ʿIyāḍ, *Tartīb*, 4:56.

with political leaders. In one narrative, Sahnun is subtly connected to the Prophet as he rides through the streets of Kairouan:

> Sulayman b. Salim said: when the appointment of Sahnun was completed, the people went out to meet him, and I saw him on a riding animal, without cloak or cap. His face was grim, and no one was running to congratulate him. He went on like this until he came to his daughter Khadija, who was among the best of women, and he said to her: "Today your father has been slaughtered without a knife."[76]

This account is rife with allusions for the attentive reader. The Prophet was famous for rejecting fine clothes, just as Sahnun rides without cloak or cap,[77] and Sahnun's words are actually those of a *ḥadīth* attributed to the Prophet.[78] Even his daughter Khadija plays a role not dissimilar to that of her namesake, Muhammad's first wife, as both recognize the weight of leadership and offer comfort. These symbols add significantly to Sahnun's power. While governors and caliphs derive some of their authority from Prophetic example, jurists, such as Sahnun, are no less heirs of the Prophet.

As I suggested above, the very insularity of the scholarly community may be seen as a source of their power; masters of large bodies of information, they delve into obscure discussions that only al-Shafiʿi's elite can understand. Yet this very mastery also gives them access to a symbolic language that they can wield to their advantage, as demonstrated by carefully constructed accounts of both Sahnun's and Ibn Hanbal's altercations with civil authority, in which their disciples turned their experiences into didactic tales for future generations. The scholar, therefore, is much more than the possessor of sacred knowledge; through the actions of his disciples he becomes a hero, an exemplary figure whose life is to be emulated. While a cursory examination of these five manuscripts might give the impressions that these elite scholarly communities were isolated from one another, this is manifestly not the case. In fact, the manuscript evidence suggests a highly mobile population, where scholars travelled widely, bringing back the latest books from abroad, which, in turn, further burnished the reputations of those scholars.

[76] Ibid., 4:57.

[77] This is just one of numerous stories that emphasize Sahnun's simplicity, and it is worth noting that Malik b. Anas himself also emulated these aspects of the Prophet's behavior.

[78] Al-Tirmidhī, *al-Jāmiʿ al-Ṣaḥīḥ* 3:614 (*kitāb al-aḥkām*, 5). See also Wensinck, *Concordance*, 2:495.

"Seek Out Knowledge, Even in China"

This well-known *ḥadīth* of the Prophet Muhammad is usually retrospectively cited as the basis for the institution of *riḥla*, or travel in search of knowledge.[79] While the *ḥadīth* itself is not attested from this early period, three of the five manuscripts surveyed in this chapter bear the marks of travel. *Gharīb al-Ḥadīth* is written on eastern paper with western script, and al-Basri's *Tafsīr* cites sources from the eastern end of the Islamic world, though it was composed in Kairouan. Even Sahnun's *Mudawwana* bears evidence of travel to Egypt, if not to Medina. But scholars from provincial capitals, such as Kairouan, did not do all the travelling; rather, both the manuscripts and the biographical dictionaries reveal that Kairouan was itself a destination along a path that connected Cordoba to Medina across the southern Mediterranean in a series of short jumps from one major center of knowledge to another. The mosque-library of Kairouan was a great beneficiary of these trips. For example, Abd al-Malik b. Habib (d. 238/852), one of the greatest scholars of ninth-century Cordoba, wrote several books on law and history, but all that has survived is what happens to have arrived in Kairouan and Fez via scholarly travels. Ibn Habib lived during the initial flourishing of scholarship in al-Andalus that accompanied the reestablishment of Umayyad power under Abd al-Rahman II (r. 206/822–238/852). According to literary sources, he left Cordoba in search of knowledge when he was around twenty-five in the year 824, returning three years later. Along the way, he studied with a host of famous scholars in Kairouan, Fustat, and Medina, engaging in debate and sharpening his knowledge. Upon his return to Cordoba, he wrote his monumental *al-Wāḍiḥa fī l-fiqh* (*The Clarification of Jurisprudence*), which served as a major text of the new teaching institutions in Cordoba.[80]

Ibn Habib's slightly older colleagues, Isa b. Dinar (d. 212/827) and Yahya b. Yahya al-Masmudi (d. 234/848), also travelled to Medina in search of knowledge. Famously, Yahya b. Yahya, who came from an Arabized family of Berbers of the Masmuda, met Malik b. Anas in Medina and transmitted the most widely known version of Malik's

[79] In his analysis of literary accounts of the *riḥla*, Touati suggests that the institution began only in the second Islamic century (*Islam and Travel*, 11–15).

[80] Beatrix Ossendorf-Conrad, *Das "K. al-Wāḍiḥa" des ʿAbd al-Malik b. Ḥabīb: Edition und Kommentar zu Ms. Qarawiyyīn 809/40 (Abwāb al-Ṭahāra)*, Beiruter Texte und Studien, vol. 43 (Stuttgart: Franz Steiner Verlag, 1994). Ossendorf-Conrad did not make use of the Kairouan manuscripts; however, she does describe the major Kairouan fragment on pp. 149–153. For additional fragments, see Muranyi, *Materialien*, 15–29.

*Muwaṭṭa*ʾ in the Islamic west.[81] The words of Malik b. Anas and other Medinan scholars loom large in texts by these Cordoban jurists, just as they did for Sahnun in Kairouan. In both cities, the jurists' authority rested not merely in their own erudition, personal charisma, or mastery of religious sources, but also in the fact that they had been to *Madīnat al-nabī* (the city of the Prophet) and had brought back "relics" in the form of ideas, interpretive strategies, and even texts from that city.

In calling these items relics, I am suggesting a parallel between the *riḥla* and the pilgrimage.[82] Just as pilgrims will see themselves transformed as the result of a process of travel, ritual activity, and return, so also these scholars are transformed in a rite of passage that was considered essential for their acceptance as legal authorities in al-Andalus. But pilgrims also commonly bring back relics – the clay of Karbala, medals from Santiago de Compostela, water from the well of Zamzam, etc. Sometimes, these keepsakes themselves form new places of pilgrimage.[83] Similarly, when scholars go to Medina to gain knowledge, they bring this knowledge back to Kairouan and Cordoba and teach in the Great mosques of those cities. Normal Cordobans need not travel to Medina to gain this knowledge, for it is available through the mediation of these great scholars. Further, the very mosques of Cordoba and Kairouan evoke the great mosques of the east,[84] and in Kairouan and Fez, the relics of these trips, the books of famous scholars, were stored within the mosque itself. In this way, royal architecture and scholarly knowledge worked together to create an experience of a new Medina in southern Spain and northern Africa.

For North African and Andalusian scholars, the choice of Medina is no accident as this "radiant city" of the Prophet Muhammad is both cause and effect of legal legitimacy in the Maliki school of law. Unique among legal scholars, Maliki jurists argued that the practice of the living Muslim community in Medina was a far better source of religious knowledge than the vogue of depending on stories (*ḥadīth*) passed on from one person to

[81] Maribel Fierro, "El alfaquí beréber Yaḥyà b. Yaḥyà, 'el inteligente de al-Andalus,'" in María Luisa Ávila and M. Marín (eds.), *Estudios onomástico-biográphicos de al-Andalus. VIII* (Madrid: CSIC, 1997), 269–344.

[82] Touati (*Islam and Travel*, 207–212) discusses some aspects of pilgrimage, especially as it related to jihad, but he does not make the connections I am suggesting here.

[83] Just as when St. Louis brought the Crown of Thorns back from Jerusalem and built around it the gorgeous Sainte-Chapelle in the middle of the Île de la Cité, Parisians need not go to Jerusalem to see the site of Christ's passion, but can appreciate this relic in Paris, and thereby Paris in a small way becomes a new Jerusalem.

[84] Nina Safran, "The Sacred and Profane in Islamic Cordoba," *Comparative Islamic Studies* 1 (2007), 21–41, at 26.

another. In other words, stories alone were of little value unless they were backed up by the authoritative practice of an individual scholar. Therefore, one of the pillars of Maliki thought – the authority of the living community – would seem to be diametrically opposed to the authority of a written text. This helps explain why we have so many versions of Malik's *Muwaṭṭa'*. Not only had Muslim scholars not yet developed the techniques for ensuring verbatim transmission of texts, there was little interest in doing so. If authority resided in the living example of Medina, then every audition from Malik is as good as any other.[85] This preference for the living teacher helps to explain why actual books are so rare during the earliest period, but that situation begins to change as we move to the following generation.

For men like Sahnun, Ibn Habib, and Yahya b. Yahya, the portable authority of the written text proved to be an important enhancement of their personal authority. This generation began to see Malik as something more than just one great teacher among many, but rather as the primary conduit to the Prophet and his *Sunna*, his righteous path. This is the meaning of a dream recounted by one of Sahnun's students: "I saw in a vision the Prophet (God's blessings and peace be upon him) walking on a path, and Abu Bakr behind him, and Umar behind Abu Bakr, and Malik behind Umar, and Sahnun behind Malik."[86] For this generation – Sahnun who focused on collecting Malik's every utterance, Yahya b. Yahya who brought the *Muwaṭṭa'* to Cordoba, and Ibn Habib who gave a triumphal history to those early jurists – their authority was linked to that of Malik, whose importance was raised above that of his peers. Because Malik's knowledge could no longer be accessed orally, but only through texts, the teachers of those texts became vital conduits to sacred knowledge. Identifying a key individual authority from the past was essential to building a Maliki school, but it was dependent on the rituals of travel, which in turn drove the methods of disciplined textual transmission that would lead to the rise of book culture.[87]

[85] Further, fragments of texts from al-Majishun, Ashhab and Ibn Wahb demonstrate that Malik was only one of the creative minds of this period. Without the Kairouan collection, we would not know that so many other scholars were pursuing their own inquiries at the same time.

[86] 'Iyāḍ, *Tartīb*, 4:87.

[87] While I limit my discussion here to the Maliki school of law, following the evidence of our earliest manuscripts, I believe that my connection of book culture to the rise of schools holds for the other legal and theological schools.

As I will describe in Chapter 5, one of the interesting results of this focus on written texts is that the manuscripts themselves start to gain an intrinsic value. Legal texts start to become illuminated, with varied colors of ink and even gold, in ways similar to that of early Qur'ans. Moreover, the trade in manuscripts crosses cultural divides, with Byzantine emperors sending the gift of important Greek manuscripts, along with scholars to interpret them, to their sometime rivals in Cordoba. It should be no surprise then that all these cultures – Umayyad, Byzantine, and later Fatimid – built renowned libraries as they shared in a common Mediterranean history. Just as the Maliki school can be thought of as a Mediterranean school, depending on the possibility of both near and distant connectivities to maintain coherence, so also these civilizations can be thought of as loose confederations of local cultural niches that promoted the development of regional scholarly clusters in Constantinople, Cairo, Kairouan, and Cordoba.[88] Travel among these centers, along with the translation of texts and scholars, allowed for local schools to flourish, while also providing sites for productive interaction among various kinds of Muslims, Jews, and Christians who shared in a broader scholarly world.

[88] For further definition of technical terms such as "connectivity" and "niches" see Horden and Purcell, *Corrupting Sea*, 123–171.

5

The Mature Scholarly Community of Kairouan, 880–950

A mature scholarly community is a dynamic configuration of individuals and texts that can only come into being once a suitable past has been established, in our case an Islamic past. Proto-scholars, such as Wahb b. Munabbih, were not part of such a community precisely because, by the Umayyad period, a uniquely Islamic past had not yet evolved. Like Ibn Ishaq, Wahb connected Muhammad to King David and other exemplary individuals in a line that derived more from Judaism and Christianity than it did from Islam. A century later, however, Islamic history had come into its own: Muhammad's life story was suffused with miracles, and the Qurʾan was defended not as just one more piece of God's creative activity in the world, but as His very own speech, uncreated. Scholars after 880 could look back at a mature, independent religious tradition, one that placed them in the position of *ʿulamāʾ*, those who have God-given knowledge. At this point, the lives of proto-scholars such as Wahb and Ibn Ishaq (and also figures such as Zayd b. Thabit and Ibn Abbas) were subjected to selective memory to bring them in line with the Muslim imagination of what an exemplary scholar should look like. Historically, they were proto-scholars, but the later tradition reimagined them as scholars.

In this chapter, I continue my argument that historians of scholarship, especially Ibn Habib (d. 238/852 in Cordoba) and Abu l-Arab al-Tamimi (d. 333/944 in Kairouan), collected biographical information precisely to solidify the position of scholars as arbiters of correct Islamic identity. This activity corresponds with a shift in scholarly texts, which, already in the previous period, began to focus on exemplary individuals, with Sahnun b. Saʿid collecting the views of Malik b. Anas and Abu Dawud al-Sijistani collecting Ibn Hanbal's *responsa*. As the schools of law and theology become established, these individuals move from being members of a broader intellectual community to paragons of correct actions, second only to the Prophet himself. This shift certainly occurred across the Muslim world, perhaps even earlier in some places where communities coalesced around Abu Hanifa and the Shiite Imams, but only in Kairouan can we see the specific ways that the community of scholars worked together to solidify these reputations by building up an entire library devoted to their texts.[1]

Only in the Kairouan collection can we directly observe the scholarly processes by which the words and ideas of scholars from previous generations were preserved and passed on during this period. Here we can see the rigid control of terminology, careful attention to detail, and the process of oversight that produced a disciplined community of scholars, devoted to study. Of course, it is only the accidents of history that bring us to Kairouan, since, as I detail in the Appendix, twenty-three of the thirty Arabic/Islamic manuscripts dated before the year 900 come from Kairouan, and many more Kairouan manuscripts may be dated to the tenth century. The scholars of North Africa and Andalusia, therefore, offer us a controlled experiment of sorts, a smaller stage on which we can observe developments and interactions on the basis of the extraordinary documentary evidence that I began to describe in Chapters 3 and 4.

Still, it must be admitted that the material evidence from Kairouan is limited. First, it is at odds with historical reports, which record Baghdad, Kufa, Nishapur, and many other sites as both more active and more sophisticated than centers in Egypt and the Maghrib. To be sure, these centers were interconnected through the institution of the *riḥla*, yet consider the fact that almost all the early Kairouan manuscripts are written on parchment, with only two of the very earliest manuscripts on paper (*kāghidh*), one quite coarse with "bits of cloth and linen,"[2] a far cry from

[1] The question of when, precisely, this community became "Maliki" or when the legal schools were founded is beyond the scope of this book, but the evidence from Kairouan is instructive. While there is no denying the importance of Malik b. Anas in the Kairouan collection, the existence of so many other scholars' writings in Kairouan (see the Appendix) certainly suggests that these communities supported a wide variety of intellectual commitments. Attempts to draw bright lines between schools can be documented in the ninth century, but their success was limited.

[2] Miklos Muranyi, "Das Kitāb Aḥkām Ihn Ziyād über die Identifizierung Eines Fragmentes in Qairawān (qairawāner Miszellaneen V)," *Zeitschrift der Deutschen morganländischen Gesellschaft* 148, no. 2 (1998), 241–260, at 241, n.1, referring to Ashhab's *Kitāb*

the fine paper used in al-Baghdadi's *Gharīb al-Ḥadīth*. Similarly, it must be assumed that the sophistication of scholarly methods that we see in Kairouan is but a shadow of the institutions that must have obtained in wealthier centers in the east and probably Cordoba to the west. A second limitation is the fact that the Kairouan manuscripts focus almost exclusively on texts written by and for jurists, virtually excluding philosophers, physicians, historians, and theologians. In his catalogue *(fihrist)* of books from 377/987, Ibn al-Nadim records having seen many texts in these and other fields,[3] so focus on the Kairouan manuscripts could give us a skewed understanding of the interconnectedness of these fields. Finally, the Kairouan collection excludes Christian and Jewish texts.

Material culture, therefore, still plays the leading role in this chapter, as we delve deeply into the rich manuscript collection of the ancient mosque-library of Kairouan. Yet the limitations of this source must always be kept in mind. Fortunately for our analysis of the rise of the *ʿulamāʾ*, however, we can now use literary sources in a new way to gain further information about the scholarly community of Kairouan; because our earliest historians of North African scholars write on the basis of first- and second-hand accounts, their narratives are much more trustworthy. Abu l-Arab, for example, was himself the student of some of Sahnun's students, and so his entry on Sahnun includes significant details on his life, the memory of which would still have been fresh in Abu l-Arab's lifetime.[4] Further, to a limited extent, we can test Abu l-Arab's account against information in the manuscripts: Abu l-Arab's list of Sahnun's students can be compared with the names of individuals who actually transmitted Sahnun's manuscripts, for example, and Abu l-Arab's own hand is visible in the Kairouan collection via manuscripts that he himself copied. Finally, we can compare these near contemporary accounts with those of later compilers, such as the much more extensive entries on Sahnun in Iyad b. Musa's *Tartīb al-Madārik*.[5] This long history of biographical writing in the Maliki school allows us to trace specific patterns of addition and excision, as details are shaped to conform to the expectations of the exemplary scholar.

In Chapter 3, I recalled a well-known story from the biographical texts, that of Sahnun competing with Asad for the correct version of Ibn

al-Daʿwā wa l-Bayyināt. See description in the Appendix, manuscript number 12. In that list, number 17, dated before AH 283, is also on paper.

3 Ibn al-Nadīm, *Fihrist*, Flügel (ed.).

4 Ben Cheneb, *Ṭabaqāt*.

5 ʿIyāḍ, *Tartīb*, 4:45–88; see also Mohamed Talbi's partial edition, *Tarājim Aghlabiyya (Biographies Aghlabides)* (Tunis: University of Tunis, 1968), 86–136.

al-Qasim's *responsa*. Whatever else we may learn from this story, it encapsulates a keen anxiety about the accurate transmission of textual knowledge. This continues to include our current knowledge of the Kairouan manuscripts, which is still based on oral and written sources. During the period discussed in this chapter, after 880, we have a much larger array of dated manuscripts from Kairouan other than the two that I discussed in Chapter 4, but no one has yet published a list of these manuscripts – for good reasons. First, we still do not have an accurate sense of the contents of the collection; many fragments are still unidentified or wrongly identified. Second, there is no accurate system for cataloguing even the identified manuscripts.[6] With these important caveats in mind, I attempt a preliminary list in the Appendix only to give some sense of the magnitude of this collection and the significant work that remains to be done. While I have made several research trips to work with the collection, now housed at the National Laboratory for the Restoration of Parchment Manuscripts, behind the Museum of Islamic Arts in Raqqada, I remain dependent on publications by Joseph Schacht, Nejmeddine Hentati, and Miklos Muranyi (as well as private correspondence with Dr. Muranyi) for much of my information. It will become quickly obvious, however, that the Kairouan collection is nonpareil and that the size and quality of this collection can support a method of dating manuscripts based on paleography, codicological details, and biographical information that would potentially add dozens of additional fragments to my list, which is limited to the appearance of a specific date on a manuscript, either in the colophon, the incipit, or a marginal remark.[7] The arguments to justify this broader approach, pioneered by Muranyi, have never been made explicitly, so the first step is to lay out as clearly as possible the large number and variety of manuscripts that can be securely dated and that therefore give us the foundation for further speculation.

Before turning to analysis of the manuscripts, however, it is necessary to place this collection within its historical context. The great wealth of the Kairouan collection, after all, is not in any single manuscript, but in

[6] See here Muranyi, *Beiträge*, xxxv, and idem, "Visionen des Skeptikers," *Der Islam* 81, no. 2 (2004), 206–217, which is a response to Andrew Rippin's criticism.

[7] For the purposes of this investigation, I use a more stringent set of criteria for dating manuscripts than does Muranyi. Further, this date must be consistent with other evidence both internal (names mentioned in the text, other marginal remarks) and external (orthography, age of parchment). These strict criteria match those of François Déroche and so are useful in comparing the Kairouan collection with early Arabic manuscripts from other libraries.

the fact that it presents an intact archive, somewhat similar to the famous Cairo Geniza in giving us insight into the daily lives of scholars. This context is all the more important to describe since it is so little known. Just as Ibn al-Nadim barely mentions the scholars of Kairouan, so also modern historians focus far more on the central Islamic lands to the exclusion of provincial towns. Kairouan's history may not be unique, but it is different enough from that of Cordoba, Cairo, or Baghdad that it is worth recalling in some detail.

Taken together, manuscripts, mosques, and historical accounts help us to discern in Kairouan the same three-stage process that I have outlined for Islamic history in general. First, we see an early bifurcation of the learned class into a professional chancery and individual proto-scholars. This is the difference between specialized knowledge that is of use to the interests of the ruling class and charismatic individuals who maintain an authority apart from that of the state through the attaining of religious knowledge and through their acts of piety. Second, these proto-scholars gradually give way to the rise of a true scholarly class. This class is a phenomenon of interlinked urban areas, marked by books and the communities of inquiry that passed books on, intact, to future generations. Finally, the position of scholars as rightful defenders of the tradition is solidified through the shaping of a historical narrative that depicts scholars as heroic figures, heirs of the Prophet. In this stage, scholars continue to assert their independence from the ruling class, while depending on them for the establishment of teaching institutions, and for maintaining the vast trans-regional networks of trade that facilitate scholarly travel.

A BRIEF HISTORY OF THE KAIROUAN COLLECTION

The discovery of so many manuscripts from the provincial capital of Kairouan may come as a surprise to those who do not know the history of this area. In fact, the province of *Africa* (as it was known to the Romans) was rich and prosperous long before the Arabs arrived; its cities of Carthage, Sufetula, and Hadrumentum were well-established and provided with an organized network of resistance to enemies.[8] This helps to explain the fact that the "conquest" of North Africa was not an event but a century-long process. It began with the battle of Sufetula (Sbeitla)

[8] Denys Pringle, *The Defense of Byzantine Africa from Justinian to the Arab Conquest* (Oxford: Oxford University Press, 1981), 44.

in 647[9] and continued when Uqba b Nafi was forced to recapture "Ifriqiya" in 670. Over the next five years, Uqba built up the city of Kairouan, in the middle of a plain, outlining the place for the mosque and other buildings. Al-Baladhuri (d. 279/892) wrote our first history of the conquests, but he barely mentions the military events, preferring to spend pages telling the reader about the character and deeds of Uqba b Nafi, including the magical driving out of wild beasts and scorpions from the site of Kairouan.[10] He also includes a vision in which Uqba saw the completed mosque that now bears his name; upon awaking, he immediately went and laid out the foundation.[11] This account, in which Kairouan was founded on a miracle, is an essential basis for the creation of a divinely ordained history that helps to justify the authority of the *ʿulamāʾ*.[12] In fact, however, Byzantine and Berber attacks continued for decades, and not until the reign of Abd al-Malik b. Marwan was North Africa finally conquered, with the defeat of Byzantine forces in Carthage around 697.[13] In 705, the *wilāya* (province) of Ifriqiya was established with Kairouan as its capital.[14]

From these literary accounts, as well as what we know from the rest of the Near East, it is clear that establishing *Ifrīqiya* as an official *wilāya* is neither a reflection of actual Muslim/Arab control nor a wholesale conversion to Islam. Uprisings continued, including an insurrection of Berber tribes and former Byzantine citizens led by a queen known to the Arabs as the *kāhina* (priestess). Such uprisings were possible because the coasts were not secured, and the rural population (perhaps largely Christian) maintained ties to the rest of the Mediterranean; in the Sahel, the majority Berber population had been nominally Christian, but came under the

9 Politics and religion, it seemed, played a role in the fact that Constantinople failed to reinforce local militias; before the battle, in 646, the councils of Numidia, Byzaceum, Mauritania, and Proconsularis unanimously condemned Monothelitism, and shortly thereafter the African patrician Gregory proclaimed himself emperor, effectively cutting himself off from aid (ibid., 46).

10 Aḥmad b. Yaḥyā al-Balādhurī, *Futūḥ al-Buldān*, 317–322. Translated by Philip K. Hitti as *The Origins of the Islamic State (Kitāb futūḥ al-buldān)* (New York: Columbia University Press, 1916), 356–361.

11 Ibid.

12 See also the *ḥadīth* of the Prophet mentioned in Chapter 1, where he foresees that "On the day of resurrection there will arise a people from my community from Africa; their faces will be strongly illuminated, like the light of the moon when it is full."

13 Pringle, *Defense*, 49–50 and 120. The specific date is disputed.

14 Jamil Abun-Nasr, *A History of the Maghrib in the Islamic Period* (Cambridge: Cambridge University Press, 1987), 32. Up until this time, the entire Maghrib had been under the administration of the *wilāya* of Egypt.

influence of Ibadi Kharijism.[15] Arabs from the east (some of whom may also have been Christian) were a definite minority, and, as outlined in previous chapters, the boundaries of "Islam" were still poorly defined.

It is at this point that Abu l-Arab al-Tamimi, our early North African historian of the *ʿulamāʾ*, makes some specific claims about the rise of a scholarly class. He opens his account by dutifully listing the Prophet's Companions who spent time in North Africa,[16] but it is not until the caliphate of Umar b. Abd al-Aziz that his story really takes shape. Umar, we are told, appointed Ismaʿil ibn Abdallah ibn Abi l-Muhajir as governor over the Maghrib in 720, and Ismaʿil "invited the Berbers to Islam."[17] Abu l-Arab credits Umar with "sending ten members of the Follower generation to teach the people of Africa."[18] As we have already seen in Chapter 1, this general verb for "teaching" (*yufaqqihūna*) seems to suggest the teaching of Islamic jurisprudence (*fiqh*), but the specific activities recorded by Abu l-Arab are more in line with setting up a bureaucracy. For example, he tells us that one of the ten, Ismaʿil b. Ubayd, served as overseer of a market and of endowments (*aḥbās*).[19] Another, Abd al-Rahman b. Rafi, served as *qāḍī*, a position that likely had more to do with administration of government than with heading up an independent judiciary.[20] Only in one case does Abu l-Arab record a *ḥadīth*, transmitted through Sahnun himself, that mentions a specific instance of religious instruction:

Jabla b. Hammud told me on the authority of Sahnun from Muʿawiya al-Sumadihi from Abd al-Rahman b. Ziyad [who said] that among the people of North Africa, wine was permitted until Umar b. Abd al-Aziz sent these *fuqahāʾ*, and they made known (*ʿarrafū*) that it was forbidden. Another [account has it] that when "the overseen" (*al-musawwada*) arrived, meaning the army, word

[15] Abdallah Laroui, *A History of the Maghrib: An Interpretive Essay*, Ralph Mannheim (trans.) (Princeton: Princeton University Press, 1977), 117. T. Lewicki, "Al-Ibāḍiyya," in *The Encyclopaedia of Islam*, 2nd ed., 3:655.

[16] Ben Cheneb, *Ṭabaqāt*, 16–18. See also Miklos Muranyi, *Die Prophetengenossen in der frühislamischen Geschichte* (Bonn: Orientalistisches Seminar der Universität Bonn, 1973), 158ff.

[17] Balādhurī, *Futūḥ al-Buldān*, 323–324. Note that this seems to continue a policy initiated by Abu al-Muhajir in the 670s (Mohamed Talbi, "al-Ḳayrawān," in *The Encyclopaedia of Islam*, 2nd ed., 4:826).

[18] Abu l-Arab suggests that the first of Kairouan's renowned Muslim scholars came from this group (Ben Cheneb, *Ṭabaqāt*, 20–21).

[19] Ibid., 20. Just a paragraph later, Abu l-Arab says that Ismaʿil b. Ubayd was not one of the ten sent by Umar.

[20] Ibid. Governors applied justice in their courts at this time; see ibid., 21.

spread that [wine] was forbidden; this spread among the people of the east when they came [to North Africa].[21]

North Africa was known for its wine production since ancient times, an agricultural history that clearly continued under Byzantine Christian rule, so it is hard to imagine a better example of the long process by which Islam came to differentiate itself from other religions than this evidence that in North Africa, one hundred years after the *hijra*, Muslims did not know that wine was forbidden. This story also clarifies the limits of what served as scholarly knowledge at this time (simple food prohibitions, not complex legal or theological speculation), and it reinforces the nonspecialized nature of this knowledge: virtually anyone could be expected to know this and other basics of the faith; no specialized training was required or available.[22] What Abu l-Arab is describing in this report, therefore, is precisely the social role of the proto-scholar that I described in Chapter 2: individuals with some expertise and local authority instructed small groups, but there is no evidence of training or organization.

Abu l-Arab's story of Umar sending a delegation of Followers to Kairouan is a second founding of the city, this one based on knowledge and direct connections with the Prophet as opposed to force of arms and miracles. Even so, Umar's mission to the Berbers was not a success, further demonstrating the limits of these projects. Not only were the mountainous, interior regions of the area closed to the Arab elite, the conquests along the coastline, including the campaigns of 711–732 that would bring the Iberian peninsula under nominal Umayyad control, also did not result in anything like a unified empire. Abu l-Arab's account ignores this political context and continues, rather, by establishing the lineage that would connect scholars of his generation to these original teachers supposedly sent in the eighth century who were themselves connected to the Prophet. Again, the details are important. We are told, for example, that Yahya b. Saʿid b. Qays al-Ansari (whom Malik himself quoted on occasion) came to Africa to teach there (*jālasa bi-hā*) and that

[21] Ibid., 21. As Wael Hallaq points out, wine drinking served as a marker for the general lack of Islamic legal regulation during this period; he relates the story of Shurayh b. al-Harith (d. 80/699–700?) who was a respected *qāḍī* despite his devotion to wine (Hallaq, *Origins*, 40–41).

[22] Al-Shafiʿi's three levels of knowledge (discussed in Chapter 4) are interesting to consider at this point. This fits into his most basic level, which al-Shafiʿi required of all Muslims. While he is referring to three classes in society, it may also mirror a historical evolution.

ḥadīth were collected from him that did not appear in Malik's *Muwaṭṭa*ʾ.[23] Another early teacher is remembered as having writings:

In Tunis [lived] Khalid b. Abi Imran al-Tujibi. He had heard [*ḥadīth*] from al-Qasim b. Muhammad, the grandson of Abu Bakr al-Siddiq, and from Salim b. Abdallah, the grandson of Umar b. al-Khattab, and from Sulayman b. Yasar. [Khalid] had a large *kitāb* [where he recorded his transmissions] from them. Abdallah b. Abi Zakariya al-Hafri told me about it, on the authority of his father, from Abd al-Malik b. Abi Karima, from Kalid b. Abi Imran [himself], who said: "I asked al-Qasim b. Muhammad, Salim b. Abdallah and Sulayman b. Yasar ..." Khalid was trustworthy and reliable (*thiqa wa maʾmūn*).[24]

There are several points worth noting from these stories. First, the criteria for being in this group appears to consist of (1) personal connections to important members of the Prophet's Companions, (2) collecting unspecified stories (*ḥadīth*) from them, and (3) passing these stories on to others. Oral transmission appears to be the rule, though it seems reasonable that some collections would be written; these, of course, are not books and no community is mentioned that would have an interest in passing down these writings intact. It is also interesting to note that the content of these *ḥadīth* is not defined – we do not know if they referred to history, law, theology, or some other subject. We also find no mention of the Qurʾan or of other books in these descriptions.

Abu l-Arab's account shifts significantly in the generation before Sahnun, scholars who would have been rough contemporaries with Malik b. Anas. Compared with earlier entries, Abu l-Arab now provides much richer detail. Further, in some cases, we can cross-check his information with manuscript evidence. For example, Abu l-Arab writes:

Abu l-Hasan Ali b. Ziyad was from the people of Tunis. He was trustworthy (*thiqa*), reliable, insightful (*faqīhan*), decisive, devout, and proficient in jurisprudence. He took auditions from Malik b. Anas, Sufyan al-Thawri, al-Layth b. Saʿd, Ibn Lahiʿa and others – he had no equal in his generation ... [Abu l-Arab] said: it has reached me that Asad b. al-Furat said "I entreat God both for Ali b. Ziyad and my father, because [Ali b. Ziyad] was the first to teach me *ʿilm*. Abu l-Arab also said that Sahnun preferred no one in *Ifrīqiya* to [Ali b. Ziyad].[25]

Later in this entry, Abu l-Arab tells us that Ali b. Ziyad died in 183 (799 CE). Ali b. Ziyad's brief biography is altogether similar to those of many other scholars from his generation that Abu l-Arab records. The

[23] Ben Cheneb, *Ṭabaqāt*, 25.
[24] Ibid., 245.
[25] Ibid., 251.

difference is that we happen to possess a manuscript of Ali b. Ziyad's transmission of the *Muwaṭṭa'* as passed down through Sahnun. As I detail in the Appendix, this fragment (number 20) may have been written in Sahnun's lifetime; it was certainly written before AH 288 and is therefore an older witness to Ali b. Ziyad's scholarly activity than Abu l-Arab's entry. This manuscript, along with quotations attributed to Ali b. Ziyad in Sahnun's *Mudawwana* and in other early legal texts, corroborates Abu l-Arab's description in two ways. First, Ali b. Ziyad does indeed appear in Sahnun's texts as a source and, second, he definitely passed on Malik's *Muwaṭṭa'* in Kairouan.[26] Whether we should therefore treat all of Abu l-Arab's accounts from this generation as factual is open to debate, but this entry at least seems to accord with the material evidence.

The notion of an emerging scholarly community in Tunis and Kairouan in the last quarter of the second/eighth century is slightly behind our evidence from Egypt and Medina. But the transmission of Malik's text to Ali b. Ziyad and to Sahnun is direct evidence that scholars already in this period travelled in search of knowledge from North Africa to Medina. There is every reason to suspect that these travels were common throughout the eastern Mediterranean. The fact of travel is important, because it provides evidence of political stability in the region where scholars and merchants (often the same individual) could travel land and sea routes in safety. In Baghdad, this stability had to do with the rise of the Abbasid caliphs, but in the Mediterranean, it was dependent upon new, quasi-independent political entities: the Umayyads in Spain, the Idrisids in *al-Maghrib al-Aqṣā* (the "far west"), and the Aghlabid amirate in modern-day Tunisia.

The Aghlabid amirate is well-documented in literary as well as artistic, architectural, and numismatic evidence.[27] Al-Baladhuri recounts the advent of the Aghlabids in an almost conversational style, which is indicative of his personal familiarity with the events. He writes that Ibrahim b al-Aghlab ran away from Kairouan to a region called the Zab (in present-day Algeria), after raiding the treasury. He assumed command of the troops in this frontier area and demonstrated his fealty to the governor of Kairouan, Harthama. Al-Baladhuri continues:

When Harthama's resignation from the governorship of [*Ifrīqiya*] was accepted, he was succeeded by Ibn al-Akki, whose rule was so bad that the people rose up

[26] It is interesting that Abu l-Arab calls this a *samā'* from Malik, not his *Muwaṭṭa'* per se, even though this manuscript must have been in Kairouan when Abu l-Arab wrote his text.

[27] Muhammad Abu l-Faraj al-'Ush, *Monnaies Aġlabides étudiées en relation avec l'histoire des Aġlabides* (Damascus: Institut Français de Damas, 1982).

against him. [Abbasid Caliph Harun] al-Rashid consulted Harthama regarding a man whom he could assign to that post and entrust to him its management, and Harthama advised him that Ibrahim be reconciled, won over and appointed over the region. Accordingly, al-Rashid wrote to Ibrahim, stating that he had forgiven him his crime, excused his fault and thought it wise to assign him to the governorship of al-Maghrib as an act of favor, expecting to receive from him loyalty and good counsel. Ibrahim became ruler of the region and managed its affairs thoroughly.[28]

This statement suggests that strong ties between Baghdad and Kairouan were at the root of this arrangement between caliph and vassal. It conceals, however, a significant change in status for Kairouan and its province. Coins from the period show that the Aghlabid amirs first minted money under the name of the Abbasid caliph but later substituted their own names, with no mention of their overlord.[29] The story presented by these coins is repeated in architecture, bureaucratic structure, and scholarship. In all these areas the template established in the east is first copied and then locally developed.

Under the Aghlabids, Kairouan's intellectual life, architecture, and economy all flourished during a time of general prosperity with merchants who travelled extensively.[30] Because manuscripts are expensive to produce, economic prosperity is a prerequisite for a scholarly community based on written texts. Local scholars also appear to have been independent of the Aghlabids, leading to a number of confrontations between the citizens of Kairouan and their rulers;[31] it could be due to their increasing criticism that the government palace, originally located to the east of the grand mosque, was abandoned. Instead, the amirs moved their seat of administration outside of Kairouan to a new city, called al-Abbasiyya, a few kilometers to the south.[32] The name of the city, as well as the very idea of moving the seat of government outside of the capital, are among the several ways that the Aghlabids mimicked their Abbasid suzerains in building what was essentially an independent polity.[33]

[28] Al-Balādhurī, *Futūḥ*, 370.

[29] Al-ʿUsh, *Monnaies*, 18.

[30] Laroui, *History*, 107. Just as in earlier decades, revolts challenged the government from time to time, but Arab rule had finally begun to settle in, at least in the limited region of the amirate.

[31] See J. Schacht, "Aghlabids," in *The Encyclopaedia of Islam*, 2nd ed., 1:249.

[32] Al-Balādhurī, *Futūḥ*, 371.

[33] The Abbasids moved from Baghdad to Samarra in 836. Georges Marçais, *Manuel d'art musulman: l'architecture* (Paris: A. Picard, 1926), 9, where he also mentions that the Aghlabids supposedly established an African guard, as did the Abbasids.

The move to al-Abbasiyya is evidence of an autonomous citizenry in Kairouan. Not only did the city no longer depend on the government for its existence, it proved strong enough to force the amir to move out, and numismatic evidence confirms both local wealth and an active commerce with Europe, central Africa, and the East.[34] Under the third amir, Ziyadat Allah I (r. 817–838) the conquest of Sicily, led by the scholar Asad b. al-Furat in 827, ushered in a long period of peace for the amirate.[35] The pursuit of jihad by the government helped quell murmurings by religious leaders and gave the restless troops an outlet for their aggressions. Before his death, Ziyadat Allah also completely demolished and rebuilt the grand mosque of Kairouan in the year 836,[36] creating the beautiful structure that Sahnun himself taught in, and which has remained almost completely intact to this day.[37]

According to Ibrahim Shabbuh, the historian who published the first description of the collection in 1956, it was after the completion of these renovations that the library of the Sidi Uqba mosque was established within the arcade, to the north of the massive minaret (Figure 5.1).[38] Shabbuh suggests that it was the community of scholars, not the Aghlabid rulers, who endowed the library with their own books,[39] perhaps including precious Qurʾan manuscripts that had been brought to Kairouan from the Near East.[40] We have some evidence of this early stage of the library from endowment notes on the manuscripts themselves (though they often simply list the fact of endowment, not the place). More direct evidence is found in an extraordinary handlist (*sijill*), dating to the year 693/1294, that records 125 manuscripts in the library at that point.[41] While the descriptions of the

[34] Al-ʿUsh, *Monnaies*. 20. Laroui, *History*, 119.

[35] Laroui, *History*, 118. See Asad's speech, discussed in Chapter 3.

[36] Marçais, *Manuel*, 16.

[37] Ibid, 14. Ironically, Marçais calls the mosque "a museum of Christian and pagan art," as its columns were taken from Roman and Byzantine sites, and its capitals reflect the work of artists from Constantinople and Italy.

[38] Ibrāhīm Shabbūḥ, "Sijill qadīm li-maktabat jāmiʿ al-Qayrawān," *Revue de l'Institut des Manuscrits Arabes* 2 (1956), 339–372, at 339.

[39] Ibid.

[40] According to Mr. Saleh al-Mehdi, the chief conservator of the Kairouan collection, the laboratory sent out some Qurʾan fragments for radiocarbon dating, and the oldest have been dated to the first quarter of the second Islamic century (private communication, December, 2015).

[41] Shabbūḥ, "Sijill." The number 125 is somewhat misleading, since the handlist groups many texts together. See also Werner Schwartz, "Die Bibliothek der großen Moschee von al-Qayrawān, Tunesien: Vorarbeiten zu ihrer Geschichte," Unpublished thesis. Fachhochschule für Bibliotheks- und Dokumentationswesen, Cologne, 1986 (my thanks to Thomas Eich for this reference).

Figure 5.1: Photograph of Kairouan mosque, *circa* 1929,

texts are laconic, they give some evidence that these manuscripts have resided in the same location for centuries. Among these manuscripts is listing number 67: "Seven notebooks (*dafātir*) of Ibn Abd al-Hakam's *Compendium*."[42] The collection today contains both more and less than that note would indicate.

THE STUDY OF IBN ABD AL-HAKAM'S TEXTS IN KAIROUAN

To demonstrate the benefits of working with Kairouan's interlinked collection of manuscripts, I again take up the history of Ibn Abd al-Hakam's texts. While none of the manuscripts of Ibn Abd al-Hakam's works appears on my list of the most ancient dated manuscripts in the Appendix, they were all produced in the same milieu. Therefore, Ibn Abd al-Hakam's texts offer us an excellent test case to show how the collection of dated manuscripts can help us understand patterns of usage regarding undated manuscripts written down in the ninth and tenth centuries.

[42] Ibid., 360.

Interestingly, many of the Kairouan manuscripts, including those of Ibn Abd al-Hakam's books, were actually produced during the Fatimid period, demonstrating that the Fatimids respected the independence of the scholarly community, or perhaps that scholars were not directly dependent on government sponsorship. The story of the spectacular rise of the Fatimid state (and the equally ignominious fall of the Aghlabids) need not detain us, other than to point out that the last Aghlabid amir Ziyadat Allah III, who is said to have despaired and walled himself up in the castle of Raqqada, received the ridicule of scholars, who recorded him crying out: "Fill me up and give me to drink! what enemy will hurt me?"[43] Abu Abd Allah al-Shi'i and Ubayd Allah al-Mahdi ceremoniously entered Raqqada together in January of 910.[44] This may have been the height of Fatimid influence over the scholars of Kairouan, who were not exactly overwhelmed with enthusiasm for the Mahdi.[45] Ubayd Allah quickly moved out of Kairouan, founding the city of Mahdiyya around the year 912, and in 921 he inaugurated it as his new capital.[46] After his arrival there, Ubayd Allah began constructing a large navy and conducted several invasions of Egypt.

For the next few decades (at least until the Kharijite rebellion of 943), Kairouan was left to flourish on its own, and despite the political turmoil, its scholars apparently maintained close links with active centers in Egypt and Andalusia, bringing both the latest texts from these centers as well as older texts that had not been transmitted by Sahnun. Among these were Ibn Abd al-Hakam's two *Compendia*, as witnessed by several manuscripts, all of which I have examined in person: (1) five fragments of the *Major Compendium*, (2) a single fragment of the *Minor Compendium* (currently distributed in three separate folders), and (3) a single page from Abu Bakr al-Abhari's commentary on the *Major Compendium*. It is very

[43] Arīb b. Sa'd [d. Cordoba, AH 977], *An Account of the Establishment of the Fatemite Dynasty in Africa*, John Nicholson (trans.) (Tübingen: Ludwig Fues, 1840), 74–75. De Lacy O'Leary (*Short History of the Fatimid Khalifate* [London: Kegan Paul, 1923], 262) identified Nicholson's manuscript (falsely attributed to al-Mas'udi) as belonging to Ibn Sa'd.

[44] Paula Saunders, *Ritual, Politics, and the City in Fatimid Cairo* (Albany: State University of New York Press, 1994), 13–14.

[45] Ibn Sa'd, *Account*, 110. On pp. 117–118 Ibn Sa'd records the following poem composed by "a young fellow of Qayrawān:" "We could have borne with tyranny; but not with blasphemy and stupidity! Oh thou who boastest thy knowledge of mysteries, who wrote this note?"

[46] For the architecture, see Marçais, *Manuel*, 100.

likely that more fragments are to be found in Kairouan, but this is what we know of at the present time.

Description of the Manuscripts

Of the five fragments of *al-Mukhtasar al-kabir fi l-fiqh* in Kairouan, only the largest has been fully described. This is the twenty-three-folio fragment located under serial number (*rutbī*) 85, written in typical North African Kufi, on parchment measuring 29 cm by 18 cm, with twenty-six lines per page (see Figure 5.2).[47] As Joseph Schacht noted in his article, this manuscript belonged to a certain "Ṣūlād b. Abi l-Qāsim," who cannot otherwise be identified. Schacht also provided section titles but did not record an important piece of marginalia that I discuss below. The remaining fragments have not previously been fully described.[48]

Serial number 1662 is in folder (*milaff*) 13; it is a single parchment folio, 30 cm by 18 cm with thirty-four lines per page in North African Kufi; it begins with "the second book on business transactions" and also belonged to Sulad b. Abi l-Qasim. It has an endowment remark "to the mosque of the city of Kairouan." Serial number 3/498 (in folder 47) is also a short fragment of only two folios (with the back page entirely blank); it is on parchment measuring 29 cm by 18 cm and has the same ownership and endowment remarks as serial number 1662. It covers part of the chapters on drinks (*ashriba*) and rites of sacrifice at the birth of a child (*ʿaqīqa*). Serial number 342/5 is a heavily damaged manuscript of eight folios in folder 23, now 10 cm by 16 cm, since only the top third remains, the bottom having rotted away. The contents has to do with *zakat*. It is also on parchment in *naskhī* script with about ten lines remaining on a page.

Finally, serial number 1646 (in folder 13) is made of a single *kurrāsa* of 16 folios (eight parchment leaves folded and bound in the middle to make a notebook); the pages measure 25 cm by 16 cm, and the script is fine North African Kufi with few dots or vowel marks, rather compact, with thirty-four lines on a page.[49] The text is that of the *jāmiʿ*, the appendix to the *Major Compendium* that contains an unorganized discussion of

[47] This is the only one described by Schacht, "On Some Manuscripts," 239–240.

[48] I identified these manuscripts with the assistance of al-Sadiq Malik al-Gharyani during a research trip to Tunisia in 1996.

[49] Folio 1a is a title page; the text begins on 1b. The text then ends of 15b, where a new unidentified text begins, continuing on 16a–b.

Figure 5.2: Folios 22b–23a of *al-Mukhtaṣar al-kabīr fi l-fiqh* by Abdallah b. Abd al-Hakam. Serial number 85, collection of the National Laboratory for the Restoration of Parchment Manuscripts, Raqqada, Tunisia.

several different legal topics.[50] While the manuscript is badly damaged (the bottom third of the front page is entirely missing, and there is water and other damage inside), some pages are nearly complete. Importantly, it has a reader's remark from Ali al-Dabbagh, dated to AH 355, that I will discuss below.

In addition to these five fragments of the *Major Compendium*, there are fragments of two other texts worth noting. First, with the assistance of Dr. Mourad Rammah, I identified a single folio as al-Abhari's commentary on *al-Mukhtaṣar al-kabīr fi l-fiqh*.[51] This manuscript is catalogued by the serial number 6400 and is an unusually small size of 15.5 cm by 16 cm (Figure 5.3). Only the first page of the "third part of the [chapter on]

[50] Brockopp, *Early Maliki Law*, 93–95.

[51] This was during a research trip in the spring of 2000. I am grateful to the Fulbright Foundation for supporting this trip.

Figure 5.3: Folios 1a–1b of al-Abhari's commentary on *al-Mukhtaṣar al-kabīr fī l-fiqh*. Serial number 6400, collection of the National Laboratory for the Restoration of Parchment Manuscripts, Raqqada, Tunisia.

manumission and clientage from the Compendium of Abd Allah b. Abd al-Hakam [with the] commentary of Abu Bakr al-Abhari, the Maliki" is preserved. Along with this title, the obverse contains an endowment notice: "Shaykh and jurist Abu Muhammad Abd al-Aziz b. Abd al-Jalil dedicated [this manuscript] as an endowment for the search for knowledge at the Madrasa of . . ." The manuscript is damaged at this point, but Abd al-Aziz b. Abd al-Jalil (d. 702/1302–1303) is a well-known figure in the Kairouan collection, according to the late Shaykh al-Sadiq Malik al-Gharyani, who helped me decipher this passage.[52] The script is strikingly similar to that found on manuscripts of Ibn Abd al-Hakam's *Minor Compendium*, which I discuss next.[53] As noted in Chapter 3, al-Abhari was from Baghdad, and his commentary was well-known in the East, but this manuscript demonstrates a continuing connection between scholars in Kairouan and Baghdad well beyond the period covered in this chapter.

[52] In a private communication from September 2013, Miklos Muranyi confirmed that Abd al-Aziz b. Abd al-Jalil appears in many endowment notes in the Kairouan collection. His father, Abdallah b. Ali, died in 636/1238.

[53] If correct, that provides a rough *terminus post quem* for these manuscripts, since al-Abhari died in 375/985. My earlier conjecture that the manuscripts of the *Minor Compendium* might be dated "as early as the 280s/890s" (Brockopp, "*Minor Compendium*," 158) could therefore be a century too early.

The final manuscript of interest to us here is that of Ibn Abd al-Hakam's *Minor Compendium (al-Mukhtaṣar al-ṣaghīr)*. This text is of tremendous importance for the history of early Islamic scholarship; it has been capably edited based, unfortunately, on a much later manuscript with no regard for the Kairouan fragments.[54] Currently, only about one-third of the text is known to exist in Kairouan, eight folios from a single original, now found in three different locations. Using the later manuscript as a guide, I have tentatively reconstructed the Kairouan manuscript as follows: folios 1a–4b are missing; 5a–b are found in serial number 94/14 located in folder 35 (or 23 according to the new computer catalog); 6a–b are missing; 7a–b are in 915/2 (folder 49); 8a–b are in a third fragment, without a *rutbī* designation, in folder 75; 9a–10b are also in 915/2; 11a–b are in the folder 75 fragment; 12a–b are in 915/2; 13a–b are missing, and 14a–b are in 94/14.[55] The remainder of the manuscript, probably four more folios in this *kurrāsa* and an additional ten folios, may yet emerge from the folders of loose folios in the collection.

Analysis of the Ibn Abd al-Hakam Manuscripts

In Chapter 3, I used these manuscripts, along with manuscript witnesses from Fez, Gotha and al-Azhar, to demonstrate that Ibn Abd al-Hakam's *Major Compendium* was a book, written within his lifetime (he died in 214/829) and passed on, intact, to later generations. What interests me here, however, is the activity of those later generations. For example, Ibn Abd al-Hakam's texts appear to have been brought to Kairouan by scholars in the generation after Sahnun. The beginning of serial number 85 (the fragment that Schacht described in 1967) states: "*qāla Muḥammad b. Abd Allāh b. Abd al-Ḥakam ʿan abīhi Abd Allāh, qāla* (Muhammad, the son of Abdallah b. Abd al-Hakam said on the authority of his father, Abdallah, who said . . .)."[56] From this incipit, we do not know who heard and copied the text from Muhammad; for that we can turn to a student's remark that Schacht did not record, perhaps because it appears on the manuscript after the colophon (see Figure 5.2):

[54] *Al-Mukhtaṣar al-ṣaghīr li ʿAbd Allāh b. ʿAbd al-Ḥakam*, ʿUmar ʿAlī Abū Bakr Zāryā (ed.) (Al-Riyāḍ: Dār Ibn al-Qayyim li l-Nashr wa-l-Tawzīʿ, 2013).

[55] For a full description and analysis, see Brockopp, "*Minor Compendium*."

[56] Kairouan 85, fol. 1b. Elsewhere this formula is dropped, and it simply states: Abdallah b. Abd al-Hakam said . . .

أخبرنا به ابو جعفر احمد بن محمد القصري[57] قال حدثنا به محمد[58] ابو علي الحسن بن محمد بن رمضان عن ابيه محمد بن رمضان بن شاكر عن محمد بن عبد الله عن ابيه عبد الله بن عبد الحكم وقابلته بكتابه وصحّ بحمد الله.

We do not know who penned this statement. I read it as "Abu Jaʿfar Ahmad b. Muhammad al-Qasri taught us from [this manuscript], saying that he heard it from Abu Ali al-Hasan b. Muhammad b. Ramadan from his father Muhammad b. Ramadan b. Shakir from Muhammad b. Abdallah from his father Abdallah b. Abd al-Hakam and I compared [Abu Jaʿfar's copy] with [Abu Ali al-Hasan's] writing and it is correct, praise God." The script and ink of this note match that of correction remarks throughout the manuscript, while they do not match the writing of the text itself.

By itself, this note demonstrates that this manuscript was subject to a combination of oral and written transmission in which our anonymous scholar took care to compare this manuscript with another copy and record his corrections. Added to other information in the Kairouan collection, we can say with some confidence both that this manuscript was written and studied in the early fourth/tenth century, and also that this method of disciplined transmission was not unusual. For example, Abu Jaʿfar Ahmad b. Muhammad al-Qasri, the first name in this chain, is known to the literary sources as a collector of books in Kairouan who died in 321–322/933–934.[59] This is prima facie evidence that Ibn Abd al-Hakam's text was taught in Kairouan at the beginning of the Fatimid period. Our source for this biographical information is Abu l-Arab al-Tamimi, who was a contemporary of Abu Jaʿfar al-Qasri. But we do not have to depend solely on literary texts for our information, since Abu Jaʿfar al-Qasri is mentioned in an important colophon on a page of Yahya b. Umar al-Kinani's writings. This unusual comment has already been analyzed by Muranyi,[60] but it bears repeating here because these two individuals, al-Qasri and al-Kinani, virtually unknown in the modern study of Islamic law, play significant roles in the Kairouan collection.

[57] My correction; the original script reads more like القلهنى

[58] Crossed out in original. In a private communication, September 2013, Miklos Muranyi suggested that the crossing out is evidence of a *Schreibfehler*, not a *Hörfehler*, and so evidence that the scribe here is copying a note, though I am not entirely convinced.

[59] Ben Cheneb, *Ṭabaqāt*, 170; Muranyi, *Beiträge*, 177–183, though Muranyi does not mention his appearance in this manuscript. Compare Brockopp, *Early Mālikī Law*, 85n, at which point I had not yet identified the author.

[60] Muranyi, *Beiträge*, 101–103.

Al-Kinani, who lived from 213/828 to 289/902,[61] appears in many of our earliest dated Kairouan manuscripts (see numbers 8 to 11 in the Appendix). One of the most important scholars in the generation of Sahnun's students,[62] he was a key conduit through whom new works by Egyptian scholars Ashhab b. Abd al-Aziz (d. 204/819) and Asbagh b. al-Faraj (d. 225/839) came to Kairouan. Originally from Andalusia, he is said to have spent his youth in Cordoba, where he had sporadic contact with Ibn Habib. His travels are mentioned specifically in manuscripts: in Dhu l-Qaʿda 234/May 849, he studied *ḥadīth* in Mecca, and he was in Qulzum (ancient Clysma) in Shawwal 262/June–July 876.[63] I provide more details in the Appendix, but among our earliest dated fragments is one of al-Kinani's own texts, *Kitāb al-Ḥujja fi l-radd ʿalā al-Shāfiʿī.* It is dated to AH 271, eighteen years before al-Kinani's death.[64]

Returning to the unusual colophon, it appears that in 387/997, a scribe made a copy of a text by al-Kinani and in his colophon transcribed the colophon as it appeared on the original manuscript, which reads as follows:

Ahmad b. Muhammad b. Abd al-Rahman [al-Qasri] said: I heard [this text] from Yahya b. Umar [al-Kinani] in the year 271, comparing [my notes] with his own book, and it is correct, God willing. I wrote out this, my copy here (*nasakhtu ana kitābī hādhā*), from Yahya's own copy and compared [mine] to [his] and it is correct, God willing. But I also heard it from Abu Bakr Muhammad b. Muhammad and compared it twice with his book and it is correct according to it, God willing. I heard it from Yahya in Shawwal of 271.[65]

[61] Sezgin, *Geschichte*, 1:475; Ben Cheneb, *Ṭabaqāt*, 134–136, Muranyi, *Beiträge*, 92–117. His *Aḥkām al-Sūq* (based on a much later manuscript) has been edited by Maḥmūd ʿAlī Makkī (Cairo: Wizārat al-Tarbiya wa-l-Taʿlīm, al-Idārah al-ʿĀmma lil-Thaqāfa, 1956); also edited by Ḥasan Ḥusnī ʿAbd al-Wahhāb (Tunis: al-Sharika al-Tūnisīya li l-Tawzīʿ, 1975). See also Muranyi's description of some fifteen folios (dated to 387/997) of a lost text by Yahya b. Umar in *Beiträge*, 95–103.

[62] Muranyi, *Beiträge*, 62.

[63] Ibid., 92, 179, and 103.

[64] Sezgin, *Geschichte*, 1:475. François Déroche, "Manuscrits," 347 (number 18). Schacht described this manuscript in 1967 ("On Some Manuscripts," 249), where he transliterated the incipit, including the *samāʿ* remark of Muhammad b. Umar (Yahya's brother) who wrote this down (*dawwana*) from Yahya b. Umar in his lifetime. See also Muranyi, *Beiträge*, 95.

[65] My translation of the Arabic that appears in Muranyi, *Beiträge*, 102. In my view, the repetition of phrases here suggests that the unnamed scribe of 387 may have combined two different colophon remarks.

These notes reinforce the impression from the literary sources that Abu Ja'far Ahmad al-Qasri was a particularly punctilious scholar,[66] and from the evidence of serial number 85, it appears that he passed on this love of precision to his students. These specific methods of textual discipline (recitation, correction, collation) have been noted before, but they are of especial interest with regard to Ibn Abd al-Hakam's *Major Compendium.* I have already demonstrated, through analysis of the content, that this text is a book, but here in these marginalia we learn of the specific means used to ensure the accurate transmission of this text. A book can be passed on intact only when there exists a disciplined group of individuals who are schooled in these methods of transmission.

Other notations can help specify precisely when this text was transmitted by Ibn Abd al-Hakam's Egyptian students to members of Kairouan's scholarly community. According to statements at the beginning of chapters, three other Kairouan manuscripts (serial numbers 1646, 1662, and 3/498) were also transmitted along the same initial path as that of serial number 85, from Muhammad b. Abdallah b. Abd al-Hakam to Muhammad b. Ramadan b. Shakir, but from here they diverge, following the path of Ibn Shakir to Ali b. Muhammad b. Masrur al-Dabbagh (d. 359/970).[67] From our literary sources, we know that Muhammad b. Abdallah b. Abd al-Hakam and Ibn Shakir taught in Egypt, while al-Dabbagh travelled from Kairouan to Egypt, a fact corroborated in serial number 3/498, which states in the incipit that Ali b. Muhammad b. Masrur obtained his copy in Egypt: "Ali b. Muhammad transmitted to us, saying: Muhammad b. Ramadan b. Shakir transmitted to us in Egypt, saying: Muhammad b. Abdallah b. Abd al-Hakam transmitted to us on the authority of his father, Abdallah ..."[68]

Notations on serial number 1646 of the *Major Compendium* are even more informative. As mentioned above, 1646 is made of a single *kurrāsa* of sixteen folios and is badly damaged, yet two clear sets of margin notes are visible, one in the same dark ink as the text proper (simple corrections of one or two words) and a second set with substantial additions of a line or two.[69] The text begins with a long chain of transmission:

[66] As noted by Muranyi, ibid., 177, though his remark there that Ahmad was not known for his knowledge of *fiqh* is to be corrected, based on the evidence of serial number Kairouan 85. For Ahmad's other appearances in the Kairouan collection, see ibid., 177–183.

[67] 'Iyāḍ, *Tartīb*, 2:525–528; Muranyi, *Beiträge*, 48.

[68] 3/498, fol. 1b.

[69] In one case (14a) actually written around an earlier margin note.

Abu l-Hasan Ali b. Muhammad transmitted to us, saying: Muhammad b. Ramadan ^ b. Shakir transmitted to us, saying: Muhammad b. Abdallah b. Abd al-Hakam transmitted to us on the authority of his father, saying: Abdallah b. Wahb said that Malik b. Anas said . . .[70]

The change in language here from the verb *ḥaddathanā* (he transmitted to us) to *qāla* (he said) seems to correspond with a shift from oral to written text. But what is particularly interesting here is the caret (^) inserted in the line that corresponds with a remark in the left margin ("in the year 310"). I take this to mean that the transmission of the text from Muhammad b. Ramadan to Ali b. Muhammad b. Masrur took place in the year 310; it may be that the scribe has copied this fact from an earlier manuscript, or else he received it orally from Ibn Masrur.[71] At the end of the chapter, on fol. 15b, a simple colophon is added in the same hand as the rest of the manuscript, decorated with round marks:

() The chapter on miscellaneous subjects (lit. the collection of collections) from the *Compendium* is completed ()
() Praise be to God for His help and favor ()

To the left side of this is found an anonymous note that the text was collated and corrected. Below this on the same page another remark is appended in yet a different hand: "I heard all of it from Ali b. Muhammad b. Masrur in the year 355."

In other words, in AH 355 an anonymous studied the manuscript with Ibn Masrur; not only does this give us a *terminus ante quem* for the writing of the manuscript, it also verifies the incipit as a correct representation of the chain of transmission for this manuscript. That is to say, the scribe wrote this manuscript upon hearing it directly from Ibn Masrur; this incipit was not simply copied from an older manuscript as might be the case with other manuscripts. The final Kairouan manuscript of Ibn Abd al-Hakam's *Major Compendium* (serial number 5/342) verifies the role of Muhammad b. Ramadan b. Shakir as the primary conduit of Ibn Abd al-Hakam's texts to Kairouan. It was transmitted not to Ibn Masrur, but to another jurist of the same generation, Abu Bakr Masarrah b. Muslim b. Yazid al-Hadrami (d. 373/983).[72] This confirms the desires of Kairouan scholars to travel great distances in order to

70 Serial number 1646, fol. 1b.

71 Cf. Muranyi, *Beiträge*, 224, where he suggests that al-Dabbagh was in Egypt sometime "in the first two decades of the fourth century," based on his analysis of the literary sources.

72 ʿIyāḍ, *Tartīb*, 2: 533–535; Muranyi, *Beiträge*, 233–234.

ensure both their own reputation as well as to compare their notes with a faithful copy of an important text.

To summarize, the manuscripts of Ibn Abd al-Hakam's *Major Compendium* in Kairouan offer us a plausible basis for reconstructing the dates of this text and the paths of its transmission without recourse to any literary text whatsoever. It appears that the author, Abdallah b. Abd al-Hakam, transmitted the text to his son, Muhammad, who transmitted it to Muhammad b. Ramadan b. Shakir, who was teaching it in Egypt at the beginning of the fourth/tenth century. Muhammad b. Ramadan b. Shakir apparently taught this text to a couple of different scholars (Ali b. Muhammad b. Masrur al-Dabbagh and Abu Bakr Masarrah b. Muslim b. Yazid al-Hadrami) who brought it to Kairouan, where we know it was studied in 355, though it very likely came there shortly after 310, at the beginning of the Fatimid period.

As it turns out, Masarrah b. Muslim is known to the Kairouan collection only through his transmission of the *Major Compendium.* But the Kairouan native, Ali b. Muhammad b. Masrur al-Dabbagh (the tanner), is well-known to the collection for passing on manuscripts of the *Mudawwana*, the *Muwaṭṭaʾ* in the recension of Ibn al-Qasim, and also Ibn Wahb's *Muwaṭṭaʾ*.[73] His father, Muhammad b. Masrur al-Assal ("the beekeeper"; d. 346/957), was himself a scholar who appears in many important manuscripts as a key transmitter. We have no evidence that either father or son wrote texts of their own, but their transmission of others' writings is quite evident. For example, in the above list of dated manuscripts, Muhammad b. Masrur appears as a transmitter of one of our oldest dated manuscripts, Abu Zayd Abd al-Rahman b. Abi l-Ghamr's *Majālis* (Appendix, number 10), passing this text on from Yahya b. Umar al-Kinani. He also appears on manuscripts of both the *Mudawwana* and the *Muwaṭṭaʾ*.[74] Importantly, he was connected with the Andalusian scholarly community, passing on both the *Samāʿ* of Ibn Habib (as an old man in 343/954–955 and 344/955–956) and also his *Wāḍiḥa* in 342/953–954.[75] Finally, in the preface to his *Kitāb al-nawādir wa-l-ziyādāt*, the illustrious scholar Ibn Abi Zayd al-Kairouani (d. 386/996) mentions Ibn Abd al-Hakam's *Compendium* as one of his most important sources and specifically states that he used this text in a

[73] Muranyi, *Beiträge*, 221–224.
[74] Ibid., 216–217.
[75] Ibid., 214–216, where Muranyi includes the Arabic text of colophons and *samāʿ* remarks. Cf. Ossendorf-Conrad, *Das "K. al-Wāḍiḥa."*

recension that went back through Muhammad b. Masrur.[76] In his *Mukhtaṣar al-Mudawwana*, Ibn Abi Zayd also lists him as his conduit to the (now lost) writings of Muhammad b. Sahnun.

The manuscripts of the Kairouan collection, therefore, not only corroborate information recorded by local historians, they also allow for an extensive history of manuscript transmission far beyond what can be gleaned from the literary sources. From this evidence, we know far more than simply that Ibn Abd al-Hakam's texts were studied in Kairouan; we can also determine who brought them there from Egypt, when they arrived, and who read them. This analysis offers solid evidence of a lively scholarly community in this provincial capital from 850 on, but when this is combined with work already done by Muranyi and others, it opens up significant new lines of research. For example, most work on the Kairouan collection has been thus far restricted to a focus on individual scholars,[77] but the evidence indicates that these scholars – Sahnun, al-Kinani, Ibn Habib – were all related, both directly and indirectly. Muranyi has laid the foundation for a network analysis of this community, but much more work remains to be done. A second key project is the accurate dating of every manuscript in the Kairouan collection from the third and fourth centuries. Not only can Muranyi's methods of analyzing marginal remarks be developed and refined, a thorough paleography can be established based on the morphology of the scripts used. Such work will likely result in increasing the size of the known collection, since Muranyi has already discovered one important manuscript of Kairouani origins in the British Library;[78] more are likely strewn throughout other libraries in Europe, Istanbul, and elsewhere.

If carried out, these projects have the potential to significantly increase the number Arabic manuscripts securely dated to before AH 300, possibly leading to new insights into the development of Muslim scholarship in Egypt, Cordoba, and beyond. Already, I have mentioned that the Kairouan collection contains works that originated in Baghdad; Muranyi's preliminary work on Isma'il b. Ishaq, the great Maliki Qadi of Baghdad, is an example of how to mine the Kairouan manuscripts for first-hand information on the Baghdadi intellectual community.[79] A solid paleography

[76] Muranyi, *Materialien*, 47.
[77] This is largely due to restrictions placed on researchers by local authorities, but that situation could change.
[78] Muranyi, "A Unique Manuscript."
[79] Muranyi, *Beiträge*, 371–376. See also numbers 18–19 in the Appendix.

could also have a spill-over effect for dating similar manuscripts from Andalusia and Egypt. Finally, a thorough understanding of the interconnectedness of this provincial town would help us in assessing scholarly communities in other parts of the Islamic world of the time. The Aghlabids and the Fatimids benefited from a flourishing Mediterranean society, one that took advantage of the "connectivity" provided by both sea and land routes.[80] Muslim scholarly communities developed their unique characteristics within this broader society; the concentration of wealth in "niches" like those of Kairouan provided the means to produce manuscripts. That wealth, combined with secure trade routes enabled travel, both east and west, that kept these niches in contact. This combination of stability and movement is clearly represented in the manuscripts, and the sophistication of texts and methods available in Kairouan in the late ninth century argues strongly for an equal or greater level of sophistication in other parts of the Islamic world.

MANUSCRIPT RELIQUARIES

When surveying the establishment of a scholarly community in Kairouan, I noted that the same process of development in the Near East also obtained in North Africa. Literary accounts, archeological remains, and numismatic evidence all concur that after the initial arrival of Arab soldiers, the process of differentiation from the local population was slow. The first generation of "scholars" produced no books; they appear in the literary accounts either as individual savants or as government bureaucrats. The situation started to change under the energetic Aghlabid amirs (800–909 CE), whose rise to power coincided with the appearance of our first evidence of Muslim scholarly communities in Egypt.

The great mosque of Kairouan, rebuilt by the Aghlabids in 836 (Figure 5.1), is an ideal representation of these various relationships. On the one hand, the structure, shape, and monumental size of the edifice all echo similar mosques in Eastern capitals. This is consistent with a program of representing Abbasid power in North Africa, including naming their new administrative capital al-Abbasiyya. On the other hand, the very stones and pillars of the mosque were taken from Roman and Byzantine ruins, demonstrating that this new culture was very much a pastiche of previous civilizations. But the most striking feature of the

[80] Hordon and Purcell, *Corrupting Sea*, 123–171. David Abulafia, "Mediterranean History as Global History," *History and Theory* 50 (May 2011), 220–228.

Kairouan mosque is its minaret, which had no predecessor in the East but was itself a model for the unique minarets in the Muslim West.

Likewise, our manuscript evidence demonstrates both imitation and innovation. Imitation is perhaps most important in terms of understanding the rise of scholarly communities across the Muslim world. We see in Kairouan the same pattern of development (with a delay of a few decades). We also note that Kairouan scholars kept close tabs on developments in other parts of the Muslim world, and travelers both spread texts from Kairouan and also brought eastern and western texts to Kairouan. Specifically, techniques of transmitting books verbatim, first identified in Egypt, were then brought to Kairouan. From this evidence, we may surmise that scholarly communities were first established in Iraq, but then spread rapidly.

Yet, in making this observation, innovative techniques are also extremely valuable. Our manuscripts demonstrate that Kairouan was not only the recipient of information, but also a producer. Paper serves as a material example. Already in the ninth century we find both imported paper in the Kairouan collection as well as locally produced paper. To be sure, Sahnun's *Mudawwana* lacks the sophistication and polish of earlier Egyptian texts, but its exhaustive cataloging of remote legal opinions is unusual. More important, Sahnun's text regards the Egyptian legal expert Ibn al-Qasim as little more than a conduit to Malik b. Anas, and in this way his work is a key step in the process of establishing the Maliki school as the premier form of legal authority in North Africa and Andalusia.

The intense focus on the opinions (and the practices) of Malik b. Anas by both Sahnun and also other scholars from North Africa and Andalusia can easily be seen in the contents of texts from this period. We also see this focus in the development of the biographical dictionaries, that began to organize scholars into lineages that all lead, in some way, back to Malik. Eventually, these literary texts regard Malik (and also Ibn Hanbal and al-Shafiʿi) as something of a saint, a direct conduit to Muhammad's own semi-divine practices. But in the Kairouan manuscripts, we start to see something new: the physical representation of the manuscript as something more than a utilitarian vessel for knowledge. In addition to the obvious signs of wear and intense study, we also have a few highly decorated title pages as well as some unusual formats. These suggest to me another level of devotion that is indicative of a mature scholarly community.

At the end of Chapter 4, I suggested that scholars were like pilgrims, travelling in search of divine knowledge and bringing that knowledge back home as a relic. Like all relics, the power of this knowledge is greatly enhanced by the stories that accompany it, and so the narratives of its acquisition and the chains of scholars who were involved in its transmission are duly recorded, both in the manuscripts themselves and also in the biographical dictionaries that became popular during this period. But here I want to take that analogy further and suggest that if Malik is a saint and his knowledge is a relic, then fine decorated manuscripts, such as the beautiful copy of Yahya b. Yahya's transmission of Malik's *Muwaṭṭa'* preserved in the Chester Beatty library, are reliquaries. Like the silver and gold reliquaries that fill cathedrals all over Spain, they are seemingly useless products of excess wealth that transform the text from a utilitarian vessel of language and ideas into a thing that demands awe and worship. Despite its age, the Chester Beatty manuscript (Figure 5.4 and cover illustration) is in excellent condition – indeed, while it contains marginal remarks, it is quite in contrast with manuscripts of similar age from Kairouan, which are covered with readers' remarks and students' notes, dog-eared and edge-worn. The Kairouan manuscripts were produced in the class as a course of study, and daily wear is visible on every page. The Chester Beatty manuscript was perhaps produced for royalty as a symbol of power relations between the ruling class and the scholars.

Chester Beatty Ar. 3001 has been the subject of some controversy. According to its colophon, it should be one of the oldest dated manuscripts known, completed in AH 277. Like many manuscripts collected by the Irish-American mining magnate Chester Beatty, it is physically beautiful, with liberal use of gold dust ink as well as an unusual amount of red ink. Even its marginal remarks are written in a decorative, zig-zag pattern. Despite its age and beauty, though, Arthur Arberry did not include a photograph in his extensive catalogue of the Arabic manuscripts in the library, a lacuna that François Déroche has suggested was purposeful.[81] Déroche goes further to express serious doubts that the date on the colophon is accurate, based on his analysis of the script and the paper.[82]

My own examination of the marginalia confirms this suspicion, as it seems clear that at least some of the notes were written by the same scribe who wrote the text. Further, these notes refer to scholars who died well after AH 277, so the manuscript was most likely written around AH 400.[83]

[81] Déroche, "Manuscrits," 350–351 (number 28).
[82] Ibid.
[83] The colophon could have been copied from an earlier exemplar, and since this manuscript preserves only the middle third of the text, an explanation might have been found in the final colophon, now missing.

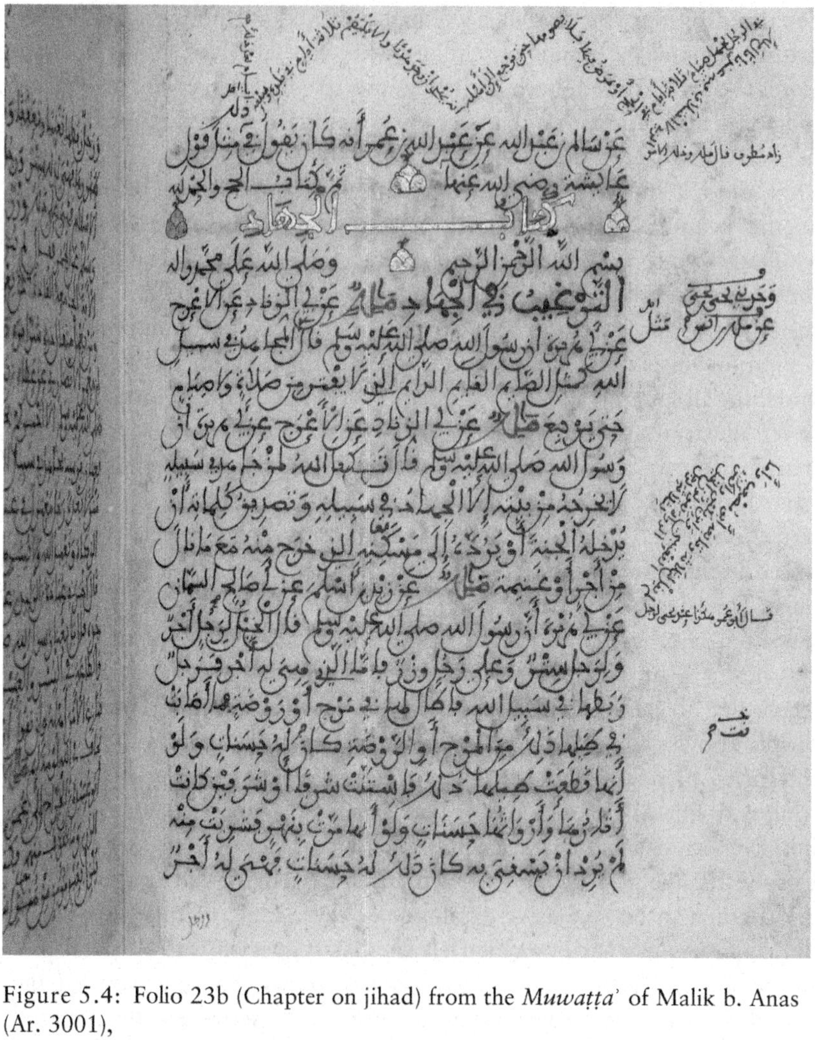

Figure 5.4: Folio 23b (Chapter on jihad) from the *Muwaṭṭa'* of Malik b. Anas (Ar. 3001),

What interests me here, though, is not the questionable date of the manuscript, but the way it treats Malik b. Anas, the namesake of the Maliki school of law. In other early manuscripts of this text, paragraphs have this heading: "Yahya told me that Malik said that . . ." or "Yahya reported to me that Malik related to him that . . ." The "Yahya" here is al-Masmudi, the famous Andalusian Berber scholar, and his transmission of Malik's text is the one most widely known today. However, as is visible in this image

(Figure 5.4), the Chester Beatty manuscript literally marginalizes Yahya's name, excising it from the text, to begin paragraphs with Malik's name or the phrase "Malik said . . ."[84] Furthermore, Malik's name in these cases is written in bold red ink, leaving no doubt as to who is the key authority in this text.

With this use of ink color, the luxurious gold of the headings, and the decorative marginal commentary, not to mention the fine quality of its paper and large size, Chester Beatty Ar. 3001 gains attributes that make it similar to Qur'ans produced around this period. If scholars are heirs to the prophets, then their books (the vessels of their knowledge) are also in a line of descent from prophetic books such as the Qur'an. Given this is the case, Malik's *Muwaṭṭa'*, which we know was not originally produced as an actual book, now becomes one. That is, texts can change their status over time, depending on the communities that use them. What was once a *hypomnena* now becomes a *syngramma*, subject to the same rules of disciplined transmission that ensure verbatim transmission of all *syngrammata*. This fact, then, helps to explain the mistaken dating of this manuscript, since in this new world, even important colophons are dutifully copied, passed down as part of the text. For much of the Muslim world today, Yahya b. Yahya's version of the *Muwaṭṭa'* has become the authoritative edition,[85] and in North and West Africa, it is considered one of the six *ṣaḥīḥ*s, the true collections of Muhammad's *sunna*.

The power of a mature scholarly community, then, outweighs any authority exercised by an individual scholar. Regardless of authorial intent, the difference between text and book ultimately resides with the community of scholars that enforces these boundaries. The Qur'an itself, given its many styles of drafting, can hardly qualify as a book written in a single redactional effort, yet the proto-scholars who devoted themselves to the careful, verbatim transmission of this text made it into a book. Likewise, the *Muwaṭṭa'* of Malik, al-Shafi'i's *Risāla*, and many other works become, over time, books, subjected to the same scholarly attention, even the same decorative arts, that we find in early Qur'an manuscripts.

[84] I am grateful to Dr. Elaine Wright and the staff at the Chester Beatty library for their kind assistance during my research trip in July 2015 and their help in providing me with this photograph.

[85] This is why we have dozens of ancient manuscripts of this recension, in comparison with only one or two for other recensions.

Conclusion

In a recent book, Asma Afsaruddin discusses a treatise written by the late Ayatullah Khomeini titled *Jihād al-nafs aw al-jihād al-akbar*.[1] According to Afsaruddin, Khomeini's conceptualization of jihad is as a social and political struggle against injustice and oppression:

> [Khomeini] addresses his treatise primarily to the scholars who are to be the vanguard of the coming revolution against unjust rulers. He says to them, "On your necks lie a heavy duty," and "you are not like other people." Their responsibility differs from the rest of humanity, for the scholar who is righteous in his behavior with people is the primary cause of the well-being of the people. According to Abū 'Abd Allāh (the Imām), the Prophet had narrated that the apostles had asked Jesus, "O spirit of God, who should we mix with?" The latter replied, "Those whose presence reminds you of God, whose deeds cause you to desire the next world, and whose speech causes you to increase in knowledge." The converse is also true; in an interesting play on words in Arabic, Khomeini comments that if "the scholar is corrupt, then the world becomes corrupt" (*idhā fasada al-ʿālim fasada al-ʿālam*).[2]

In Khomeini's understanding, then, the scholars truly are the heirs of the prophets, those who are sent by God to prevent the world from falling into corruption. By studying and passing on *ʿilm*, sacred knowledge, they keep the community of Muslims on the straight path of justice. Khomeini,

[1] Ruhollah Khomeini, *Jihād al-nafs aw al-jihād al-akbar*, with an introduction by Hasan Hanafi (Cairo, 1980?).

[2] Asma Afsaruddin, *Striving in the Path of God: Jihād and Martyrdom in Islamic Thought* (New York: Oxford University Press, 2013), 218. My quotation is from a prepublication version of Prof. Afsaruddin's book that she was kind enough to share with me; only the first part made it into print.

of course, is speaking at our end of a centuries-old tradition in which the heroes of the *ʿulamāʾ* have been long celebrated. From the great imams (Jaʿfar al-Sadiq, Abu Hanifa, Malik b. Anas, al-Shafiʿi, and Ibn Hanbal) to the great Companions (Abdallah b. Umar, Ibn Abbas, Zayd b. Thabit, etc.) to the rightly guided caliphs, these exemplary individuals have been understood as perfectly mirroring the Prophet's own actions, making their words and actions nearly equivalent to his in setting precedents.

In part, the rise of the Muslim scholar is closely tied to the rise of that heroic narrative. By the time of al-Isfahani (d. 430/1038), who recorded the miracles associated with Ibn Hanbal's trial at the hands of the Abbasid Caliph's chief judge, this narrative was well established. Likewise, Iyad b. Musa (d. 544/1149), who extolled the virtues of Malik and Sahnun, sees the scholars as part of a virtual salvation history; he cannot imagine a time when the *ʿulamāʾ* did not exist. However, in the work of earlier historians, such as Abu l-Arab (d. 333/944) and Ibn Habib (d. 238/852), we can see that this narrative is still in the process of being established. While they gather information on scholars, especially those of their own period, they have not yet created a convincing narrative for previous generations. Abu l-Arab, for example, suggests that Muslims in North Africa did not know that wine was forbidden until the late Umayyad period, hardly evidence for an influential cadre of scholars. For his part, Ibn Habib is hard pressed to name more than a few "scholars" in the first century, and details of what they may have accomplished is thin.

This line of development is mirrored in the physical evidence, which offers no sign of scholarly writings before 150/767. Further, some of those earliest texts that have come down to us are hard to distinguish from Jewish or Christian writings. As I argued in Chapter 2, Abbasa's tombstone, along with new statements on coins and on the Dome of the Rock, do suggest the increasing influence of private religious experts, but this influence was limited and shows no evidence of organization. Further, when we take sociological data into account, we realize that Muslims, to the extent that they existed at all, were but a small part of most communities in the Near East. It is reasonable to suggest that any Muslim proto-scholars would pattern their activities after those of scholars in more established religious traditions, especially those of Judaism and Christianity.

Establishing the identity of the Muslim scholar, therefore, depended on splitting off from two closely connected forerunners: (1) the influential scholars of other religious traditions and (2) trained bureaucrats serving the state. The popularity of stories that have Malik, al-Shafiʿi, and Ibn Hanbal all resisting the state, I would argue, is indicative of the effort put into separating the identity of scholars from bureaucrats. Similarly, the stories denouncing Zayd b. Thabit's connections to Judaism (as well as the silence on relationships to Jewish scholars in later biographical texts) could be seen as a similar separating mechanism. History, in my view, is part of the formation of identity for Muslim scholars – those stories that have utility in this regard are remembered, while others are forgotten. To discern the workings of these narratives, however, we must have a solid understanding of the material evidence, which is not subject to the same processes of emphasis and forgetting.

The material documents provide clear evidence of a mature scholarly community in Kairouan, demonstrating intense study of texts by a large number of scholars beginning in the mid-third/ninth century and extending well into the Fatimid period. From these manuscripts, we know that similar communities were flourishing in Andalusia, Egypt, Syria, Medina, Iraq, and Khurasan, but we do not have nearly the same level of evidence about those communities. The surviving texts further indicate a shifting relationship between oral and written sources by the end of the second/eighth century. Our earliest texts (from Ibn Lahiʿa, al-Majishun, and Malik) seem to indicate a secondary role for writing as simply a means of recording oral transmissions, whether of Prophetic *ḥadīth* or authoritative statements of important individuals. In the next generation, though (Ashhab, Ibn Wahb, and Ibn Abd al-Hakam), we see written texts taking a primary role, as these authors explicitly use writing to formulate and organize ideas based on material gathered by the previous generation. This new use for writing arises from and depends on the rise of scholarly communities: students devoted to the study of law, theology, and history who traveled the world in search of knowledge; they, in turn, developed sophisticated means to pass on books, intact, to subsequent generations. The rise of the authority of the written text was a process, one that rivaled oral authority but never eclipsed it. It coincides, I would argue, with a broader change of attitude toward Arabic as a literary language at the end of the second/eighth century.

It has been suggested that the reason we have no manuscripts of literary Arabic from earlier than AH 229 is because of a pious notion that only the Qurʾan should be written down. But even if this were true, it does not explain the lack of Christian texts in Arabic. François Déroche lists twelve of these from before 300, the earliest of which is a fragment of John's Gospel, dated to AH 245.[3] There is no doubt that significant Arab

[3] Déroche, "Manuscrits," 346.

Christian communities existed long before the rise of Islam, and it is possible that their Arabic texts have been lost, yet the scholars among them appear to have preferred Greek, Syriac, and Coptic languages as the vehicles for their writings. The inclusion of Arabic in the third/tenth century indicates, in my view, both an increase in literacy as well as a recognition of this language as an appropriate vessel for scholarly thought.

In making this argument, it is important to remember the limited nature of our evidence. While it is quite reasonable to compare Kairouan with Cairo, Cordoba, and Constantinople as a local niche within a larger Mediterranean world, this provincial capital could not possibly rival the wealth and sheer size of these three seats of power – nor that of Baghdad. The rough-hewn mosque of Kairouan is one of the most impressive examples of North African architecture to survive, relatively intact, from its renovation in 836, yet it pales in size and splendor compared to the great mosques of Cordoba (784–987), Samarra (848–851), or the al-Azhar in Cairo (972–973). Likewise, we have a precious example of North African paper production (*kāghidh*) with a reader's remark from 273/886–887, but its coarse paper is a far cry from the fine paper used in eastern manuscripts also dated to the third/ninth century. It seems reasonable to draw an analogy from these physical artifacts to the scholarship of the period. It may well be that the scholarship produced in North Africa, much like the great mosque of Kairouan, was impressive in its own right, but coarse and unrefined compared to the sophisticates of Andalusia, Egypt, Iraq, and Khurasan. With greater wealth, a larger population, and significant Jewish and Christian scholarly communities, these other centers must have had scholarly communities both larger and more advanced than what we know to have existed in Kairouan.

Therefore, the evidence from North Africa is our best argument for accepting, prima facie, many sophisticated works of scholarship attributed to the late second/eighth century as authentic until proven otherwise, including texts attributed to al-Shaybani, Abu Yusuf, Ibn Qutayba, and al-Shafiʿi. But the Kairouan collection also cautions us against making too many presumptions based on this finding. First, we cannot know when these early texts reached their present form. Like Malik's *Muwaṭṭaʾ*, they may well have begun as student recordings of oral texts, only later reduced to an accepted, written form. Second, we need to read these texts with the presumption that they represent rare survivals of a rich scholarly environment. Just as the Kairouan collection has yielded many early texts once thought to be lost and some unknown to literary accounts, so also we should accept that most of the scholarly production from these other centers has vanished. When we read the words of al-Shafiʿi and his students al-Muzani and al-Buwayti, for example, we read what later generations chose to preserve for us, surely only a small portion of the lively scholarly discussions that these texts partially reflect.

Finally, while this book is dependent on understanding newly available material sources, which require a great deal of specialized knowledge to comprehend, I believe that our inquiry can progress no further without embracing an interdisciplinary approach to these sources. People of knowledge had (and have) divine gifts, intrinsic personal qualities of intelligence and discernment, and were also part of a broad social phenomenon. Their texts are vital to our work, but alone they can give us only a narrow insight into their worlds. Literary accounts, contemporary artifacts and documents, and also sociological theory are essential to reconstructing the story of how these individuals made the transition from being heirs to the prophets to becoming Muhammad's heirs, continuing his work of establishing the religion of Islam in the centuries after his death.

Appendix

This appendix contains an annotated list of all the known Arabic literary manuscripts that can be confidently dated to before AH 300; Qur'ans and Christian manuscripts are excluded. More than three-quarters of these manuscripts (twenty-three of thirty) come from the ancient mosque-library of Kairouan, making this the most important repository of early Islamic manuscripts in the world. The appendix is therefore split into two sections, the twenty-three Kairouan manuscripts first, followed by the remaining seven. I compiled this list from several of Miklos Muranyi's publications, as well of those of Joseph Schacht and Nejmeddine Hentati, combining their notes with information gleaned from my own research. I then returned to Kairouan in December of 2015 in an attempt to verify these references first-hand. As for the remaining seven, they are far better known, and I depend largely on secondary publications for their description. However, I make no claim that this list is complete, since new discoveries are being reported all the time.[1]

Because the Kairouan collection lacks a proper catalog, I have tried to provide basic codicological information for as many manuscripts as possible; most of this information has never before been published. Because of various factors, described below, I was not able to personally

[1] In fact, an anonymous reviewer of this book referred me to a footnote in Ayman Fu'ad Sayyid's new edition of Ibn al-Nadim's *Kitāb al-Fihrist*, 4 vols. (London, 2009), volume 2, part 1, p. 120, n. 2, where he mentions a manuscript of al-Tabari's *Ikhtilāf al-fuqahā'* in Tanta (number 490) that includes a reader's remark saying that a student read the text to al-Tabari himself in the year 294/907. I have not included this manuscript in my account here because I have not been able to personally verify the information, nor have I found any scholarly study of this manuscript. But it serves as an excellent reminder of the many discoveries yet to be made.

see all of the manuscripts in my list; also, there is every reason to believe that more manuscripts with very early dates will emerge with further research. Despite these limitations, I hope that this list will prompt more scholars to make use of this unparalleled collection.

This work would not have been possible without the support of the current director of the National Laboratory for the Restoration of Parchment Manuscripts in Raqqada, Dr. Jalel Alibi, and the previous director, Dr. Mourad Rammah. They and the entire staff at the laboratory, especially Mr. Saleh al-Mehdi, chief conservator, have my profound thanks.

THE KAIROUAN MANUSCRIPTS DATED BEFORE AH 300[2]

1–5 The oldest dated fragments in the Kairouan collection are from Sahnun's *Mudawwana.* Sahnun b. Saʿid (d. 240/854) was a Kairouan native, and he taught a generation of scholars. As witnessed by the Kairouan collection, he evidently taught several important works from Egyptian scholars, in addition to his own text.

1 The oldest dated manuscript in Kairouan is a single folio; it was written before AH 235, when a student wrote a note on the bottom, stating that he had studied this text with Sahnun in that year. I discuss the importance of this manuscript in Chapter 4 and published a photograph, description, and partial transcription in 2014.[3] Muranyi does not mention this manuscript in his published works, though he alerted me to its existence. Because of the sheer number of *Mudawwana* fragments, I was not able to find this one again in 2015. Like all Kairouan manuscripts, it has no proper catalog number, but this fragment also has no serial (*rutbī*) number, making it that much more difficult to locate; when I saw it in April of 2000, it was located with dozens of other loose parchment pages in folder (*milaff*) number 69.

2 The next two *Mudawwana* fragments differ significantly from most Kairouan manuscripts in that they are dated by colophons, not by *samāʿ* remarks.[4] I saw both of these in 1996 and again in

[2] Again, this appendix contains only literary manuscripts. There is also a dated Qurʾan fragment in Kairouan (dated before AH 295) according to Déroche, "Manuscrits," 349.

[3] Brockopp, "Saḥnūn's *Mudawwana.*"

[4] These are both mentioned in Muranyi, *Rechtsbücher*, 18, though he does not offer full descriptions of the manuscripts there. He also notes that the AH 256 manuscript has a secondary remark from 292.

2015. The first fragment contains the chapter on *kirāʾ al-arḍīn;* it is located in *milaff* 29 under serial number 38 and was written by Zaydayn b. Ismaʿil in Rajab of AH 256. It is seventeen folios long, with around twenty-eight lines per page on heavy parchment with measurements that vary between 24–24.5 × 15.5–17 cm. Like many early Kairouan manuscripts, margins follow the natural shape of the animal skin to maximize the use of space, resulting in some unusual page shapes. The manuscript consists of four bifolios, loosely nested together, followed by a single loose folio, and then a second *kurrasa* of four bifolios. The chapter title on 1a is unusually decorated, and the script (compact North African Kufi) appears to match that of the main text.

3 The next fragment contains the chapter on *ṭahūr;* it is located in *milaff* 46 under serial number 1/1786 and was written by Aḥmad b. al-Budhdhār [?][5]al-Madanī in AH 258. It is eight folios long, with twenty-six to twenty-seven lines per page on heavy parchment with measurements of around 29 × 18 cm. The pages are loose and out of order, so that the end of the chapter appears on 7a, with the colophon; the script is very distinctive, with a morphology that betrays Eastern influences.

4–5 Muranyi mentions two more dated manuscripts of Sahnun's *Mudawwana* with readers' remarks from AH 279 and 294 (collection numbers and size unknown). It was not possible to verify these observations in 2015, though I have no doubt that they are accurate and that there are, in fact, many more early dated fragments of the *Mudawwana* amid the hundreds of loose folios.[6]

6–7 Important remains from the intellectual activity of Yahya b. Sallam al-Basri (d. 200/815). Yahya b. Sallam was from Iraq, lived in Kairouan, and died in Egypt.

6 *Tafsīr al-Qurʾān*. Before 260/873–874. The Kairouan collection contains very many complete parts and other loose fragments,[7]

[5] My thanks to the anonymous reviewer for this suggestion.

[6] Muranyi, "„man ḥalafa ʿalā minbarī āṯiman . . .," 94–95; idem, *Materialien*, 3-4; idem, *Beiträge*, 33–39 (on p. 79 Muranyi describes a small fragment that he argues must be dated before 276). Wesley Thiessen's dissertation (*Formation of the* Mudawwana) does not include analysis of the Kairouan manuscripts, though he has now begun that work.

[7] First described by Schacht, "On Some Manuscripts," 233, though he only recorded later marginalia, evidence that this manuscript was still in use at the end of the fourth/tenth century. Muranyi, *Beiträge*, 16–20, describes the earlier *samāʿ* remark and includes an excerpt on pages 390–396. See also Cerrahoğlu, "Yaḥyā b. Sallām ve tafsirdeki metodu."

too many to go through during my limited trip in 2015. There is some question as to whether this is the oldest manuscript of a text devoted to Qur'an interpretation in Kairouan.[8] I discuss this text in Chapter 4, where I provide further references.

7 Fragments of Yahya b. Sallam's texts on *fiqh* have also survived, offering a valuable opportunity to compare two distinct genres from a single author. A single folio from his *Kitāb al-ashriba* is located in *milaff* 30 under serial number 109 with readers' remarks from 273 and 275. 1a is the title with reader's remarks, 1b has forty-one lines of compact North Africa Kufi on heavily damaged parchment with measurements of around 25.5 × 15 cm.

8-11 Four manuscripts that exemplify the intellectual range of Yahya b. Umar al-Kinani (213/828–289/902). As discussed in Chapter 5, he was one of the most important scholars in the generation of Sahnun's students.

8 Yahya b. Umar is mentioned in a *samāʿ* remark (from Shawwal 262/July 876) on a manuscript of a collection of *ḥadīth* attributed to Sufyan b. Uyayna (d. 196/811), our earliest witness to the works of this key scholar.[9] This single bifolio (two folios) is located in *milaff* 30 under serial number 110. It has twenty-nine lines on folio 1b, fourteen lines on 2a, on parchment that is heavily damaged with measurements of around 26 × 16 cm. The script is compact Kufi with some unusual flourishes. This is an especially important text, because *ḥadīth* collections are poorly represented in Kairouan, and so it helps challenge the presumption that Maliki jurists were uninterested in *ḥadīth* as a source for law. The many *samāʿ* remarks testify to its heavy use.

9 A fragment (12 fol.) of one of Yahya b. Umar's own texts, demonstrating his engagement with the methods of al-Shafiʿi, *Kitāb al-ḥujja fi l-radd ʿalā al-Shāfiʿī*. It is dated to AH 271, eighteen years before al-Kinani's death.[10] This manuscript is located in *milaff* 10 under serial number 242. It has thirty to thirty-eight lines per

[8] See Muranyi's claim in *'Abd Allāh b. Wahb*, 53–54, regarding an undated 24 fol. manuscript under serial numbers 1779 and 1781; this is a *tafsīr* attributed to Ibn Wahb from the *Jāmiʿ*.

[9] Muranyi, *Beiträge*, 103. As usual, Muranyi does not provide codicological details or catalog numbers.

[10] Sezgin, *Geschichte*, 1:475. Déroche, "Manuscrits," 347, manuscript number 18 in Déroche's list. Schacht described this manuscript in 1967 ("On Some Manuscripts," 249), where he transliterated the incipit, including the *samāʿ* remark of Muhammad

page with narrow margins on heavy parchment that is around 25 × 14.5–15.5 cm. The twelve folios comprise five bifolios with the two outside folios stitched together. The script is compact Kufi. There is at least one other "response" to al-Shafiʿi,[11] whose works were apparently known in Kairouan, though we have no trace of them today.[12]

10 Yahya b. Umar's name also appears in a manuscript of Abu Zayd Abd al-Rahman b. Abi l-Ghamr's *Majālis* in a *samāʿ* remark from 272.[13] This manuscript is thirteen folios long, comprising five bifolios and three single folios; it is located in *milaff* 3 under serial number 3/84. It has twenty-eight to thirty-three lines per page on good quality parchment that is around 30.5 × 17–19 cm. The script is an angular North African Kufi. Ibn Abi l-Ghamr was an Egyptian who died in 234/848, and his text is devoted to auditions from Ibn al-Qasim (d. 191/806) who is also the main authority in Sahnun's *Mudawwana*. The text was taught in the circles of Muhammad b. Masrur al-Assal (d. 346/957), whom I discuss in Chapter 5.

11 Yahya b. Umar al-Kinani also transmitted a *Kitāb al-daʿwā wa-l-bayyināt* by Ashhab b. Abd al-Aziz (d. 204/820). Ashhab's works are only known through the Kairouan collection; while he is often classified as part of the Maliki school, his texts reveal a sharp, independent mind. This manuscript is unusual as it is the oldest dated manuscript in Kairouan on *kāghidh* (a coarse, locally produced paper) and the second-oldest Arabic manuscript on paper in the world; it totals eighteen folios, with eight paper bifolios inside a parchment bifolio. It is located in *milaff* 10 under serial number 1648. It has twenty-eight to twenty-nine lines per page on the paper, twenty-four on the parchment, and measures 27 × 16.5 cm. A reader's remark is from 273/886–887, well before Yahya b. Umar's death in AH 289.[14]

b. Umar (Yahya's brother) who wrote this down (*dawwana*) from Yahya b. Umar in his lifetime. See also Muranyi, *Beiträge*, 95.

11 By one Abu Bakr b. Muhammad; a bifolio is found in *milaff* 10, serial number 1637.

12 On folio 6a there is a reference to al-Muzani's *Mukhtaṣar*, for example.

13 See Schacht, "On Some Manuscripts," 240–241; number 19 in Déroche, "Manuscrits," 347; Muranyi, *Beiträge*, 83–85.

14 Miklos Muranyi, "Das Kitāb Aḥkām Ihn Ziyād," 241, n.1, where Muranyi suggests that this is the oldest datable manuscript on paper that we possess, but see the *Gharīb al-Ḥadīth*, number 25 below, discussed in Chapter 4.

12 Several other texts by Ashhab b. Abd al-Aziz are found in Kairouan, including *Kutub al-Hajj* (twenty folios), which has numerous *samāʿāt*, the oldest of which is 276/889, transmitted through Sahnun;[15] I was not able to locate this particular fragment when in Kairouan in December 2015, though I looked at several other fragments, some of which may be from the same manuscript.[16] In Muranyi's comparison of Ashhab's texts with Sahnun's *Mudawwana* he notes a curious lack of understanding on Sahnun's part.[17] This preliminary assessment indicates the possibilities presented by this collection for the analysis of school activity during this period. See also number 15 below.

13 Fragments of legal writings by Abd al-Aziz b. Abdallah b. Abi Salama al-Majishun (d. 164/780–781) are among the most important finds in Kairouan.[18] Al-Majishun was a contemporary of Malik b. Anas who also taught in Medina, and this manuscript was written down by Abd al-Jabbar b. Khalid b. Imran al-Surti (d. 281/894), who transmitted it from Sahnun and taught it in 275/888.[19] I was not able to locate this particular fragment when in Kairouan in December 2015.

Appended serial number 1648 is an undated copy of a thirty-six-line letter from Sahnun b. Saʿid to Muhammad b. Ziyad, a judge in Cordoba. Because the letter appears to have been written during Sahnun's appointment as Qadi of Kairouan, Muranyi has dated the original to between 234–238/848–852 (*Beiträge*, 46). While we have other legal correspondence preserved in literary sources, this is the oldest example of such a letter; it concerns the function of the courts of complaint (*maẓālim*). Compare Qadi Iyad, *Tarājim aghlabiyya* (M. Talbi, ed.) (Tunis, 1968), 111. My thanks to Miklos Muranyi for this reference.

15 Number 24 in Déroche, "Manuscrits," 348, extensively described in Schacht, "On Some Manuscripts," 233–235, including transliteration of the first part of the text and a list of Ashhab's works.

16 Muranyi, *Beiträge*, 54, mentions discovery of a *Kitāb al-ghasb* and a *Kitāb al ʿitq* from Ashhab.

17 Muranyi, *Rechtsbücher*, 29, where he writes: "Saḥnūn bleibt sowohl in der Vielfalt wie auch in der inhaltlichen Tiefe der einzelnen ritualrechtlichen *masāʾil* oft hinter dem Fiqhbuch des Ašhab – seiner Primärquelle – zurück."

18 Muranyi, *Beiträge*, 53, calls it the oldest example of Medinan jurisprudence we possess, and suggests that it was probably finished before 152/769.

19 An excerpt was published and analyzed in Muranyi, *Ein altes Fragment medinensischer Jurisprudenz aus Qairawān* (Stuttgart: Franz Steiner, 1985). Since then, a *Kitāb al-buyūʿ* and a *Kitāb al-ṭalāq* have been uncovered (Muranyi, "Fiqh," 312). In 1999, Muranyi shared an additional chapter on pilgrimage with me, which I analyzed in "Competing Theories of Authority". This chapter has now been published by Muranyi, together with the chapter on pilgrimage from the *ʿUtbiyya* (Beirut: Dār Ibn Ḥazm, 2007).

14 Asad b. al-Furat (d. 213/828), *Kitāb al-sariqa wa-qaṭʿ al-ṭarīq* from the *Asadiyya* (twelve folios) with two *samāʿ* remarks, one dated to 278/891.[20] I was not able to see this manuscript directly in 2015 but was able to consult a digital image at the Laboratory. Nejmeddine Hentati describes it as serial number 264, 18 × 32 cm written in old Naskhi.[21] While the tale of Asad and Sahnun may be a fiction, this manuscript is clear evidence that Asad was the conduit for Hanafi learning in Kairouan. The text names al-Shaybani, Abu Yusuf, and Abu Hanifa as sources. Schacht also described an additional twenty-three-folio fragment on manumission.[22]

15 A fragment of the *Majālis* by Ashhab b. Abd al-Aziz (see numbers 11 and 12 above) is dated to before AH 279 by a reader's remark. I do not believe this manuscript is mentioned directly by Muranyi; I happened across it in 1996. Its fourteen folios are located in *milaff* 4 under serial number 1651. It has thirty-nine lines per page; the parchment measures 28 × 16 cm.

16–17 Two fragments of Sahnun's *Mukhtaliṭa*, neither of which I have seen personally. Muranyi mentions an eight-folio fragment that he argues must have been written before 282/895 in Kairouan; he has published the colophon but provides no further information.[23] Hentati discusses several fragments, including two folios from the *kitāb al-ḥajj*, located in *milaff* 16 under serial number 333. On the second folio appears a remark by Ibrahim b. Dawud al-Qadi who heard the text in Muharram of 284.[24] The precise relationship between the *Mudawwana* and the *Mukhtaliṭa* is hard to ascertain based on these few fragments.[25]

[20] Number 25 in Déroche, "Manuscrits," 348; described in Schacht, "On Some Manuscripts," 238–239. According to Muranyi (*Beiträge*, 22–23), a few other undated fragments are in Kairouan – Muranyi says these appear to have been studied in the third/ninth century.

[21] Nejmeddine Hentati, "Min al-Asadiyya ilā l-Mukhtaliṭa fa-l-Mudawwana" in Hentati (ed.), *Dirāsāt Ḥaḍāriyya ḥawla l-Qayrawān* (Tunis: Imprimerie Officielle de la République Tunisienne, 2015), 39–52, at 40.

[22] Schacht, "On Some Manuscripts," 238.

[23] Muranyi, *Rechtsbücher*, 18.

[24] Hentati, "Min al-Asadiyya," 46–47.

[25] Muranyi, *Rechtsbücher*, 11, writes that it presents "lediglich eine *Titelvariante* der *masā'il*-Sammlung Saḥnūn's mit einer inhaltlich teilweise anderen Struktur als die *Mudawwana*."

18–19 The wide geographical range of this manuscript collection is demonstrated by the appearance of two fragments from texts by the famous Baghdad scholar Isma'il b. Ishaq al-Qadi (d. 282/895), an important representative of the Baghdad Maliki school. Manuscripts of his writings are unknown outside of Kairouan.

18 A nine-folio fragment of his *Aḥkām al-Qur'ān* is the second-oldest manuscript on paper in Kairouan (compare number 11 above); this one is in large Kufi on fine paper that has been beautifully restored by the staff at the national laboratory. It is located in *milaff* 22 under serial number 1/221 with a reader's remark from Jumada I, 282, that is before the author's death.[26]

19 The second text is part five of a *Musnad Ḥadīth Mālik b. Anas* that includes a secondary remark from 283.[27] It is located in *milaff* 1 under serial number 516 and comprises seven bifolios (fourteen folios) with matching binding holes, measuring 24–25 × 16 cm with twenty-eight lines per page (fewer on folios that are smaller).

20 Fragment of the *Muwaṭṭa'* by Malik b. Anas (d. 179/795), written before 288 (nine folios).[28] This is the oldest dated manuscript of this famous text. The transmission is from Malik to Ali b. Ziyad (d. 183/799) to Musa b. Mu'awiya (d. 225 or 226); Muranyi speculates it was actually written within Sahnun's lifetime (d. 240/854), since the date is derived from a secondary *samā'* remark.[29] Because of the sheer number of *Muwaṭṭa'* fragments, however, I was unable to locate this specific manuscript in 2015.

21–23 Muranyi has done an extensive study of the several Kairouan manuscripts that derive from the Egyptian scholar Abdallah Ibn

[26] Now edited by 'Āmir Ḥasan Ṣabrī (Beirut: Dār Ibn Ḥazm, 2005), who mentions this fragment in his introduction (pp. 55–56). My thanks to Miklos Muranyi for this information.

[27] Muranyi, *Beiträge*, 206–207. Now published by Muranyi in a facsimile edition (Beirut: Dār al-Gharb al-Islāmī, 2002).

[28] Number 30 in Déroche, "Manuscrits," 349; described in Schacht, "On Some Manuscripts," 227–228. Published as *Qiṭ'a min Muwaṭṭa' Ibn Ziyād*, Muḥammad b. Shādhilī al-Nayfar (ed.) (Tunis: al-Dār al-Tūnisiyya li-l-Nashr, 1978, and Beirut: Dār al-Gharb al-Islāmī, 1980). Al-Nayfar does not analyze the marginalia, nor does he address another fragment (one folio, maghribi script, transmitted through Ibn Sahnun, perhaps third century) found in Damascus; see Sourdel-Thomine and Sourdel, "Nouveaux documents,"15–16.

[29] Muranyi, *Beiträge*, 7–8. For Musa b. Mu'awiya, see ibid., 28–30.

Wahb (d. 197/812); three of these are dated before AH 300. I was not able to independently verify this information.

21 *Kitāb al-qaḍā' fi l-buyū'* from his *Muwaṭṭa'* (serial number 1019, twenty-two folios). This *Muwaṭṭa'* is an independent work that has little in common with Malik's book of the same title; the manuscript has a secondary *samā'* remark from 290, though Muranyi argues that it must have been written before 282/895.[30]

22 Chapters on poetry and song (*al-shi'r wa-l-ghinā'*) from Ibn Wahb's *Jāmi'* (serial number 266, fourteen folios). The manuscript was transmitted by Isa b. Miskin (d. 295) from Sahnun from Ibn Wahb. The incipit mentions that it was copied by (lit. "belonged to") Abd Allah b. Masrur (d. 346/958), and a *samā'* remark says: "I [*viz.* Ibn Masrur] heard this from Ibn Miskin in his house in 290."[31] Another manuscript, serial number 246 (twenty-six folios), contains the chapter on *'ilm* from the *Jāmi'*; it was written by the same copyist, Abd Allah b. Masrur, though it is otherwise undated.[32]

23 *Kitāb al-Tafsīr* or *Tafsīr gharīb al-Muwaṭṭa'*, serial number 96 (nine folios). Before 293/906. Muranyi explains that these are the oldest fragments from literature surrounding Ibn Wahb's *Muwaṭṭa'*.[33]

[30] Published with an analytical study as 'Abd Allāh b. Wahb, *al-Muwaṭṭa', kitāb al-qaḍā' fī al-buyū'*. See Muranyi, *Beiträge*, 36 and 51–52; on 77–79 Muranyi mentions the *samā'* remark from 290, but argues that the manuscript must have been produced before 282, the date given for the death of the last transmitter, Abd al-Rahman b. Muhammad b. Imran. I am less sanguine about mixing literary and material evidence, but the secondary *samā'* remark from 290 makes this a reasonable conjecture. For a full description of all the Kairouan manuscripts for Ibn Wahb see Muranyi, *'Abd Allāh b. Wahb*, 50–54; this book includes an edition of serial number 244, a twenty-folio fragment of the "Kitāb al-Muḥāraba" from Ibn Wahb's *Muwaṭṭa'*.

[31] Number 33 in Déroche, "Manuscrits," 349; described in Schacht, "On Some Manuscripts," 231. Muranyi, *'Abd Allāh b. Wahb*, 51.

[32] Described in Schacht, "On Some Manuscripts," 231, though the similarity is only pointed out by Muranyi, *'Abd Allāh b. Wahb*, 50. Much of the *Jami'* has been published by Muranyi in three volumes as 'Abd Allāh b. Wahb, *al-Ǧāmi': die Koranwissenschaften*, Miklos Muranyi (ed.) (Wiesbaden: Harrassowitz, 1992); idem, *al-Ǧāmi': tafsīr al-Qur'ān (die Koranexegese)*; and idem, *al-Ǧāmi': tafsīr al-Qur'ān, Koranexegese 2. Teil.* See also the study and edition of a papyrus fragment (dated before AH 276; see number 28 below) of Ibn Wahb's *Jāmi'* by J. David-Weill: *Le Djāmi' d'Ibn Wahb*, 2 vols. (Cairo: Institut Français d'Archéologie Orientale, 1939–1948).

[33] The *samā'* remark shows it was taught in circle of Yahya b. Aun (in 293), from Aun, from Ibn Wahb. Interlinear remark (in the same script as rest of manuscript) looks to be a

The importance of these twenty-three manuscripts can hardly be overstated. Not only do they make up the most extraordinary collection of early Arabic manuscripts known, they are full of textual notations that demonstrate interweaving lines of connection among authors, students, and copyists.

OTHER EARLY MANUSCRIPTS

To complete this review, I add here a list of all the other dated Arabic manuscripts of similar age from the rest of the Islamic world. Excluding Qur'ans and Christian texts, there are only seven, two of which connect directly with the scholarly communities of Egypt and North Africa.

24 Wahb b. Munabbih (d.110/728 or 114/732), *Ḥadīth Dāwūd*. Heidelberg, P. Schott-Reinhardt, Arab. 23 (twenty-nine folios). Incipit dates the manuscript to *dhū l-qaʿda* 229 (July of 844).[34] I discuss this text in Chapter 4 (see Figure 2.5).

25 *Gharīb al-Ḥadīth* by Abu Ubayd al-Qasim b. Sallam al-Baghdadi (d. 223/837), Dated Dhu al-Qa'da 252 (866). Leiden Or. 298. (241 folios).[35] Discussed in Chapter 4 (see Figure 4.1).

26 *Masāʾil ibn Ḥanbal*. Collected by Abu Dawud (d. 275/889) and dated to AH 266, well before his death. Damascus, Zahiriyya, *ḥadīth* 334 (eighty-six folios).[36] Discussed in Chapter 4.

27 *Kitāb al-siyar* by Abu Ishaq al-Fazari (d. 186/802). Fez, Qarawiyin, AH 270. This is the earliest dated source for al-Awzaʿi's thought as al-Fazari quotes extensively from al-Awzaʿi on the subject of war and international relations.[37] The law of war, of

collation remark, naming Muhammad b. Umar (d. 310/922). Muranyi, *Beiträge*, 30–32. See also Muranyi, *ʿAbd Allāh b. Wahb*, 54.

34 Number 2 in Déroche, "Manuscrits," 345; Khoury, *Wahb b. Munabbih*. Volume 1 is Khoury's study and edition with facing German translation. Volume 2 is a facsimile edition.

35 Number 6 in Déroche, "Manuscrits," 346; see bibliographic references there. Edited by Muhammad Azim al-Din in 3 vols. (Hyderabad: Osmania Oriental Publications Bureau, 1964).

36 Number 12 in Déroche, "Manuscrits," 346. First described by Ritter, "Philologika II," 250. See a partial translation by Spectorsky in *Chapters on Marriage and Divorce*, 60–90.

37 Number 15 in Déroche, "Manuscrits," 347. Muranyi, "Das Kitāb al-siyar von Abū Isḥāq al-Fazārī." Now edited by Fārūq Ḥammādah as *Kitāb al-Siyar* (Beirut: Mu'assasāt al-Risāla, 1987). Sezgin, *Geschichte*, 1:292, knows of this text, but incorrectly places it under prophetic biography, also known as *siyar*.

great interest to early jurists, is extensively covered in the Kairouan manuscripts.[38]

28 A substantial papyrus fragment of Ibn Wahb's *Jāmiʿ* (ninety-one folios) found in Edfu. A reader's remark dates it to before AH 276.[39] See further discussion of Ibn Wahb's works above, numbers 21–23.

29 *Gharīb al-Ḥadīth* by Ibn Qutayba (d. 270/884 or 276/889). AH 279; Chester Beatty, Ar. 3494 (136 folios).[40] Compare with number 25 above.

30 *Kitāb al-maʾthūr fīmā ittafaqa lafẓuhu wa-ikhtalafa maʿnāhu.* Abu l-Amaythal (d. 240/854). AH 280; Istanbul, Bayazit, Veliüddin Effendi 3139 (size unknown).[41]

[38] For an overview, see Mathias von Bredow, *Der heilige Krieg (Ǧihād) aus der Sicht der mālikitischen Rechtsschule* (Beirut: Fritz Steiner Verlag, 1994).

[39] David-Weill (ed.). Number 23 in Déroche, "Manuscrits," 348; Sezgin, *Geschichte*, 1:466. As for Chester Beatty Arab 3497 (61 ff.), Muranyi questions Arberry's dating to the third century, suggesting rather a date from the first quarter of the fifth century; see Muranyi: *ʿAbd Allāh b. Wahb*, 56–57.

[40] Number 26 in Déroche, "Manuscrits," 348.

[41] Number 28 in Déroche, "Manuscrits," 348. Edited by F. Krenkow (London: Probsthain, 1925).

Bibliography

Abbott, Nabia. *The Kurrah Papyri from Aphrodito in the Oriental Institute*, Studies in Ancient Oriental Civilization 15. Chicago: University of Chicago Press, 1938.

"A Ninth-Century Fragment of the 'Thousand Nights.' New Light on the Early History of the Arabian Nights." *Journal of Near Eastern Studies* 8, no. 3 (1949), 129–164.

Studies in Arabic Literary Papyri. 3 vols. Chicago: University of Chicago Press, 1955–1972.

Abd-Allah, Umar F. *Mālik and Medina: Islamic Legal Reasoning in the Formative Period*. Islamic History and Civilization, 101. Leiden: E. J. Brill, 2013.

Abou El Fadl, Khaled. *Conference of the Books: The Search for Beauty in Islam*. Lanham, MD: University Press of America, 2001.

Abulafia, David. "Mediterranean History as Global History." *History and Theory* 50 (May 2011), 220–228.

Abu l-Amaythal. *Kitāb al-maʾthūr fīmā ittafaqa lafẓuhu wa-ikhtalafa maʿnāhu*. F. Krenkow (ed.). London: Probsthain, 1925.

Abu l-ʿArab, Muḥammad b. Aḥmad al-Tamīmī. *Kitāb Ṭabaqāt ʿUlamāʾ Ifrīqīya*. Mohammed ben Cheneb (ed.). Beirut: Dār al-Kitāb al-Lubnānī, n.d.

Kitāb al-Miḥan. Yaḥyā Wahīb al-Jabbūrī (ed.). Beirut: Dār al-Kitāb al-Lubnānī, 1983.

Abun-Nasr, Jamil. *A History of the Maghrib in the Islamic Period*. Cambridge: Cambridge University Press, 1987.

Abū ʿUbayd al-Qāsim b. Sallām al-Baghdādī. *Gharīb al-Ḥadīth*. Muḥammad ʿAzīm al-Dīn (ed.). 3 vols. Hyderabad: Osmania Oriental Publications Bureau, 1964.

Afinogenov, Dmitry, Patrick Andrist, and Vincent Déroche. "La recension γ des Dialogica Polymorpha Antiiudaica et sa version slavonne, Disputatio in Hierosolymis sub Sophronio Patriarcha: une première approche." In Constantine Zuckerman (ed.), *Constructing the Seventh Century*, 27–103. Paris: Assocation des Amis du Centre d'Histoire et Civilisation de Byzance, 2013.

Afsaruddin, Asma. "Obedience to Political Authority: An Evolutionary Concept." In M. A. Muqtedar Khan (ed.), *Islamic Democratic Discourse: Theory, Debates, and Philosophical Perspectives*, 37–60. London: Lexington Books, 2006.

"Where Earth and Heaven Meet: Remembering Muḥammad as Head of State." In Jonathan E. Brockopp (ed.), *The Cambridge Companion to Muḥammad*, 178–195. New York: Cambridge University Press, 2010.

Striving in the Path of God: Jihād and Martyrdom in Islamic Thought. New York: Oxford University Press, 2013.

Ahmed, Shahab. *What Is Islam? The Importance of Being Islamic*. Princeton: Princeton University Press, 2015.

Andrist, Patrick. "Questions ouvertes autour des Dialogica polymorpha antiiudaica." In Constantine Zuckerman (ed.), *Constructing the Seventh Century*, 9–26. Paris: Assocation des Amis du Centre d'Histoire et Civilisation de Byzance, 2013.

al-Balādhurī, Aḥmad. *Futūḥ al-buldān*. *ʿAbdallāh Anīs al-Ṭabbāʾ and ʿUmar Anīs al-Ṭabbāʾ*. Beirut: Muʾassasat al-Maʿārif, 1987. Philip K. Hitti (trans.). *The Origins of the Islamic State (Kitāb futūḥ al-buldān)*. New York: Columbia University Press, 1916.

Bates, Michael. History, Geography, and Numismatics in the First Century of Islamic Coinage. *Revue Suisse de Numismatique* 65 (1986), 231–263.

Ben Ashur, Al-Fāḍil. *Al-Tafsīr wa-rijāluh*. Tunis: [n.p.], 1966 [reprint Cairo, 1970].

Ben Cheneb, Mohammed (ed.). *Ṭabaqāt*. *See* Abu l-ʿArab, Muḥammad b. Aḥmad al-Tamīmī.

Berg, Herbert. *The Development of Exegesis in Early Islam: The Authenticity of Muslim Literature from the Formative Period*. Curzon Studies in the Qurʾān. Richmond, Surrey: Curzon, 2000.

(ed.). *Method and Theory in the Study of Islamic Origins*. Leiden: E. J. Brill, 2003.

Booth, Phil. "The Muslim Conquest of Egypt Reconsidered." In Constantine Zuckerman (ed.), *Constructing the Seventh Century*, 639–729. Paris: Assocation des Amis du Centre d'Histoire et Civilisation de Byzance, 2013.

Brock, Sebastian. "Syriac Views of Emergent Islam." In G. H. A. Juynboll (ed.), *Studies on the First Century of Islamic Society*, 9–21. Carbondale: Southern Illinois University Press, 1982.

Brockopp, Jonathan. "Re-reading the History of Early Mālikī Jurisprudence." *Journal of the American Oriental Society* **118** (1998), 233–238.

Early Mālikī Law: Ibn ʿAbd al-Ḥakam and His Major Compendium of Jurisprudence. Studies in Islamic Law and Society 14. Leiden: E. J. Brill, 2000.

"Competing Theories of Authority in Early Mālikī Texts." In Bernard Weiss (ed.), *Studies in Islamic Legal Theory*, 3–22. Leiden: E. J. Brill, 2001.

"The *Minor Compendium* of Ibn ʿAbd al-Ḥakam (d. 214/829) and Its Reception in the Early Mālikī School." *Islamic Law and Society* **12**, no. 2 (2005), 149–181.

"Theorizing Charismatic Authority in Early Islamic Law." *Comparative Islamic Studies* **1**, no. 2 (2005), 129–158.

"Contradictory Evidence and the Exemplary Scholar: The Lives of Sahnun b. Saʿid (d. 854)." *International Journal of Middle East Studies* **43**, no. 1 (2011), 115–132.

"The Formation of Islamic Law: The Egyptian School, 750–900." *Annales Islamologiques* **45** (2011), 123–140.

"Saḥnūn's *Mudawwanah* and the Piety of the 'Sharīʿah-Minded'." In Kevin Reinhart and Robert Gleave (eds.), *Islamic Law in Theory: Studies on Jurisprudence in Honor of Bernard Weiss*, 129–141. Leiden: E. J. Brill, 2014.

"Interpreting Material Evidence: Religion at the 'Origins of Islam'." *History of Religions* **55** (2015), 121–147.

Brunschvig, Robert. "Polémiques médiéval autour du rite de Malik." *al-Andalus* **15** (1950), 377–435.

Bulliet, Richard. *Conversion to Islam in the Medieval Period: An Essay in Quantitative History*. Cambridge, MA: Harvard University Press, 1979.

Burrell, David. *Knowing the Unknowable God: Ibn Sina, Maimonides, Aquinas*. South Bend, IN: University of Notre Dame Press, 1992.

Calder, Norman. "Ikhtilāf and Ijmāʿ in Shāfiʿī's Risāla." *Studia Islamica* **58** (1983), 55–81.

Studies in Early Muslim Jurisprudence. Oxford: Clarendon, 1993.

Cameron, Averil, and Lawrence I. Conrad (eds.), *The Byzantine and Early Islamic Near East, Vol. 1, Problems in the Literary Source Material*, 215–275. Princeton: Princeton University Press, 1992.

Cerrahoğlu, Ismail. "Yaḥyā b. Sallām ve tafsirdeki metodu." *Ankara universitesi Ilāhiyat Fakultesi Yayinlari* **89** (1970), 3–211.

Cooperson, Michael. *Classical Arabic Biography: The Heirs of the Prophets in the Age of al-Ma'mun*. Cambridge: Cambridge University Press, 2000.

"Ibn Ḥanbal and Bishr al-Ḥāfī: A Case Study in Biographical Traditions." *Studia Islamica* **86** (1997), 71–101.

Crone, Patricia. *Hagarism: The Making of the Islamic World*. Cambridge: Cambridge University Press, 1980.

"Two Legal Problems Bearing on the Early History of the Qur'ān." *Jewish Studies in Arabic and Islam* **18** (1984), 1–37.

Roman, Provincial and Islamic Law. Cambridge: Cambridge University Press, 1987.

Slaves on Horses: The Evolution of the Islamic Polity. Cambridge: Cambridge University Press, 2003.

Dakake, Maria. *The Charismatic Community: Shi'ite Identity in Early Islam*. Albany: State University of New York Press, 2008.

de Goeje, M. J. "Beschreibung einer alten Handschrift von Abû 'Obaid's Ġarîb-al-ḥadîṯ." *Zeitschrift der Deutschen morgenländischen Gesellschaft* **18**, no. 4 (1864), 781–807.

Demiri, Lejla, and Cornelia Römer. *Texts from the Early Islamic Period of Egypt: Muslims and Christians at Their First Encounter; Arabic Papyri from the Erzherzog Rainer Collection, Austrian National Library, Vienna*. Vienna: Phoibos, 2009.

de Prémare, Alfred-Louis. "Wahb b. Munabbih, une figure singulière du premier islam." *Annales: histoire, sciences sociales* **60** (2005), 531–548.

Déroche, François. "Les manuscrits arabes datés du IIIe/IXe siècle." *Revue des Études Islamiques* **55–57** (1987–1989), 343–379.

"Manuscripts of the Qur'ān." In Jane Dammen McAuliffe (ed.), *Encyclopaedia of the Qur'ān*. Leiden: E. J. Brill, 2001–2005.

Islamic Codicology: An Introduction to the Study of Manuscripts in Arabic Script. London: Al-Furqān Islamic Heritage Foundation, 2006.

Qur'ans of the Umayyads: A First Overview. Leiden: E. J. Brill, 2014.

Donner, Fred. *Narratives of Islamic Origins: The Beginnings of Islamic Historical Writing*. Studies in Late Antiquity and Early Islam, No. 14. Princeton: Darwin Press, 1998.

"From Believers to Muslims: Confessional Self-Identity in the Early Islamic Community." *Al-Abhath: Journal of the Faculty of Arts and Sciences of the American University of Beirut* **50–51** (2002–2003), 9–53.

Muhammad and the Believers: At the Origins of Islam. Cambridge, MA: Harvard University Press, 2010.

Duri, Abd al-Aziz. *Early Islamic Institutions: Administration and Taxation from the Caliphate to the Umayyads and 'Abbāsids*. New York: Tauris, 2011.

Dutton, Yasin. *The Origins of Islamic Law: The Qur'an, the Muwaṭṭa' and Madinan 'Amal*. Culture and Civilization in the Middle East. Richmond, Surrey: Curzon, 1999.

"An Umayyad Fragment of the Qur'an and Its Dating." *Journal of Qur'anic Studies* 9, no. 2 (2007), 57–87.

El-Hawary, Hassan Mohammed. "The Second Oldest Islamic Monument Known, Dated A.H. 71 (A.D. 691). From the Time of the Omayyad Calif 'Abd-el-Malik ibn Marwān." *Journal of the Royal Asiatic Society of Great Britain and Ireland* 2 (Apr. 1932), 289–293.

El Shamsy, Ahmed. *The Canonization of Islamic Law: A Social and Intellectual History*. Cambridge: Cambridge University Press, 2013.

Eshragh, A. S. "An Interesting Arab-Sasanian Dirhem." *Oriental Numismatic Society Newsletter* 178 (2004), 45–46.

al-Fazārī, Abū Isḥāq. *Kitāb al-Siyar*. Fārūq Ḥammāda (ed.). Beirut: Mu'assasāt al-Risāla, 1987.

Fierro, Maribel. "El alfaquí beréber Yaḥyà b. Yaḥyà, 'el inteligente de al-Andalus'." In María Luisa Ávila and M. Marín (eds.), *Estudios onomástico-biográphicos de al-Andalus. VIII*, 269–344. Madrid: Consejo Superior de Investigaciones Científicas, 1997.

Gaube, Heinz. *Arabosasanidische Numismatik*. Braunschweig: Klinkhardt & Biermann, 1973.

George, Alain and Andrew Marsham (eds.). *Power, Patronage, and Memory in Early Islam.* Oxford: Oxford Universtiy Press, forthcoming 2017.

Gilliot, Claude. "'Ulamā'." In *Encyclopaedia of Islam*, 2nd ed. Leiden: E. J. Brill, 1962–2001.

"Le Commentaire Coranique de Hud b. Muhakkam/Muhkim." *Arabica* 44 (1997), 179–233.

Goldziher, Ignacz. *The Ẓāhirīs. Their Doctrine and Their History, a Contribution to the History of Islamic Theology*. Wolfgang Behn (trans.). Leiden: E. J. Brill, 1971.

Grob, Eva Mira. *Documentary Arabic Private and Business Letters on Papyrus: Form and Function, Content and Context*. New York: De Gruyter, 2010.

Grohmann, Adolf. "Aperçu de papyrologie arabe." *Études de papyrologie* 1 (1932), 77–79.

Gruendler, Beatrice. *The Development of the Arabic Scripts: From the Nabatean Era to the First Islamic Century According to Dated Texts*. Harvard Semitic Series, 43. Atlanta: Scholars Press, 1993.

Guest, Rhuvon. *Introduction to al-Kindī, Kitâb el umarâ (el wulâh) wa Kitâb el qudâh*. Leiden: E. J. Brill, 1912.

Guillaume, Alfred (trans.). *The Life of Muhammad According to Ibn Ishaq*. Karachi: Oxford University Press, 1978.

Gutas, Dimitri. *Greek Thought, Arabic Culture: The Graeco-Arabic Translation Movement in Baghdad and Early 'Abbasad Society (2nd–4th/8th–10th c.)*. New York: Routledge, 1998.

Halevi, Leor. "The Paradox of Islamization: Tombstone Inscriptions, Qurʾānic Recitations, and the Problem of Religious Change." *History of Religions* **44**, no. 2 (Nov. 2004), 120–152.

Hallaq, Wael. "Was al-Shafii the Master Architect of Islamic Jurisprudence?" *International Journal of Middle East Studies* **25** (1993), 587–605.

The Origins and Evolution of Islamic Law. Cambridge: Cambridge University Press, 2005.

"Qurʾānic Constitutionalism and Moral Governmentality: Further Notes on the Founding Principles of Islamic Society and Polity." *Comparative Islamic Studies* **8**, nos. 1–2 (2012), 1–51.

Heffening, W. "Zum Aufbau der islamischen Rechtswerke." In W. Heffening and W. Kirfel (eds.), *Studien zur Geschichte und Kultur des nahen und fernen Ostens*, 101–118. Leiden: E. J. Brill, 1935.

Heidemann, Stefan. "The Evolving Representation of the Early Islamic Empire and Its Religion on Coin Imagery." In Angelika Neuwirth et al. (eds.), *The Qurʾān in Context*, 149–195. Leiden: E. J. Brill, 2010.

Hentati, Nejmeddine. "Min al-Asadiyya ilā l-Mukhtaliṭa fa-l-Mudawwana." In Hentati (ed.), *Dirāsāt Ḥaḍāriyya ḥawla l-Qayrawān*, 39–52. Tunis: Imprimerie Officielle de la République Tunisienne, 2015.

Hermosilla, M. J. "Corán 22,52 en el tafsīr de Yaḥyà b. Salām." *Al-Qanṭara: Revista De Estudios Árabes* **12**, no. 1 (1991), 271–272.

Hilali, Asma. "Le palimpseste de Ṣanʿāʾ et la canonisation du Coran: nouveaux éléments." *Cahiers du Centre Gustave Glotz* **21** (2010), 443–448.

Horden, Peregrine, and Nicholas Purcell. *The Corrupting Sea: A Study of Mediterranean History*. Oxford: Blackwell, 2000.

Hoyland, Robert. "The Content and Context of Early Arabic Inscriptions." *Jerusalem Studies in Arabic and Islam* **21** (1997), 77–102.

Seeing Islam as Others Saw It. A Survey and Analysis of the Christian, Jewish and Zoroastrian Writings on Islam. Princeton: Darwin Press, 1997.

"New Documentary Texts and the Early Islamic State." *Bulletin of the School of Oriental and African Studies* **69**, no. 3 (2006), 395–416.

Humbert, Geneviève. "Le Kitāb de Sībawayhi et l'autonomie de l'écrit." *Arabica* **44**, no. 4 (Oct. 1997), 553–567.

Humphreys, R. Stephen. *Islamic History: A Framework for Inquiry*, rev. ed. Princeton: Princeton University Press, 1991.

Hurvitz, Nimrod. "Miḥna as Self-Defense." *Studia Islamica* **92** (2001), 93–111.

Formation of Hanbalism: Piety into Power. London: RoutledgeCurzon, 2002.
Ibn ʿAbd al-Ḥakam, ʿAbdallāh, *Sīrat ʿUmar b. ʿAbd al-ʿAzīz*. Aḥmad ʿUbayd (ed.). Cairo: al-Maktaba al-ʿArabiyya, 1927.
Al-Mukhtaṣar al-ṣaghīr li ʿAbd Allāh b. ʿAbd al-Ḥakam. ʿUmar ʿAlī Abū Bakr Zāryā (ed.). Al-Riyāḍ: Dār Ibn al-Qayyim lil-Nashr wa-'l-Tawzīʿ, 2013.
Ibn Abī Zamanīn, Muḥammad. *Mukhtaṣar tafsīr Yaḥyá ibn Sallām li-Abī 'Abd Allāh Muḥammad ibn Abī Zamanayn*. ʿAbd al-Salām b. Aḥmad al-Kanūnī (ed.). Tetouan(?), 2001.
Ibn al-Nadīm, Muḥammad b. Isḥāq. *Kitāb al-Fihrist*. Gustav Flügel (ed.). 2 vols. Leipzig: Vogel, 1872.
Kitāb al-Fihrist. Ayman Fu'ad Sayyid (ed.) (4 vols.) London: Al-Furqan Islamic Heritage Foundation, 2009.
Ibn al-Qāsim, ʿAbd al-Raḥmān. *al-Muwaṭṭaʾ*. Miklos Muranyi (ed.). Beirut: Dār al-Bashāʾir al-Islāmī, 2012.
Ibn Ḥabīb, ʿAbd al-Malik. *Kitāb al-Ta'rīj (La historia)*. Jorge Aguadé (ed.). Madrid: Consejo Superior de Investigaciones Científicas, 1991.
Ibn Hishām, ʿAbd al-Malik. *Sīrat sayyidinā Muḥammad Rasūl Allāh*. F. Wüstenfeld (ed.). Göttingen: Dieterichsche Universitäts-Buchhandlung, 1859.
Ibn Khaldun, ʿAbd al-Raḥmān b. Muḥammad. *The Muqaddimah: An Introduction to History*. Franz Rosenthal (trans.). 3 vols. Princeton: Princeton University Press, 1958.
Ibn Māja, Muḥammad b. Yazīd, *Sunan Ibn Māja*, 5 vols. Lahore: Kazi Publications, 1993–1996.
Ibn Saʿd, Arīb. *An Account of the Establishment of the Fatemite Dynasty in Africa*. John Nicholson (trans.). Tübingen: Ludwig Fues, 1840.
Ibn Wahb, ʿAbdallāh. *Le Djâmiʿ d'Ibn Wahb*. J. David-Weill (ed.). 2 vols. Cairo: Institut Français d'Archéologie Orientale, 1939–1948.
al-Ǧāmiʿ: die Koranwissenschaften. Miklos Muranyi (ed.). Wiesbaden: Harrassowitz, 1992.
al-Ǧāmiʿ: tafsīr al-Qurʾān, Koranexegese 2. Teil. Miklos Muranyi (ed.). Wiesbaden: Harrassowitz, 1995.
al-Muwaṭṭaʾ, kitāb al-qaḍāʾ fī al-buyūʿ. Miklos Muranyi (ed.). Beirut: Dār al-Gharb al-Islāmī, 2004.
Ibn Ziyād, ʿAlī al-Tūnisī. *Qiṭʿa min Muwaṭṭaʾ Ibn Ziyād*. Muḥammad b. Shādhilī al-Nayfar (ed.). Tunis: al-Dār al-Tūnisiyyah li-l-Našr, 1978 and Beirut: Dār al-Gharb al-Islāmī, 1980.
Ismāʿīl b. Isḥāq. *Musnad Ḥadīth Mālik b. Anas*. Miklos Muranyi (ed.). Beirut: Dār al-Gharb al-Islāmī, 2002.
Aḥkām al-Qurʾān. ʿĀmir Ḥasan Ṣabrī (ed.). Beirut: Dār Ibn Ḥazm, 2005.

ʿIyāḍ b. Mūsā al-Yaḥṣubī. *Tartīb al-madārik*. ʿAbd al-Qādir al-Saḥrawī et al. (eds.). 8 vols. Rabat: Wizārat al-Awqāf, 1982.

Jankowiak, Mark. "The First Arab Siege of Constantinople." In Constantine Zuckerman (ed.), *Constructing the Seventh Century*, 237–320. Paris: Assocation des Amis du Centre d'Histoire et Civilisation de Byzance, 2013.

Johns, Jeremy. "Archaeology and the History of Early Islam. The First Seventy Years." *Journal of the Economic and Social History of the Orient* 46, no. 4 (2003), 411–436.

Jones, Alan. "The Dotting of a Script and the Dating of an Era: The Strange Neglect of PERF 558." *Islamic Culture* 72, no. 4 (1998), 95–103.

Judd, Steven. *Religious Scholars and the Umayyads: Piety-Minded Supporters of the Marwānid Caliphate*. New York: Routledge, 2014.

Kennedy, Hugh, "Egypt as a Province in the Islamic Caliphate, 641–868." In Carl F. Petry (ed.), *The Cambridge History of Egypt*, 1:62–85. Cambridge: Cambridge University Press, 1998.

Kern, Linda. *The Riddle of ʿUmar b. al-Khaṭṭāb in Bukhārī's* Kitāb al-Jāmiʿ al-ṣaḥīḥ *(and the Question of the Routinization of Prophetic Charisma)*. Unpublished Ph.D. thesis, Harvard University, 1996.

Khadduri, Majid. *Islamic Jurisprudence: Shafiʿi's Risala*. Baltimore: Johns Hopkins University Press, 1961.

Khalek, Nancy. *Damascus after the Muslim Conquest: Text and Image in Early Islam*. Oxford: Oxford University Press, 2011.

Khomeini, Ruhollah. *Jihād al-nafs aw al-jihād al-akbar*, with an introduction by Hasan Hanafi. Cairo: n.p., 1980(?)

Khoury, Raif Georges. *ʿAbd-Allāh Ibn-Lahīʿa, [97–174/715–790]: juge et grand maître de l'école égyptienne*. Wiesbaden: Harrassowitz, 1986.

Wahb b. Munabbih. 2 vols. Wiesbaden: Harrassowitz, 1972.

"L'Apport spécialement important de la papyrology dans la transmission et la codification des plus anciennes versions des *Mille et une nuits* et d'autres livres des deux premiers siècles islamiques." In Petra Sijpesteijn and Lennart Sundelin (eds.), *Papyrology and the History of Early Islamic Egypt*. Leiden: E. J. Brill, 2004.

"Les papyrus arabes de Heidelberg disparus. Essai de reconstruction et d'analyse." In Alexander T. Schubert and Petra Sijpesteijn (eds.), *Documents and the History of the Early Islamic World*. Boston: Brill Academic Publishers, 2014.

al-Kinānī, Yaḥyā b. ʿUmar. *Aḥkām al-Sūq*. Maḥmūd ʿAlī Makkī (ed.). Cairo: Wizārat al-Tarbiya wa-l-Taʿlīm, al-Idārah al-ʿĀmma lil-Thaqāfa, 1956. Also Ḥasan Ḥusnī ʿAbd al-Wahhāb (ed.). Tunis: al-Sharika al-Tūnisīya li l-Tawzīʿ, 1975.

Kohut, Heinz. *The Analysis of the Self: A Systematic Approach to the Psychoanalytic Treatment of Narcissistic Personality Disorders*. Chicago: University of Chicago Press, 1971.

Laroui, Abdallah. *A History of the Maghrib: An Interpretive Essay*. Ralph Mannheim (trans.). Princeton: Princeton University Press, 1977.

Lecker, Michael. "Ḥudhayfa b. Al-Yamān and 'Ammār B. Yāsir, Jewish Converts to Islam." *Quaderni di Studi Arabi* **11** (1993), 149–162.

Muslims, Jews, and Pagans: Studies on Early Islamic Medina. Leiden: E. J. Brill, 1995.

"Judaism among the Kinda and the Ridda of the Kinda." *Journal of the American Oriental Society* **115**, no. 4 (1995), 635–650.

"Zayd b. Thābit, 'A Jew with Two Sidelocks': Judaism and Literacy in Pre-Islamic Medina (Yathrib)." *Journal of Near Eastern Studies* **56**, no. 4 (October 1997), 259–273.

"Glimpses of Muhammad's Medinan Decade." In Jonathan E. Brockopp (ed.), The Cambridge Companion to Muḥammad, *61-79*. New York: Cambridge University Press, 2010.

Lecomte, G. "A propos de la résurgence des ouvrages d'Ibn Qutayba sur le hadît aux VIe/XIIe et VIIe/XIIIe siècles. Les certificats de lecture du *K. Garīb al-Ḥadīt et du K. Islāḥ al-ġalat fī ġarīb al-hadīt* li-Abī 'Ubayd al-Qāsim b. Sallām." *Bulletin d'Études Orientales* **21** (1968), 347–409.

Leslie, D. D., Yang Daye and A. Youssef. *Islam in Traditional China: A Bibliographical Guide*. Sankt Augustin: Monumenta Serica Institute, 2006.

Lowry, Joseph E. (ed. and trans.). *The Epistle on Legal Theory. See* al-Shāfi'ī, Muḥammad b. Idrīs.

"The Legal Hermeneutics of al-Shāfi'ī and Ibn Qutayba: A Reconsideration." *Islamic Law and Society* **11**, no. 1 (2004), 1–41.

Early Islamic Legal Theory: The Risāla of Muḥammad ibn Idrīs al-Shāfi'ī. Leiden: Brill, 2007.

Luxenberg, Christoph. "A New Interpretation of the Arabic Inscription in Jerusalem's Dome of the Rock." In Karl-Heinz Ohlig and Gerd Puin (eds.), *The Hidden Origins of Islam*, 125–151. Amherst, MA: Prometheus Books, 2010.

Mālik b. Anas, *Al-Muwaṭṭa'*. Ḥasan Abdallāh Sharaf (ed.). 2 vols. Cairo: Dār al-Rayān li-l-Turāth, 1988. Also: Aḥmad Rātib 'Armūsh (ed.). Beirut: Dār al-Nafā'is, 2001; and al-Shaybani's recension. Beirut: Dār al-Yarmūk, n.d.

Marlowe, Louise. "Scholars." In Jane Dammen McAuliffe (ed.), *Encyclopaedia of the Qur'ān*. Leiden: E. J. Brill, 2001–2005.

Marçais, Georges. *Manuel d'art musulman: l'architecture*. Paris: A. Picard, 1926.

Melchert, Christopher. "The Adversaries of Aḥmad Ibn Ḥanbal." *Arabica* 44 (1997), 234–253.

The Formation of the Sunni Schools of Law, 9th–10th Centuries. CE. Studies in Islamic Law and Society. Leiden: E. J. Brill, 1997.

"The Early History of Islamic Law." In Herbert Berg (ed.), *Method and Theory in the Study of Islamic Origins*, 293–324. Leiden: E. J. Brill, 2003.

Mikhail, Maged. *From Byzantine to Islamic Egypt: Religion, Identity and Politics after the Arab Conquest*. London: I. B. Taurus, 2014.

Mochiri, Malek. "A Pahlavi Forerunner of the Umayyad Reformed Coinage." *Journal of the Royal Asiatic Society of Great Britain and Ireland* 2 (1981), 168–172.

Mojaddedi, Jawid. *The Biographical Tradition in Sufism: The ṭabaqāt Genre from al-Sulamī to Jāmī*. Richmond, Surrey: Curzon, 2001.

Morimoto, Kosei. *The Fiscal Administration of Egypt in the Early Islamic Period*. Kyoto: Dohosha, 1981.

Moritz, Bernhard. *Arabic Paleography*. Cairo: Khedivial Library, 1905.

Motzki, Harald. "The Role of Non-Arab Converts in the Development of Early Islamic Law." *Islamic Law and Society* 6 (1999), 293–317.

"The Author and His Work in the Islamic Literature of the First Centuries: The Case of ʿAbd al-Razzāq's *Muṣannaf*." *Jerusalem Studies in Arabic and Islam* 28 (2003), 171–201.

"Motzki's Reliable Transmitter: A Short Answer to P. Gledhill." *Islamic Law and Society*, 19, no. 2 (2012), 194–199.

Mourad, Suleiman. *Early Islam between Myth and History: Al-Ḥasan Al-Baṣrī (d. 110H/728CE) and the Formation of His Legacy in Classical Islamic Scholarship*. Leiden: E. J. Brill, 2006.

Muranyi, Miklos. *Die Prophetengenossen in der frühislamischen Geschichte*. Bonn: Orientalistisches Seminar der Universität Bonn, 1973.

Materialien zur mālikitischen Rechtsliteratur. Wiesbaden: Harrassowitz, 1984.

Ein altes Fragment medinensischer Jurisprudenz aus Qairawān. Stuttgart: Franz Steiner, 1985.

"Das Kitāb al-siyar von Abū Isḥāq al-Fazārī. Das Manuskript der Qarawiyyīn-Bibliothek zu Fas." *Jerusalem Studies in Arabic and Islam* 6 (1985), 63–91.

"Fiqh." In Helmut Gätje (ed.), *Grundriss der arabischen Philologie*. 2 vols., 2:229–325. Wiesbaden: Reichert, 1987.

"„man ḥalafa ʿalā minbarī āṯiman ...": Bemerkungen zu einem frühen Traditionsgut." *Die Welt des Orients* 18 (1987), 92–131.

ʿAbd Allāh b. Wahb: Leben und Werk. Al-Muwaṭṭaʾ, kitāb al-muḥāraba. Wiesbaden: Harrassowitz, 1992.

"Neue Materialien zur *tafsīr*-Forschung in der Moscheebibliothek von Qairawān." In Stefan Wild (ed.), *The Qur'an as Text*, 228–234. Leiden: E. J. Brill, 1996.

Beiträge zur Geschichte der Ḥadīṯ und Rechtsgelehrsamkeit der Mālikiyya in Nordafrika bis zum 5. Jh. d.H. Wiesbaden: Harrassowitz, 1997.

"Die frühe Rechstslitertur zwischen Quellenanalyse und Fiktion," *Islamic Law and Society* **4** (1997), 224–241.

"Das Kitāb Aḥkām Ihn Ziyād über die Identifizierung eines Fragmentes in Qairawān (qairawāner Miszellaneen V)". *Zeitschrift der Deutschen morgenländischen Gesellschaft* **148**, no. 2 (1998), 241–260.

Die Rechtsbücher des qairawāners Saḥnūn b. Sa'īd: Entstehungsgeschichte und Werküberlieferung. Stuttgart: Franz Steiner, 1999.

"A Unique Manuscript from Kairouan in the British Library: The *Samā'*-work of Ibn al-Qāsim al-'Utaqī and Issues of Methodology." In Herbert Berg (ed.), *Method and Theory in the Study of Islamic Origins*, 325–368. Leiden: E. J. Brill, 2003.

"Visionen des Skeptikers." *Der Islam* **81**, no. 2 (2004), 206–217.

Nawas, John. "A Profile of the mawālī *'ulamā'*." In Monique Bernards and John Nawas (eds.), *Patronate and Patronage in Early and Classical Islam*, 454–480. Leiden: E. J. Brill, 2005.

"The Birth of an Elite: *mawālī* and Arab *'ulamā'*." *Jerusalem Studies in Arabic and Islam* **31** (2006), 74–91.

Nevo, Yehuda D. and Judith Koren. *Crossroads to Islam: The Origins of the Arab Religion and the Arab State.* Amherst, NY: Prometheus Books, 2003.

Newby, Gordon. "Observations about an Early Judaeo-Arabic." *Jewish Quarterly Review*, New Series, **61**, no. 3 (Jan. 1971), 212–221.

A History of the Jews of Arabia: From Ancient Times to Their Eclipse under Islam. Columbia: University of South Carolina Press, 1988.

The Making of the Last Prophet. A Reconstruction of the Earliest Biography of Muhammad. Columbia: University of South Carolina Press, 1989.

Oakes, Len. *Prophetic Charisma: The Psychology of Revolutionary Religious Personalities.* Syracuse, NY: Syracuse University Press, 1997.

Ohlig, Karl-Heinz, and Gerd Puin. *The Hidden Origins of Islam.* Amherst, MA: Prometheus Books, 2010.

O'Leary, De Lacy. *Short History of the Fatimid Khalifate.* London: Kegan Paul, 1923.

Ossendorf-Conrad, Beatrix. *Das "K. al-Wāḍiḥa" des 'Abd al-Malik b. Ḥabīb: Edition und Kommentar zu Ms. Qarawiyyīn 809/40 (Abwāb al-Ṭahāra)*. Beiruter Texte und Studien, 43. Stuttgart: Franz Steiner Verlag, 1994.

Patton, Walter Melville. *Aḥmed ibn Ḥanbal and the Miḥna*. Leiden: E. J. Brill, 1897.

Pertsch, W. *Die arabischen Handschriften der herzoglichen Bibliothek zu Gotha*. 5 vols. Gotha: Perthes, 1877–1892.

Popp, Volker. "The Early History of Islam, Following Inscriptional and Numismatic Testimony." In Karl-Heinz Ohlig and Gerd Puin, *The Hidden Origins of Islam*, 17–124. Amherst, MA: Prometheus Books, 2010.

Pregill, Michael. "Isrāʾīlīyāt, Myth, and Pseudepigraphy: Wahb. B. Munabbih and the Early Islamic Versions of the Fall of Adam and Eve." *Jerusalem Studies in Arabic and Islam* 34 (2008), 215–284.

Pringle, Denys. *The Defense of Byzantine Africa from Justinian to the Arab Conquest*. Oxford: Oxford University Press, 1981.

Puin, Gerd. *Der Dīwān von ʿUmar ibn al-Ḫaṭṭāb: ein Beitrag zur frühislamischen Verwaltungsgeschichte*. Bonn: Rheinischen Friedrich-Wilhelms-Universität, 1970.

al-Qāḍī, Wadād. "Early Islamic State Letters. The Question of Authenticity." In Averil Cameron and Lawrence I. Conrad (eds.), *The Byzantine and Early Islamic Near East, Vol. 1: Problems in the Literary Source Material*, 215–275. Princeton: Darwin Press, 1992.

Rāġib, Yūsuf, "Lettres nouvelles de Qurra b. Šarīk." *Journal of Near Eastern Studies* 3, no. 40 (1981), 173–187.

"Un papyrus arabe de l'an 22 de l'hégire." In Ghislaine Alleaume, Sylvie Denoix, and Michel Tuchscherer (eds.), *Histoire, archéologies et littératures du monde musulman: mélanges en l'honneur d'André Raymond*, 363–372. Cairo: Institut Francais d'Archéologie Orientale, 2009.

"Les premiers documents arabes de l'ére musulmane." In Constantine Zuckerman (ed.), *Constructing the Seventh Century*, 679–726. Paris: Assocation des Amis du Centre d'Histoire et Civilisation de Byzance, 2013.

Rapoport, Yossef. "Malik ibn Anas (d. 179/795)." In David Powers, Susan Spectorsky, and Oussama Arabi (eds.), *Islamic Legal Thought: A Compendium of Muslim Jurists*, 27–41. Leiden: E. J. Brill, 2013.

Dwight Reynolds (ed.). *Interpreting the Self: Autobiography in the Arabic Literary Tradition*. Berkeley: University of California Press, 2001.

Rippin, Andrew. "*Tafsīr Ibn ʿAbbās* and Criteria for Dating Early *tafsīr* Texts." *Jerusalem Studies in Arabic and Islam* 18 (1994), 38–83.

Muslims: Their Religious Beliefs and Practices. 4th ed. New York: Routledge, 2011.

Ritter, Helmut. "Philologika II." *Der Islam* 17 (1928), 249–57.

Robinson, Chase. *ʿAbd al-Malik*. Oxford: Oneworld, 2005.
Rosenthal, Franz. *Knowledge Triumphant: The Concept of Knowledge in Medieval Islam*. Leiden: Brill, 1970.
"History and the Qurʾān." In Jane Dammen McAuliffe (ed.), *Encyclopaedia of the Qurʾān*. Leiden: E. J. Brill, 2001–2005.
Sadeghi, Behnam. *The Logic of Lawmaking in Islam: Women and Prayer in the Legal Tradition*. Cambridge Studies in Islamic Civilization. Cambridge: Cambridge University Press, 2013.
Sadeghi, Behnam, and U. Bergmann. "The Codex of a Companion of the Prophet and the Qurʾan of the Prophet." *Arabica* 57 (2010), 343–436.
Ṣafiyya, Jāsir Abū. *Bardiyyāt Qurra b. Sharīk al-ʿAbsī*. Riyadh: King Faysal Institute for Islamic Research and Studies, 2004.
Safran, Nina. "The Sacred and Profane in Islamic Cordoba." *Comparative Islamic Studies* 1 (2007), 21–41.
Saleh, Walid. "Marginalia and Peripheries: A Tunisian Historian and the History of Quránic Exegesis." *Numen* 58 (2011), 284–313.
Sammoud, Hamadi. "Un exégète oriental en Ifriqiya: Yahyâ Ibn Sallâm (742–815)." *Revue de l'Institut des Belles Lettres Arabes* 33 (1970), 227–242.
Saunders, Paula. *Ritual, Politics, and the City in Fatimid Cairo*. Albany: State University of New York Press, 1994.
Sayeed, Asma. *Women and the Transmission of Religious Knowledge in Islam*. Cambridge Studies in Islamic Civilization. Cambridge: Cambridge University Press, 2015.
Schacht, Joseph. *The Origins of Muhammadan Jurisprudence*. Oxford: Clarendon, 1950.
An Introduction to Islamic Law. Oxford: Clarendon, 1964.
"On Some Manuscripts in the Libraries of Kairouan and Tunis." *Arabica* 14 (1967), 225–258.
Schoeler, Gregor. "Die Frage der schriftlichen oder mündlichen Überlieferung der Wissenschaften im Islam." *Der Islam* 62 (1985), 201–230.
Charakter und Authentie der muslimischen Überlieferung über das Leben Mohammeds. Berlin: de Gruyter, 1996.
"Foundations for a New Biography of Muḥammad: The Production and Evaluation of the Corpus of Traditions from 'Urwah b. al-Zubayr." In Herbert Berg (ed.), *Method and Theory in the Study of Islamic Origins*, 21–28. Leiden: E. J. Brill, 2003.
The Genesis of Literature in Islam: From the Aural to the Read. Trans. and expanded by Shawkat Toorawa. The New Edinburgh Islamic Surveys. Edinburgh: Edinburgh University Press, 2009.
Schoeller, Marco. "Post-Enlightenment Academic Study of the Qurʾān." In Jane Dammen McAuliffe (ed.), *Encyclopaedia of the Qurʾān*. Leiden: E. J. Brill, 2001–2005.

Schultz, Warren. "The Monetary History of Egypt, 642–1517." In Carl F. Petry (ed.), *The Cambridge History of Egypt*, vol. 1, 318–338. Cambridge: Cambridge University Press, 1998.

Schwartz, Werner. Die Bibliothek der großen Moschee von al-Qayrawān, Tunesien: Vorarbeiten zu ihrer Geschichte. Unpublished thesis. Fachhochschule für Bibliotheks- und Dokumentationswesen, Cologne, 1986.

Sears, Stuart D. "The Sasanian Style Coins of 'Muhammad' and Some Related Coins." *Yarmouk Numismatics* 7 (1997), 7–17.

Sezgin, Fuat. *Geschichte des arabischen Schrifttums*. 9 vol. Leiden: E. J. Brill, 1967–1984.

Shabbuh, Ibrahim. "Sijill qadīm li-maktabat jāmiʿ al-Qayrawān." *Revue de l'Institut des Manuscrits Arabes* 2 (1956), 339–372.

al-Shāfiʿī, Muḥammad b. Idrīs. *Al-Risāla*. Aḥmad Shākir (ed.), second printing (Cairo: [n.p.], 1979. Translated as *The Epistle on Legal Theory*. Joseph E. Lowry (ed. and trans.). New York: New York University Press, 2013.

al-Sījīstānī, Abū Dāwūd. *Masāʾil al-Imām Aḥmad*. Abū Muʿādh Ṭāriq b. Awād Allāh b. Muḥammad (ed.). Cairo: Maktabat Ibn Taymiyya, 1999.

Sijpesteijn, Petra. "Arabic Papyri and Other Documents from Current Excavations in Egypt, with an Appendix of Arabic Papyri and Some Written Objects in Egyptian Collections." *Bardiyyat, Newsletter of the International Society for Arabic Papyrology* 2 (2007), 10–23.

Sinai, Nicolai. "When Did the Consonantal Skeleton of the Quran Reach Closure?" *Bulletin of the School of Oriental and African Studies* 77, no. 2 (2014), 273–292 and 77, no. 3 (2014), 509–521.

Sourdel-Thomine, Janine, and Dominique Sourdel. "Nouveaux documents sur l'histoire religieuse et sociale de Damas au moyen age." *Revue des Études Islamiques* 32 (1964), 1–25.

Spectorsky, Susan. *Chapters on Marriage and Divorce: Responses of Ibn Ḥanbal and Ibn Rāhwayh*. Austin: University of Texas Press, 1993.

Sundelin, Lennart. "Introduction: Papyrology and the Study of Early Islamic Egypt." In Sundelin and Petra Sijpesteijn (eds.), *Papyrology and the History of Early Islamic Egypt*, 1–19. Leiden: E. J. Brill, 2004.

al-Suyūṭī, Jalāl al-Dīn. *Ḥusn al-Muḥāḍara*. 2 vols. Beirut: Dār al-Kutub al-ʿIlmiyya, 1997.

al-Ṭabarī, Muḥammad b. Jarīr. *Jāmiʿ al-bayān fī taʾwīl al-Qurʾān*. 13 vols. Beirut: Dār al-Kutub al-ʿIlmiyya, 1999.

Takim, Liyakat. *The Heirs of the Prophet: Charisma and Religious Authority in Shi'ite Islam*. Albany: State University of New York Press, 2007.

Talbi, Mohamed. *Tarajim Aghlabiyya (Biographies Aghlabides)*. Tunis: University of Tunis, 1968.

Thiessen, Wesley. The Formation of the Mudawwana. Ph.D. dissertation, University of Victoria, 2014.

Thomas, David, and Barbara Roggema (eds.). *Christian Muslim Relations: A Bibliographical History. Volume 1: 600–900.* Leiden: E. J. Brill, 2009.

al-Tirmidhī, Muḥammad b. ʿĪsā. *al-Jāmiʿ al-Ṣaḥīḥ wa-huwa Sunan al-Tirmidhī.* 5 vols. Beirut: Dār al-Kutub al-ʿIlmiyya, 2000.

Touati, Houari. *Islam and Travel in the Middle Ages.* (Lydia Cochrane, trans.) Chicago: University of Chicago Press, 2010.

Toorawa, Shawkat M. *Ibn Abī Ṭāhir Ṭayfūr and Arabic Writerly Culture: A Ninth-Century Bookman in Baghdad,* Routledge Curzon Studies in Arabic and Middle-Eastern Literatures 7. London: Routledge, 2005.

al-ʿUsh, Muḥammad Abu l-Faraj. *Monnaies Aġlabides étudiées en relation avec l'histoire des Aġlabides.* Damascus: Institut Français de Damas, 1982.

al-ʿUtbī, Muḥammad. *Kitāb al-ḥajj [from the* ʿUtbiyya*].* Miklos Muranyi (ed.). Beirut: Dār Ibn Ḥazm, 2007.

van Koningsveld, P. S. *Levinus Warner and His Legacy. Three Centuries Legatum Warnerianum in the Leiden University Library.* Leiden: E. J. Brill, 1970.

von Bothmer, Hans-Casper Graf. "Architekturbilder im Koran: eine Prachthandschrift der Umayyadenzeit aus dem Yemen." *Pantheon* 45 (1987), 4–20.

"Masterworks of Islamic Book Art: Koranic Calligraphy and Illumination in the Manuscripts Found in The Great Mosque in Sanaa." In W. Daum (ed.), *Yemen: 3000 Years of Art and Civilization in Arabia Felix,* 178–181. Innsbruck: Pinguin-Verlag, 1987.

von Bredow, Mathias. *Der heilige Krieg (Ǧihād) aus der Sicht der mālikitischen Rechtsschule.* Beirut: Fritz Steiner Verlag, 1994.

Walker, J. *A Catalogue of the Muhammadan Coins in the British Museum. Volume I: Arab-Sassanian Coins.* London: British Museum, 1941.

Weber, Max. *Max Weber on Charisma and Institution Building.* S. N. Eisenstadt (ed.). Chicago: University of Chicago Press, 1968.

Wensinck, Arendt J. *Concordance et indices de la tradition musulmane.* 8 vols. Leiden: E. J. Brill, 1936–1988.

Whelan, Estelle. "Forgotten Witness: Evidence for the Early Codification of the Qurʾān." *Journal of the American Oriental Society* **118**, no. 1 (1998), 1–14.

Yaḥyā b. Sallām al-Baṣrī. *Tafsīr al-Qurʾān.* Hind Shalabi (ed.). 2 vols. Beirut: Dar al-kotob al-ilmiyah, 2004.

Younes, Khaled Mohamed Mahmoud. *Joy and Sorrow in Early Muslim Egypt: Arabic Papyrus Letters, Text and Content.* Ph.D. dissertation,

Leiden University, 2013. https://openaccess.leidenuniv.nl/handle/1887/21541.

Zaman, Muhammad Qasim. *Religion and Politics under the Early ʿAbbāsids: The Emergence of the Proto-Sunnī Elite*. Islamic History and Civilization. Studies and Texts, vol. 16. Leiden: E. J. Brill, 1997.

Zayd, Nasr Hamid Abu. *al-Imām al-Shāfiʿī wa-taʾsīs al-aydiyūlūjiyya al-wasaṭiyya*. Cairo: Sīnā li-l-Nashr, 1992.

Zellentin, Holger Michael. The Qurʾān's Legal Culture: The *Didascalia Apostolorum* as a Point of Departure. Tübingen: Mohr Siebeck, 2013.

Zuckerman, Constantine (ed.). *Constructing the Seventh Century*. Paris: Association des Amis du Centre d'Histoire et Civilisation de Byzance, 2013.

Index

N.B. The definite article (al-) has been dropped for places and names when it appears in the initial position (al-Abbasiyya, al-Abtah, etc.).

Other Titles in the Series:

Agricultural Innovation in the Early Islamic World: The Diffusion of Crops and Farming Techniques, 700–1100, Andrew M. Watson

Muslim Tradition: Studies in Chronology, Provenance and Authorship of Early Hadith, G. H. A. Juynboll

Social History of Timbuktu: The Role of Muslim Scholars and Notables 1400–1900, Elias N. Saad

Sex and Society in Islam: Birth Control before the Nineteenth Century, B. F. Musallam

Towns and Townsmen of Ottoman Anatolia: Trade, Crafts and Food Production in an Urban Setting 1520–1650, Suraiya Faroqhi

Unlawful Gain and Legitimate Profit in Islamic Law: Riba, Gharar and Islamic Banking, Nabil A. Saleh

Men of Modest Substance: House Owners and House Property in Seventeenth-Century Ankara and Kayseri, Suraiya Faroqhi

Roman, Provincial and Islamic Law: The Origins of the Islamic Patronate, Patricia Crone

Economic Life in Ottoman Jerusalem, Amnon Cohen

Mannerism in Arabic Poetry: A Structural Analysis of Selected Texts (3rd Century AH/9th Century AD–5th Century AH/11th Century AD), Stefan Sperl

The Rise and Rule of Tamerlane, Beatrice Forbes Manz

Popular Culture in Medieval Cairo, Boaz Shoshan

Early Philosophical Shiism: The Ismaili Neoplatonism of Abu Yaʿqub Al-Sijistani, Paul E. Walker

Indian Merchants and Eurasian Trade, 1600–1750, Stephen Frederic Dale

Palestinian Peasants and Ottoman Officials: Rural Administration around Sixteenth-Century Jerusalem, Amy Singer

Arabic Historical Thought in the Classical Period, Tarif Khalidi

Mongols and Mamluks: The Mamluk-Ilkhanid War, 1260–1281, Reuven Amitai-Preiss

Knowledge and Social Practice in Medieval Damascus, 1190–1350, Michael Chamberlain

The Politics of Households in Ottoman Egypt: The Rise of the Qazdağlis, Jane Hathaway

Hierarchy and Egalitarianism in Islamic Thought, Louise Marlow

Commodity and Exchange in the Mongol Empire: A Cultural History of Islamic Textiles, Thomas T. Allsen

State and Provincial Society in the Ottoman Empire: Mosul, 1540–1834, Dina Rizk Khoury

The Mamluks in Egyptian Politics and Society, Thomas Philipp and Ulrich Haarmann (eds.)

The Delhi Sultanate: A Political and Military History, Peter Jackson

European and Islamic Trade in the Early Ottoman State: The Merchants of Genoa and Turkey, Kate Fleet

The Ottoman City between East and West: Aleppo, Izmir, and Istanbul, Edhem Eldem, Daniel Goffman, and Bruce Masters

The Politics of Trade in Safavid Iran: Silk for Silver, 1600–1730, Rudolph P. Matthee

The Idea of Idolatry and the Emergence of Islam: From Polemic to History, G. R. Hawting

A Monetary History of the Ottoman Empire, Şevket Pamuk

Classical Arabic Biography: The Heirs of the Prophets in the Age of Al-Ma'mun, Michael Cooperson

Empire and Elites after the Muslim Conquest: The Transformation of Northern Mesopotamia, Chase F. Robinson

Poverty and Charity in Medieval Islam: Mamluk Egypt, 1250–1517, Adam Sabra
Culture and Conquest in Mongol Eurasia, Thomas T. Allsen
Christians and Jews in the Ottoman Arab World: The Roots of Sectarianism, Bruce Masters
Arabic Administration in Norman Sicily: The Royal Diwan, Jeremy Johns
Law, Society and Culture in the Maghrib, 1300–1500, David S. Powers
Revival and Reform in Islam: The Legacy of Muhammad al-Shawkani, Bernard Haykel
Tolerance and Coercion in Islam: Interfaith Relations in the Muslim Tradition, Yohanan Friedmann
Guns for the Sultan: Military Power and the Weapons Industry in the Ottoman Empire, Gábor Ágoston
Marriage, Money and Divorce in Medieval Islamic Society, Yossef Rapoport
The Empire of the Qara Khitai in Eurasian History: Between China and the Islamic World, Michal Biran
Domesticity and Power in the Early Mughal World, Ruby Lal
Power, Politics and Religion in Timurid Iran, Beatrice Forbes Manz
Postal Systems in the Pre-Modern Islamic World, Adam J. Silverstein
Kingship and Ideology in the Islamic and Mongol Worlds, Anne F. Broadbridge
Justice, Punishment and the Medieval Muslim Imagination, Christian Lange
The Shiites of Lebanon under Ottoman Rule, 1516–1788, Stefan Winter
Women and Slavery in the Late Ottoman Empire, Madeline Zilfi
The Second Ottoman Empire: Political and Social Transformation in the Early Modern World, Baki Tezcan
The Legendary Biographies of Tamerlane: Islam and Heroic Apocrypha in Central Asia, Ron Sela
Non-Muslims in the Early Islamic Empire: From Surrender to Coexistence, Milka Levy-Rubin
The Origins of the Shi'a: Identity, Ritual, and Sacred Space in Eighth-Century Kufa, Najam Haider
Politics, Law, and Community in Islamic Thought: The Taymiyyan Moment, Ovamir Anjum
The Power of Oratory in the Medieval Muslim World, Linda G. Jones
Animals in the Qur'an, Sarra Tlili
The Logic of Law Making in Islam: Women and Prayer in the Legal Tradition, Behnam Sadeghi
Empire and Power in the Reign of Süleyman: Narrating the Sixteenth-Century Ottoman World, Kaya Şahin
Law and Piety in Medieval Islam, Megan H. Reid
Women and the Transmission of Religious Knowledge in Islam, Asma Sayeed
The New Muslims of Post-Conquest Iran: Tradition, Memory, and Conversion, Sarah Bowen Savant
The Mamluk City in the Middle East: History, Culture, and the Urban Landscape, Nimrod Luz
Disability in the Ottoman Arab World, 1500–1800, Sara Scalenghe
The Holy City of Medina: Sacred Space in Early Islamic Arabia, Harry Munt
Muslim Midwives: The Craft of Birthing in the Premodern Middle East, Avner Giladi
Doubt in Islamic Law: A History of Legal Maxims, Interpretation, and Islamic Criminal Law, Intisar A. Rabb

The Second Formation of Islamic Law: The Hanafi School in the Early Modern Ottoman Empire, Guy Burak
Sexual Violation in Islamic Law: Substance, Evidence, and Procedure, Hina Azam
Gender Hierarchy in the Qur'an: Medieval Interpretations, Modern Responses, Karen Bauer
Intellectual Networks in Timurid Iran: Sharaf al-Din 'Ali Yazdi and the Islamicate Republic of Letters, Ilker Evrim Binbaş
Authority and Identity in Medieval Islamic Historiography: Persian Histories from the Peripheries, Mimi Hanaoka
The Economics of Ottoman Justice: Settlement and Trial in the Sharia Courts, Metin Coşgel and Boğaç Ergene
The Mystics of al-Andalus: Ibn Barrajan and Islamic Thought in the Twelfth Century, Yousef Casewit
Non-Muslim Provinces under Early Islam: Islamic Rule and Iranian Legitimacy in Armenia and Caucasian Albania, Alison Vacca
Muhammad's Heirs: The Rise of Muslim Scholarly Communities, 622–950, Jonathan E. Brockopp
The First of the Modern Ottomans: The Intellectual History of Ahmed Vasif, Ethan Menchinger

CPSIA information can be obtained
at www.ICGtesting.com
Printed in the USA
LVOW13*2117260418
575004LV00008B/158/P

9 781107 106666